The Self-Begetting Novel

The Self-Begetting Novel

Steven G. Kellman

Columbia University Press
New York   1980

PN
3503
.K4

Library of Congress Cataloging in Publication Data

Kellman, Steven G.   1947–
    The self-begetting novel.

    Bibliography: p.
    Includes index.
    1.   Fiction – 20th century – History and criticism.
I.   Title.
PN3503.K4   809.3′3   79-15700
ISBN 0-231-04782-7

Printed in Great Britain

To Mother

Contents

Preface

The clearest, most memorable and important feature of
art is how it arises, and the world's best works, in telling of
the most diverse things, are in fact narrations of their own
birth.

Boris Pasternak, *Proza 1915–1958*
(Ann Arbor, 1961), p.241

Novelists, like those who write about them, come into this world at the
initiative of others. Some, *en revanche*, grimly seek to control their exit.
Authors and parrots all have parents, though books are seldom dedicated to them. This book examines the Modernist ideal of autogeny as
embodied in a sub-genre of French, British and American fiction. That
ideal is, of course, a childish illusion, but it has been a compelling one for
those Western cultures in which meritocracy has supplanted heritocracy
as communal dream. Respect for the autonomy of the text restrains us
from speculating about Lady Macbeth's children; and the mere thought
of Jake Barnes's mother is ludicrous because it clashes with his, and our,
esteem for cool self-sufficiency. We would like to believe that *faber est
quisque fortunae suae*. This study was born of fascination with a kind of
novel whose very form demonstrates radical longing to overcome a
generation gap by merging parent and child into one enduring unit.

For the benefit of those whose French is not truly their own, I have
provided my own translations of quoted passages. Whenever practi-
cable, these supplement the French originals. Samuel Beckett has ren-
dered his own novels back into his native English, and I have quoted
from his versions.

Versions of some of my material have appeared as follows: "Imagin-
ing the Novel Dead: Recent Variations on a Theme by Proust," *Modern
Language Quarterly*, XXXV, 1 (Mar 1974), 45–55; "*La Nausée* as
Self-Begetting Novel," *Symposium*, XXVIII, 4 (Winter 1974), 303–14;
"Beckett's Fatal Dual," *Romance Notes*, XVI, 2 (Winter 1975), 268–73;
"Raising the Net: Iris Murdoch and the Tradition of the Self-Begetting
Novel," *English Studies*, LVII, 1 (Feb 1976), 43–50; "The Self-Begetting
Novel," *Western Humanities Review*, XXX, 2 (Spring 1976), 119–28;

"The Fiction of Self-Begetting," *Modern Language Notes*, XCI, 6 (Dec 1976), 1243–56; "The Self-Begetting Great American Novel: Clyde Brion Davis's Melding of Traditions," *Southwest Review*, LXII, 1 (Winter 1977), 65–72; "The Mirror and the Magic Lantern in *A la recherche*," *Neophilologus*, LXI, 1 (Jan 1977), 43–7. I would like to thank these journals for their earlier hospitality and for gracious permission to reprint.

The publishers and I wish to thank the following who have kindly given permission for the use of copyright material: Editions Gallimard for the extract from *La Nausée* by Jean-Paul Sartre ©1938 Editions Gallimard; Chatto & Windus Ltd and Random House Inc for the extracts from *Remembrance of Things Past (A La Recherche du Temps Perdu)* by Marcel Proust, translated by C. K. Scott Moncrieff and Frederick Blossom; Grove Press Inc for the extracts from *Three Novels* by Samuel Beckett; and Les Editions de Minuit for the extracts from *La Modification* by Michel Butor.

1   The Fiction of
Self-Begetting

prolem sine matre creatam
Ovid, *Metamorphoses*, II, 553

Know none before us, self-begot, self-rais'd
By our own quick'ning power
Milton, *Paradise Lost*, V, 860

I

The Oedipus myth, according to Otto Rank, is not primarily the savage
family romance projecting each son's dreadful wish to kill his father and
ravish his mother. Instead, he contends that "incest is a symbol of a
man's self-creative urge."[1] Sex is terrifying to the individual because it
means renouncing personal immortality and assuming the communal
and doomed role of sire. Laius, warned by the oracle that his son will
succeed him, avoids sex until, tricked into it, he breeds his own murderer. Oedipus likewise has immortal longings, and, when he usurps
Laius's position, he attempts to perpetuate himself as simultaneously
father and son. To be forever both begetter and begotten is one way,
short of sailing to Byzantium, to avoid those dying generations; yet
Aristotle's verdict is that the result is still tragic. That the child can take
charge of his own destiny by being father of the man is Romantic
delusion, and Rank recognizes in the House of Cadmus cycle "the
transition – accomplished in Greek civilization – from heroic self-
perpetuation to man's reluctant acceptance of his biologic rôle as father
and his perpetuation through the generations."[2] Rank's insight into the
ambivalence of masculine sexuality, as both egotistical pleasure and "a
coercion to propagate – hence, feared as a symbol of man's mortality"[3]
finds a literary echo in Temple's assertion to Stephen Dedalus that:
"The most profound sentence ever written . . . is the sentence at the end
of the zoology. Reproduction is the beginning of death."[4]

Rank was acknowledged within the Viennese cénacle as the adopted heir of Sigmund Freud. Erik Erikson was later to fashion a new name for himself which proclaims the fusion of both father and child in one autonomous figure, and Rank, né Rosenfeld, likewise invented a name and an identity for himself. The theme of birth preoccupied him throughout his career, in works like *Der Mythus der Geburt des Heldens* (1909) and *Das Trauma der Geburt* (1924). His break with Freud was as inevitable as the break with his biological parents. In collating myths of numerous heroes, from Sargon to Lohengrin, Rank noted a recurrent denial of family. The hero is often the product of a virgin birth or else abandoned in infancy. The fable of the stork, designed to account for babies while obscuring the role of parental sexuality, is reflected in Lohengrin, the hero who arrives mysteriously on a swan. American folklore, too, is filled with figures who, like the Lone Ranger or Johnny Appleseed (personification of the inseminator *ex nihilo*), arrive suddenly out of nowhere. According to Nietzsche, morals are oppressive because they have a genealogy, but *das souveräne Individuum*, like the Renaissance man who was able to be reborn as a complete heterocosm, will renounce pedigree. The popular American version of the *Ubermensch*, Capitol Comics' Superman, finds himself alone on this planet without natural parents.

Jesus is one of those whom Rank describes within the motif of the autonomous hero. In theological terms, he is preaching the early Christian heresy of modalism, the doctrine that the Son of God and the Father are identical. One of the most prominent champions of patripassianism, or modalism, was the third-century father Sabellius. In an observation as applicable to his own self-begetting fictions as to his elder's Work in Progress, Samuel Beckett shrewdly declared: "Mr Joyce does not take birth for granted,"[5] and it is instructive to find an invocation early in *Ulysses* of "the subtle African heresiarch Sabellius who held that the Father was Himself His own Son."[6] *A Portrait of the Artist as a Young Man* begins with the celebrated prenatal moocow fable and concludes with Stephen Dedalus, whom Johnny Cashman describes as "not his father's son,"[7] attempting to replace Simon Dedalus with another father, the old artificer Icarus, just as the twins Shem and Shaun attempt to usurp the role of the Titan H.C.E.

There are, of course, suggestive elements of modalism among the ancient gods, whether among the early generations of Greek divinities who devoured and replaced each other or in the Egyptian phoenix or bennu, living *sui generis* for five-hundred-year cycles until reborn out of its own ashes. The mother of Ra, Neith, was a self-created virgin goddess. However, the pagan faith of Sabellius has been reborn in the twentieth century, where it has become a central theme and structural principle of much of the most engaging literature.

II

Il y a une certaine matière qui veut se dire; et en un sens ce
n'est pas le romancier qui fait le roman, c'est le roman qui
se fait tout seul, et le romancier n'est que l'instrument de
sa mise au monde, son accoucheur.
Michel Butor[8]

Max Fleischer created a remarkable series of animated cartoons centering around the figure of Koko the Clown. Each episode began with a
distinctive prologue. A fountain pen would dip itself into an inkwell and
then proceed to sketch in the cartoon figures, who suddenly came to life.
When the film was over, Koko and his friends, almost like Beckett
characters, would return to the inkwell from whence they came.

I propose to define a sub-genre of the modern French, British, and
American novel which I call "the self-begetting novel." A fantasy of
Narcissus become autogamous, the self-begetting novel, like Fleischer's
cartoons, projects the illusion of art creating itself. Truly *samizdat,* in the
original sense of "self-publishing," it is an account, usually first-person,
of the development of a character to the point at which he is able to take
up his pen and compose the novel we have just finished reading. Like an
infinite recession of Chinese boxes, the self-begetting novel begins again
where it ends. Once we have concluded the central protagonist's story of
his own sentimental education, we must return to page one to commence
in a novel way the product of that process – the mature artist's novel,
which itself depicts the making of a novel. ... The final line, as in
Finnegans Wake, returns to the beginning.

This device of a narrative which is in effect a record of its own genesis is
a happy fusion of form and content. We are at once confronted with both
process and product, quest and goal, parent and child. Proust's *A la
recherche du temps perdu* is a history of Marcel's tortuous search for a
vocation; at the same time, the very existence of the book itself constitutes objective evidence of Marcel's eventual choice of a literary calling.
The nascent fiction gives life to the aging Marcel, who is in turn about to
create it. Galatea and Pygmalion embrace.

A circular form results, encouraging multiple readings. It would
please such modern craftsmen as André Gide, who confesses: "I write
only to be *re*read,"[9] and as Thomas Mann, who declares in his preface to
Der Zauberberg that the work is so constructed as to yield greater
enjoyment on the second reading. As in the dream vision and the
spiritual autobiography, the protagonist's transformation compels him
to return to us in the Cave with an account of his conversion. He must
re-create his experiences by putting them into words. The pattern in
each genuinely self-begetting novel resembles the concentric Quaker

Oats boxes on which Aldous Huxley's Philip Quarles wants to model his own book.

> Put a novelist into the novel. He justifies aesthetic generalization, which may be interesting – at least to me. He also justifies experiment. Specimens of his work may illustrate other possible or impossible ways of telling a story. And if you have him telling parts of the same story as you are, you can make a variation on the theme. But why draw the line at one novelist inside your novel? Why not a second inside his? And a third inside the novel of the second? And so on to infinity, like those advertisements of Quaker Oats where there's a Quaker holding a box of oats, on which is a picture of another Quaker holding another box of oats, on which etc., etc.[10]

The issue of to what extent the culminating act of giving birth to a novel is indeed *une issue* within these novels points to the heritage of French Naturalism. Joris-Karl Huysmans' *A rebours* (1884) revolves about the solitary des Esseintes, who, like the narrator of a self-begetting novel, retires to an isolated estate in Fontenay in order to reject the determinants of heredity and environment by fabricating every detail of his existence. Huysmans began his career as a disciple of Zola, and his most celebrated novel anticipates the tensions to be found in *A la recherche* between Decadence and Naturalism, between an assertion of the individual's sovereignty in forging his own identity and a reductive depiction of the forces which compel that assertion. Does the narrator's accomplishment in arriving at the stage where he can write a novel represent transcendence of his previously banal existence? Or is it in fact simply a necessary development in the chain of cause and effect operating throughout his life? And does the self-begetting novel's *mobile perpetuum* from life to art and back represent an upward spiral or is it simply a snake swallowing its own tail?

The status of the self-begetting novel as both process and product introduces an important dual perspective on each reading, a disparity between *temps passé* and *temps retrouvé*. A dialectic between naïve, questing hero and his narrator alter ego recollecting prior emotion in current tranquility suggests that the reading experience describes not so much a perfect circle as a Möbbius strip or Vico's *corsi e ricorsi*. The double helix is, after all, the fundamental shape of life.

The idea of a self-begetting novel is, of course, a conceit; poems are made by gods like Keats. What Flann O'Brien refers to as aesthoautogamy, the "dream of producing a living mammal from an operation involving neither fertilization nor conception,"[11] is a self-evident sham, whether applied to the narrative or to its main character. The paradigmatic figure in creating this illusion is Marcel Proust. His magnum opus is a confluence of several earlier traditions, notably the *Bildungsroman* and the *Künstlerroman*; at the same time, despite Ortega y Gasset's assertion that *A la recherche* is the last novel, it is the progenitor of a family of twentieth-century novels which conclude with their protagonists' decision to produce a novel.

"I can doubt the reality of everything but the reality of my doubt"[12] and "I no longer want to exist; I am because I think that I do not want to be"[13] come not from *Méditations* but from modern novels, from *Les Faux-Monnayeurs* and *La Nausée* respectively. For his M.A. from Trinity, Samuel Beckett – who reads *A la recherche* as "the Proustian *Discours de la méthode*"[14] – specialized in René Descartes, the self-begetting philosopher who is a narrator of Beckett's 1930 poem "Whoroscope." Descartes, who provisionally dismissed the universe in order to recreate it systematically, was also author of the suggestive titles *De la Formation du foetus* and *La Recherche de la vérité*. His achievement in thinking himself into existence has not gone unnoticed by recent egographic narrators, whose motto could be: *scribo, ergo sum*.

Jean-Paul Sartre's *La Nausée* (1938), Michel Butor's *La Modification* (1957) and Claude Mauriac's *La Marquise sortit à cinq heures* (1961) extend the Proustian formula in France. *La Nausée* concludes with Roquentin's decision to transform his life into a novel. Use of the jazz song "Some of These Days" echoes that of Vinteuil's *petite phrase* in *A la recherche*, and several studies can document the claim that Sartre's first novel is "a poor man's Proust."[15] Ensconced within a railway compartment traveling from Paris to Rome, Léon Delmont conceives the project of writing a novel which will transmute his banal existence and which will resemble *La Modification*. Claude Mauriac's novel, like *A la recherche*, incorporates extracts from the Goncourt journal, but it distributes Marcel's dual functions of creator and historian between its two central figures, Bertrand Carnéjoux and Claude Desprez.

Edouard is only one of several protagonists, and his narrative sovereignty in *Les Faux-Monnayeurs* (1925) is challenged by other fictive artists. Though Edouard keeps a diary of source material, much as did Gide,[16] for his projected novel, to be entitled *Les Faux-Monnayeurs*, it could only form part of the novel we read, which therefore remains somewhat peripheral to the self-begetting tradition. Aldous Huxley's *Point Counter Point* (1928), which according to André Maurois, "makes the 'sound' of *Swann* and *Les Faux-Monnayeurs* heard in English literature,"[17] occupies an analogous position in British fiction through its use of the diarist–novelist Philip Quarles. Similarly, because it is difficult to imagine Stephen Dedalus successful in authoring the entire novel in which he appears, *Ulysses* is not a self-begetting fiction; yet Joyce's work constantly raises the possibility, as seen in the famous discussion of *Hamlet*, in which Stephen seems to be praising Shakespeare as a consummate autogenist:

> When Rutlandbaconsouthamptonshakespeare or another poet of the same name in the comedy of errors wrote Hamlet he was not the father of his own

son merely but, being no more a son, he was and felt himself the father of all his race, the father of his own grandfather, the father of his unborn grandson . . .[18]

In fiction from the anglophonic side of the Channel, Flann O'Brien's *At Swim-Two-Birds* (1939), Iris Murdoch's *Under the Net* (1954), Lawrence Durrell's *The Alexandria Quartet* (1961) and Doris Lessing's *The Golden Notebook* (1962) concentrate on a figure who will beget both a self and a novel. Each author is somewhat alien to the Great Tradition of British realism and has strong allegiances to Continental reflexive fiction. Lessing was born in Persia and raised in Southern Rhodesia, and the title of her early autobiographical narrative, *In Pursuit of the English*, echoes Proust while stressing estrangement from the world of Trollope. O'Brien, Murdoch and Durrell, like Beckett and Joyce, their emissary doves who did not return, were all born in Ireland and are admitted francophiles. Gaelic in background and Gallic in orientation, Durrell, for one, told an interviewer in France: "Here I am happy: I am a Camembert."[19]

The same debt to the French could be cited in the careers of such Latin Americans as Ernesto Sábato and Julio Cortázar, whose respective novels *El túnel* (1948) and *Rayuela* (1963) have much in common with the self-begetting tradition. North American literature introduces its own distinctive elements when, as with *Leaves of Grass*, narrative self-consciousness becomes simultaneous consciousness of persona, nation and fiction. The idea of The Great American Novel is explicitly incorporated into William Carlos Williams's *The Great American Novel* (1923) – appropriately first published in Paris – and Clyde Brion Davis's neglected *"The Great American Novel – – "* (1938), which, like Henry Miller's *Tropic of Cancer* (1934) and *Tropic of Capricorn* (1939), recount the narrator's efforts to write The Great American Novel. The main character of William Demby's *The Catacombs* (1965) is named William Demby and is in Rome writing a book called *The Catacombs*, while Bernard Malamud's *The Tenants* (1971) centers on two competing novelists each attempting to subsume the other within the work he is begetting.

Perhaps it is no accident that the history of the self-begetting novel coincides with that of the automobile. Both are machines designed to generate their own locomotion. Yet, despite the illusion of self-sufficiency, self-begetting fictions demonstrate an unmistakable lineage. Novalis's *Heinrich von Ofterdingen*, which, unfinished at its author's death in 1801, was to have concluded with an account of its own composition, is exemplary, but it is the French reflexive tradition that is most germane to the authors of these novels. Their narratives are more than formally akin. Writing under the compelling influence of Proust, Jean-Paul Sartre,[20] Michel Butor,[21] Claude Mauriac,[22] and Samuel Beckett[23] have produced critical studies of him, and Iris Murdoch's first published book is a monograph on Sartre.[24] Claude Mauriac's *L'Alittérature contemporaine*

(1958, rev. 1969) emphasizes the fictional tradition with which he is associated as critic and novelist. Samuel Beckett's discipleship to James Joyce is legendary, and Henry Miller and Lawrence Durrell have enjoyed one of the more remarkable literary friendships of our time.

However, aside from the extrinsic matter of influence, the peculiar reflexive quality of the self-begetting novel permits it, as much a self-conscious culmination as is the New Testament, to make frequent and prolonged allusion to other literary works. Each narrator is intent on incorporating and surpassing his predecessors. And so a network of internal cross-reference among their fictions results: Murdoch evokes Sartre, Durrell evokes Proust, Lessing evokes Miller, etc. The spirit of "Proust's great poem," "the great academy of time-consciousness,"[25] haunts Durrell's tetralogy, and it is concurrence rather than coincidence that Miller's Henry resurrects his Brooklyn childhood among Aunt Caroline and Cousin Gene by biting into a thick slice of rye bread.[26]

III

For every man alone thinkes he hath got
To be a Phoenix, and that then can bee
None of that kinde, of which he is, but hee.
John Donne, "The First Anniversary," ll. 216–18

Thou, thine own daughter then, and Sire,
That Son and Mother art intire,
That big still with thy self dost go,
And liv'st an aged Embrio.
Richard Lovelace, "The Snayl," ll. 27–30

Folk wit has it that "Abraham Lincoln was born in a log cabin which he helped his father to build." The project of the self-begetting novel is to create a structure within which its main character and his fiction come to life. Perhaps Dædalus, the artist as builder, can serve here "as exemplum of the artist's vocation. As *construction* became more and more tyrannical in determining the life of the novel, the artist–architect who imposed the autotelic pattern built the labyrinth which was to be his own prison."[27] Whether nest or dungeon, the self-begetting novel begets both *a self* and *itself*. It recounts the creation of a work very much like itself, but it is also the portrait of a fictive artist being born. Like so much of the art of the past two centuries, it is a *self-portrait*: self-portrait not just in the sense of the portrait of a self, as with Van Gogh's myriad studies of Van Gogh, but a portrait of the portrait itself.

The self-begetting hero typically occupies center stage throughout this drama, and the story is, in several important senses, his story. It is literature as self-expression, and the acquisition of a name becomes an epic accomplishment for the author–protagonist. It is surely significant that Beckett's ultimate narrator is L'Innommable and that Proust's Marcel, Butor's Léon and Durrell's Darley are very rarely named. It is the book that becomes incarnation of the hero who grows up to write it and thereby earn a name for himself. The novel's title is what he in effect dubs himself. The development of the individual is inseparable from the development of the novel in which he appears and which he is to write. It is possible to declare, with Whitman, that who touches this book touches a man. Its fictive author can claim, with Flaubert and with justification, "c'est moi."

André Gide's characters, one of whom proclaims: "The future belongs to bastards,"[28] are frequently of illegitimate birth. The Rankian formula has the hero either a bastard or an orphan; he inherits nothing, not even a father, and must all alone create his identity. The American myth of the "self-made man," whether Andrew Carnegie or Dale Carnegie, holds the individual responsible for everything he has achieved through his own powers. Horatio Alger's innumerable orphan boys, like Charles Foster Kane or any number of robber barons, make something of themselves by first making themselves into their own fathers. At the age of seventeen, James Gatz rejects his parents, rechristens himself Jay Gatsby, and proceeds to father a new identity.

> His parents were shiftless and unsuccessful farm people – his imagination had never really accepted them as his parents at all. The truth was that Jay Gatsby of West Egg, Long Island sprang from his Platonic conception of himself.[29]

The future belongs to bastards and orphans because they choose it to and because, rejecting the claims of the past, they have nothing else to take possession of. The fantasy of being simultaneously father and son is primarily a fantasy of immortality, of timeless personal omnipotence.

In the self-begetting narrative, the hero forges his identity as novelist and through a novel. "Self-begetting" is not a merely fanciful critical label for these works, as is borne out by their own imagery, whether, as in Henry Miller, sexuality is a metaphor for everything or, as in Samuel Beckett, sexlessness is. Sex preoccupies the self-begetting novel's lonely and aging hero, who somehow succeeds in giving birth to twins – self and novel. The protagonist is typically solitary and single, yet his efforts are depicted as terminating in personal rebirth. And he conceives his projected novel through the explicit trope of gestation. As they begin writing, Beckett's Molloy returns to the bed in which he was born, Durrell's Darley is "like some timid girl, scared of the birth of her first child,"[30] and Miller's Henry explains: ". . . the book has begun to grow inside me. I am carrying it around with me everywhere. I walk through the streets big with child and the cops escort me across the street."[31] We never leave Nina Purefoy's maternity ward as, having concluded the account of the birth of an author and a novel, we are propelled back to its beginnings.

IV

Here it is of no use to have Abraham for one's father, nor to have seventeen ancestors – he who will not work must take note of what is written about the maidens of Israel, for he gives birth to wind, but he who is willing to work gives birth to his own father.
Søren Kierkegaard, *Fear and Trembling*[32]

Its central protagonist a novelist and its central action the conception of a novel, the self-begetting novel is supremely reflexive. Demonstrating "a consistent effort to convey to us a sense of the fictional world as an authorial construct set up against a background of literary tradition and convention,"[33] it easily satisfies Robert Alter's criterion for self-consciousness. Like slapstick farce in which the side of a building collapses to expose a demure gentleman at his bath, the self-begetting novel deliberately lays bare all its working parts. It is particularly suited for the analysis of literary theory and technique which a work like *Tom Jones* segregates in introductory chapters.

Ars poetica is, of course, at least as venerable as Horace, and the novelistic tradition had been reflexive long before "the age of suspicion" observed by Nathalie Sarraute after World War II. Harry Levin contends: "Cervantes continues to be the exemplary novelist . . . he created a new form by criticizing the old forms,"[34] And for Lionel Trilling, "all prose fiction is a variation on the theme of *Don Quixote*." [35] That theme is the relationship between art and reality – studied within a self-conscious work of art. In various ways, Shakespeare's play-within-a-play (*Pyramus and Thisbe, The Murder of Gonzago*, Portia's courtroom, Prospero's masque), the action of *Die Meistersinger*, and Alfred Hitchcock's ingenious cameo appearances in his own films all foreground their works and prevent us from ignoring the sophisticated artifice. The painter's signature in the corner of his canvas might alert even naïve Attic birds that these grapes are not edible.

We admittedly spend much of Sterne's *Tristram Shandy* waiting for our narrator to be born. But in extending the classical novel's ambivalent approach to art, the modern self-begetting novel inverts the quixotic pattern; instead of a progression from the fantasies of *Amadís* to the "real" world, its hero characteristically moves from the contingencies of life to apotheosis as novelist and within a novel. Yet the cycle of movement from life to literature begins anew with each ending, which, itself a consummation, directs us back to the flux from which it arose.

Calls by various versions of Formalism for an autonomous text and by dramatists for *Verfremdungseffekt* explain in part why modern literature is often metaliterature, a gloss on Coleridge's "Nothing can permanently please which does not contain in itself the reason why it is so and no other." The self-begetting novel exemplifies many of the elements most valued in recent theory. Roland Barthes, for example, has championed reflexive fiction and has even called for a kind of literary criticism which is self-begetting:

> All criticism must include within its discourse (whether it be in the most indirect and modest manner) an implicit commentary on itself; all criticism is criticism of the work and criticism of itself; to echo Claudel's pun, it is *connaissance* of the other and *co-naissance* of itself in the world.[36]

It is a veritable post-War baby boom.

V

Das macht, ich bin kein ausgeklügelt Buch.
Ich bin ein Mensch mit seinem Widerspruch.
Conrad Ferdinand Meyer, "Huttens letze Tage"

The Beckett trilogy – *Molloy* (1951), *Malone meurt* (1952) and *L'Innomm-able* (1953) – provides a thematic, but not chronological, limit to this novelistic tradition. Within the span of three decades, the self-begetting novel moves from paradigm to parody. Beginning with the wretched figure of Molloy on his death bed writing pages as they are snatched from him, Beckett's fiction rehearses the assassination of the poet presaged by Apollinaire and enacted by Charles Kinbote. Each successive narrator–author is aware of his predecessors. But all are inadequate, because onymous, avatars of an unnamable voice who scoffs at his circus animals in the act of parading them before us. When art examines itself here, both physician and patient are exposed as fools.

The self-begetting novel begins with an urge toward immortality. Mortal father yields to mortal son, but the life of the autonomous father–son can still shine bright in and through black ink. Proust proclaims the permanent triumph of literature over time; *A la recherche* succeeds in the creation of an enduring identity and fiction. However, with Beckett we move from the exuberance of Pygmalion to the despair of Frankenstein. Mauriac's novel begins with "The marquise went out at five o'clock" and concludes with the retraction "The marquise did not go out at five o'clock." Similarly, like Yves Tinguely's machine engineered to self-destruct, Beckett's Moran constructs a fiction at the outset of his narrative – "It is midnight. The rain is beating on the windows" – only to demolish it in his final lines – "It was not midnight. It was not raining."

From Proust to Sartre to Beckett, the entire project of novel-writing becomes increasingly suspect. Our revels now are ended, and we are left, like Alice, with the biblioclasmic realization that the elaborate artifice constructed before our eyes is "nothing but a pack of cards."

However, each Beckett narrator prolongs his existence and that of the work in which he appears in the very act of assailing both. The journeys of Molloy and Moran describe a circle, and their stories recount how they came to write what we read. The reader is again returned to the first page after he has reached the last, insuring eternal life for a suicidal narrative. While Marcel's faith in the powers of art perennially begets a new self and a new novel, Beckett's *Liebestod* is a cry of contempt for the individual and his fiction. Ironically and, for the narrators, frustratingly, such scorn provides no less egographic than Marcel's aesthetic creed. From Proust to Beckett, we move from the House of Cadmus to the House of Atreus, from autogamy to autophagy. But fathers and sons have always been problems for the novel. Tithonus chirping for death only demonstrates his continuing vitality. Despite and by means of its renunciations, the trilogy augments the patrimony of self-begetting fiction.

2 Marcel's Self-Begetting Novel

Freund, es ist auch genug. Im Fall du mehr willst lesen,
So geh und werde selbst die Schrift und selbst das Wesen

Angelus Silesius, "Beschluss"

I THE RETURN TO COMBRAY

At the beginning of *Le Temps retrouvé*, the final volume of Proust's massive narrative cycle, Marcel recounts his return to Combray. The visit occurs shortly before the war and the aging protagonist's retirement from the world to a sanatorium. It marks the culmination of a long series of disappointments. Marcel has ranged far beyond the homogeneous child's world of Combray, where the clock tower of Saint-Hilaire, a prefiguration of the triumphal symbiosis of time and art, "donnait à toutes les occupations, à toutes les heures, à tous les points de vue de la ville, leur figure, leur couronnement, leur consécration"[1] [provided all occupations, all hours, all views of the town with their shape, their coronation, their consecration.] He has apparently penetrated the most exclusive social circles, attracted the most desirable young women, and journeyed to the most exotic locales. Yet each stage in Marcel's conquest of the world is inevitably disillusioning, since vanquished reality is always vapid in contrast to prior illusions. "On n'aime plus personne dès qu'on aime", [You no longer love anyone as soon as you love.](I, 399–400). Just after his own version of death in Venice at the end of *La Fugitive*, Marcel, world-weary and purged of all future ambition, comes home to Combray to discover that, in ironic counterpoint to the title of the volume, *Le Temps retrouvé*, the past for him is at this moment irretrievably lost. "You can't go home again," declares Thomas Wolfe, and Marcel here is struck by the realization that the delightful, coherent realm of his youth has vanished forever.

This marks the most complete disillusionment in the entire novel. At the very outset of *Le Temps retrouvé*, we are presented with a starker image of "le temps perdu" than anything that has preceded it. Marcel's

Combray is destroyed more brutally for him in this sojourn than it later is in fact during savage combat between French and German troops. Ironically, all that Marcel is able to resurrect from the past is "le sentiment que jamais je ne serais capable d'écrire" [the feeling that never would I be able to write] (III, 691), a sense of artistic unworthiness which, along with his literary aspirations, has accompanied him throughout his life.

Gilberte, whom Marcel is visiting in Tansonville, makes three revelations to him. These intensify the alienation from the past already felt in his alarming lack of interest in old haunts. By suggesting that they take a short walk to the Guermantes chateau, Gilberte demolishes his youthful notion of Guermantes as an emblem of infinity. And she shows Marcel the source of the Vivonne river, which he had formerly envisioned as "something as extra-terrestrial as the Entrance to Hell." It stands before him now as merely "une espèce de lavoir carré où montaient des bulles" [a kind of square basin where bubbles rose to the surface.] (III, 693). Finally, evoking what has been a central tableau – that of the beautiful but inaccessible young girl behind the hedges at Tansonville during one of Marcel's walks with his father and grandfather – Gilberte now discloses that, far from having scorned him, she had actually been in love with the young Marcel and had made an erotic gesture toward him.

But Marcel's most striking disillusionment comes with the collapse of his conception of the two "ways." Guermantes and Méséglise are no longer the two fully distinct worlds the child had imagined when a road in each direction emanated from opposite corners of Combray. Robert de Saint Loup, nephew of the Duchess de Guermantes, has married Gilberte Swann, thereby uniting Guermantes and Swann. This would have been inconceivable to the younger, more naïve Marcel who was able to impose order on his limited universe precisely by formulating antinomies like the Guermantes way and Swann's way. On his return to Combray, he makes the startling discovery that it is possible to arrive at the Guermantes chateau by taking the Méséglise road. At this point, his provisional organization of the universe in terms of two principles – one correlating lofty aristocratic domains, social success, and the aquatic environment of the Guermantes road, and one linking the bourgeois world, love, and the terrestrial scenes of the Méséglise road – crumbles. He is not yet ready to replace it with a vision of the unity of life, and he is at this point left with nothing.

The opening of *Le Temps retrouvé* represents the nadir of the protagonist's spiritual progress. Marcel has attained the very center of the Inferno, but, like Dante, he must first experience the most extreme desolation before discovering that he is in fact on the road to salvation.

It is at Tansonville that Gilberte, who earlier has been a link for him with his favorite author, Bergotte, lends Marcel a copy of the Goncourt journal. He reads an account there of the Verdurin salon which portrays it as quite different from what he had known. Marcel, spending part of the night reading the Goncourt journal, just as he had done formerly with *François le champi*, is seized by profound despair; he is convinced that the disparity between his impressions and those of the Goncourts is yet another proof of his own inadequacy. And even if he could write, literature is an idle calling, and "la vie apprend à rabaisser le prix de la lecture, et nous montre que ce que l'écrivain nous vante ne valait pas grand-chose" [life teaches us to deprecate the value of reading and shows us that what the writer boasts about was not worth much](III, 720).

Yet a suggestion that "la lecture au contraire nous apprend à relever la valeur de la vie, valeur que nous n'avons pas su apprécier et dont nous nous rendons compte seulement par le livre combien elle était grande"[reading, on the contrary, teaches us to exalt the value of life, a value which we did not know how to appreciate, since it is only through a book that we realize how great it was] (III, 720), persists and represents the seed of his recovery. Even more than with the humiliation during Norpois's suave dismissal of literature in general and of his own youthful efforts in particular, Marcel's artistic aspirations are virtually extinguished. But a glimmer yet remains:

> D'abord, en ce qui me concernait personnellement, mon incapacité de regarder et d'écouter, que le journal cité avait si péniblement illustrée pour moi, n'était pas totale. Il y avait en moi un personnage qui savait plus ou moins bien regarder, mais c'était un personnage intermittent, ne reprenant vie que quand se manifestait quelque essence générale, commune à plusieurs choses, qui faisait sa nourriture et sa joie (III, 718).

> [First, in what concerned me personally, my inability to look and to listen, which the journal excerpt had so painfully illustrated for me, was not total. There was in me a character who knew more or less how to look, but it was an intermittent character, coming to life only when there was revealed some general essence, common to several things, which provided his nourishment and his joy.]

It is this other self which ultimately redeems Marcel's lost time and is responsible for producing the novel we read: an objective account of the discovery and strengthening of a self capable of presenting an objective account of itself. Marcel's vocation as novelist, dimly present from the beginning of his life and demonstrated through the existence of the life, takes definitive form at the triumphant conclusion of *Le Temps retrouvé*. The veritable return to Combray, however, occurs not in *Le Temps retrouvé* but in the introductory "Combray" section of *Du Côté de chez Swann*. To the jaded and ailing protagonist at the outset of the final volume, Combray is *le temps perdu* he is incapable of recovering. But the existence of Combray back at the beginning of the first volume demonstrates that Marcel has found his calling, his past, and his self. Protagonist and narrator, distinct throughout, finally merge.

Marcel has already lived in the idyllic Combray, and we have already read about it. But in the Proustian world, relationships, not objects, possess substantive reality,[2] and it is only through a juxtaposition of past and present, me and not-me that any of the separate terms – vacuous in isolation – acquires meaning. Thus, the quest for knowledge of the self, of the world, and of time which *A la recherche du temps perdu* both describes and exemplifies can only succeed by returning on its own tracks. Cognition requires re-cognition; as Georges Poulet affirms, "La seule connaissance de soi possible, c'est donc la re-connaissance."[3] We must become re-readers, and Marcel must write the novel which begins again at Combray, which in fact never ceases to begin again at Combray.

II EN FLAGRANT DÉLIT

A la recherche teems with a more motley cast of artists of all sorts than *Paradise Lost* does with angels. Bergotte, Vinteuil, and Elstir, representing literature, music and painting. respectively, are the three most important influences on the young Marcel. But the actresses la Berma and Rachel, the violinist Morel, the poetaster Bloch, the art critic *manqué* Swann, the cook Françoise, the diplomat Norpois, and even the various salon impressarios each represent an attempt to impose an artistic order on life. The protagonist learns his lessons from all of these sources and is ultimately able to assimilate them into a comprehensive artistic vision which is in fact *A la recherche*.

Marcel's contacts with literature in particular could be traced from beginning to end of the book. There is *François le champi*, which, significantly, his mother reads to him on the evening he takes the bold step of writing a note to her; the récit he writes in Percepied's carriage while gazing at the steeples of Martinville and Vieuxvicq; his relationship with Bergotte; his own article in *le Figaro*; the Goncourt journal; *François le champi*, which he opens in the Prince de Guermantes's library; his final determination to write his own novel. Writing, like any artistic activity, and like love, becomes for Proust emblematic of cognition. It is a means of discovering and expressing the relationship between self and world.

In any case, the pointillist profusion of artist figures and discussions about art from one end of the novel to the other, from the narrator's opening reference to falling asleep reading a book to his closing remarks about the novel he will write, introduces an element of emphatic self-consciousness. *A la recherche* is a highly sophisticated artifice which incorporates an awareness of its problematic status vis-à-vis "reality" into almost every page and certainly into its total design. The occurrence of pastiche reinforces the fact that we are voyeurs at a procreation.

Proust's and Marcel's work is thus squarely within the self-conscious novelistic tradition of Cervantes, Fielding and Flaubert. Don Quixote reads *Amadís* and then jousts with windmills, and Emma Bovary rushes into love affairs after reading sentimental novels; Marcel reads George Sand and Bergotte, but his resulting adventures transform him into a greater author than his mentors. Fielding read Richardson's *Pamela* and reacted by surpassing it with *Joseph Andrews*, a fact which, however, does not enter into the texture of the latter work as completely as does the movement in and out of art and life in *A la recherche*. Earlier novels prominently feature artist figures, and des Esseintes is a more thorough-going aesthete than even Marcel. However, *A la recherche* represents the supreme culmination of the reflexive novelist tradition. Erich Heller's comment on *Doktor Faustus* is as applicable to Proust's work: "There is no critical thought which the book does not think *about itself*."[4] It incorporates a pervasive awareness of the problems of the artist into its own structure, so that the work itself becomes explicitly the story of its own genesis.

The C. K. Scott Moncrieff English translation of the title, *Remembrance of Things Past*, lacks the resonance of *A la recherche du temps perdu*. The line from Shakespeare's Sonnet 30 conveys a poignant sense of emotion recollected in tranquillity, but it limits the implications of the work to that. Similarly, Leo Bersani, emphasizing the retrospection by which the narrator can organize his material, asserts: "The peculiar exclusion of the future from Proust's narrator's point of view on the past gives him an authorial control over the past."[5] However, there is an endless narrative future. *A la recherche du temps perdu* certainly attempts to come to terms with *le temps perdu*, but it is itself decidedly a continuing *recherche*. The novel is at once the account of a former quest and itself a current quest. It is no more possible to hypostatize reality within a fixed artifice than it is to imprison Albertine permanently. *A la recherche du temps perdu* accentuates its fidelity to flux; *à la recherche*, it is like "a dizzying kaleidoscope" (III,519), "perpetually becoming" (III, 1041).

Beyond its relationship to its own origins and goals, *A la recherche* also incorporates speculations on the nature of novelistic tradition and therefore presumably on its own relationship to the history of literature. Marcel the narrator affirms the possibility of cumulative development, if not improvement, in the arts. The world "was created not once but as often as an original artist has come along" (II, 327), and therefore "each new writer seemed to me to have progressed beyond his predecessor" (II,328).

T. S. Eliot, shrewdly pointing out that we know so much more than dead writers and it is precisely they whom we know, makes the following observation which is manifestly relevant to Proust: "But the difference between the present and the past is that the conscious present is an awareness of the past in a way and to an extent which the past's awareness of itself cannot show."[6] And Marcel likewise maintains that a new work of art is something more than the sum total of its predecessors:

> C'est ainsi que bâille d'avance d'ennui un lettré à qui on parle d'un nouveau "beau livre," parce qu'il imagine une sorte de composé de tous les beaux livres qu'il a lu, tandis qu'un beau livre est particulier, imprévisible, et n'est pas fait de la somme de tous les chefs-d'oeuvres précédents, mais de quelque chose que s'être parfaitement assimilé cette somme ne suffit nullement à faire trouver, car c'est justement en dehors d'elle (I, 656).

> [It is thus that an experienced reader yawns immediately when he hears of a new "good book," because he imagines a sort of amalgam of all the good books he has read, whereas a good book is special, unforeseeable, and not the sum total of all preceding masterpieces, but something which the most perfect assimilation of the parts would not help him to discover, since it is precisely something outside the sum.]

A la recherche is more than an amalgamation of such obvious sources as Saint-Simon and *The Arabian Nights*. It transcends them through its awareness of them. Just as this novel incorporates a consciousness of its own status as a work of art into the dramatic creation of that work of art, it also has a built-in recognition of the relationship between an individual novel and the flow of literary history.

Marcel's speculations on aesthetic issues and on the specific techniques of the work he creates are sprinkled throughout the novel. It would even be possible to cull a rich treasury of Proustian epigrams from reflections scattered through *A la recherche*,[7] a fact which might set this work apart from the mainstream of modernist literature, committed to "showing" and not to "telling" and to a situation in which "the artist, like the God of the creation, remains within or behind or beyond or above his handiwork, invisible, refined out of existence, indifferent, paring his fingernails."[8]

Yet Marcel is the author, but he is not Proust the author; the argument of *Contre Sainte-Beuve* is indeed that the writer creates a self distinct from his biographical one. The drama *shown* to us in this novel is that of the protagonist becoming the author of the novel in which he appears. *A la recherche* becomes at once an essay on literature and an essay at literature. René Girard sees the work conforming to the triangular pattern of *médiation* he traces from Cervantes to Dostoevsky, and for him "*A la Recherche du temps perdu* is a novel, and it is the exegesis of this novel."[9] At one point, in a characteristically stunning metaphorical leap, Marcel declares, "Une œuvre où il y a des théories est comme un objet sur lequel on laisse la marque du prix" [A work in which there are theories is like an object on which the price tag has been left] (III,882). But the exegesis here *is* the novel, and the price tag *is* the article. Reading the most consistently contrived exemplar of the reflexive tradition, we catch a fictive creator *flagrante delicto*. Not only are we revealed a portrait of the artist as young and old man, but we see the portrait being created by its subject, as the work becomes both process and product. We assist at a birth, and it is awesome.

III   THE SELF-BEGETTING NOVEL AND THE BEGETTING OF A SELF

After describing some of his desperate efforts to ascertain the precise nature of Albertine's conduct in the past, Marcel observes that novelists often claim the story they are about to unfold was told by someone they had met while traveling. And this tale is in fact the novel.

> Ainsi la vie de Fabrice del Dongo fût racontée à Stendhal par un chanoine de Padoue. Combien nous voudrions, quand nous aimons, c'est-à-dire quand l'existence d'une autre personne nous semble mystérieuse, trouver un tel narrateur informé! Et certes il existe (III, 551).

> [Thus the life of Fabrice del Dongo was told to Stendhal by a canon from Padua. How much would we like when we are in love, in other words when someone else's existence seems mysterious to us, to find such an informed narrator! And certainly he exists.]

These remarks on the elusive quality of the beloved are as appropriate a formulation of the narrative problems for the novel itself. The convention of a reliable outside observer, as in *La Chartreuse de Parme*, is no longer viable for a reality which is as fugitive as time and love. Throughout the novel, we are, among other things, *à la recherche d'un tel narrateur informé*. The convention that "certainly he exists" corresponds to intimations of immortality which surface at various points in Marcel's life as his "invisible vocation" attempts to assert itself. Just as the *magnum opus* – "the work which I was perhaps carrying within me" (I, 809) – has been gestating in him all his life, Marcel has been slouching back toward Combray, waiting to be born. The narrator who develops is never totally *informé*, just as the novel is never fully authoritative. Both, within the pattern of self-begetting novels and novelists, remain "perpetually becoming."

Within a spacious work providing exhaustive details on Charlus's mannerisms and each of Bloch's metamorphoses, it is bizarre that we are never provided with a direct description of the central protagonist. We are made acutely aware of his aging. At the Prince de Guermantes's reception, he is treated as a venerable ancient when he still considers himself young. But how old is he during the Combray period and his flirtations with Gilberte? We do know that Marcel suffers from an illness for most of his life, but its exact nature remains obscure. Instead, the disorder is characterized primarily by its inhibiting effects; it mysteriously impedes the young man from participating directly and vigorously in some activities, and it is ultimately responsible for his complete withdrawal from social life for several years to live in a sanatorium. For the most part, we know much more about the protagonist's acquaintances, experiences, and aspirations than about his substantial self. Marcel's identity is as elusive as that of Albertine or Odette. Marcel's ceaseless attempts to transform himself into the object of his own consciousness anticipate those of The Unnamable. Precise knowledge of any being, even the self, is unattainable.

> ... car tandis que se rectifie la vision que nous avons de lui, lui-même, qui n'est pas un objectif inerte, change pour son compte, nous pensons le rattraper, il se déplace, et, croyant le voir enfin plus clairement, ce n'est que les images anciennes que nous en avions prises que nous avons réussi à éclaircir, mais qui ne le représentent plus (I, 874).

> [... for while the vision which we have of it is adjusted, it, not being an inert object, changes for its part; we think we can catch it, it moves on, and, believing we will at least see it more clearly, we only succeed in clearing up the old images which we had acquired but which no longer represent it]

A remarkable feature of Golo, the character in the boy's magic lantern repertoire, is that he assumes the shape of his container. Marcel focuses the lantern on every corner of his bedroom, but:

> Le corps de Golo lui-même, d'une essence aussi surnaturelle que celui de sa monture s'arrangeait de tout obstacle matériel, de tout objet gênant qu'il rencontrait en le prenant comme ossature et en se le rendant intérieur, fût-ce le bouton de la porte sur lequel s'adaptait aussitôt et surnageait invinciblement sa robe rouge ou sa figure pâle toujours aussi noble et aussi mélancolique, mais qui ne laissait paraître aucun trouble de cette transvertébration (I, 10).

> [The body of Golo himself, of a substance as supernatural as his steed, would overcome any material obstacle, any obstruction he encountered, transforming it into his skeleton and absorbing it into himself – the door handle, for instance, over which his red robe would immediately adapt itself and float invincibly, or else his pale face which was always just as noble and melancholic but never betrayed any disturbance over this transubstantiation]

Marcel exhibits the same "negative capability" as does Golo. With Tennyson's Ulysses, he can declare "I am a part of all that I have met." He becomes inseparable from the novel in which he appears, an account of the quest to define him which paradoxically succeeds while it remains a quest. If the self-begetting and the begetting of the self ever cease, "il se déplace," and he escapes forever our epistemological reach.

In the dynamic unity that is *A la recherche*, provisional distinctions between the self and the external world collapse, and Marcel becomes the world of the novel. This transmutation of straw into gold is prefigured on the opening page of *Du côté de chez Swann*. The narrator describes how, falling asleep while reading a book, he dreams that he is in the universe of the book. Moreover, he projects himself into the *objects* of that universe:

> . . . je n'avais pas cessé en dormant de faire des réflexions sur ce que je venais de lire, mais ces réflexions avaient pris un tour un peu particulier; il me semblait que j'étais moi-même ce dont parlait l'ouvrage: une église, un quatour, la rivalité de François Ier et de Charles Quint (I, 3).

> [. . . I had not stopped thinking, while sleeping, about what I had just read, but these thoughts had taken a direction of their own; I imagined that I was myself the subject of the work: a church, a quartet, the rivalry between Francois I and Charles V.]

By the end of *A la recherche*, Marcel has found his vocation as writer, which has all along been his latent authentic self. And implicit in the notion of Marcel as reflexive novelist is the continuing effort to capture his own reality, to incarnate himself in his work. Marcel, in fact, only comes to life when he becomes both subject and object of the novel. "La vraie vie, la vie enfin découverte et éclaircie, la seule vie par conséquent réellement vécue, c'est la littérature" [True life, life at last discovered and clarified, the only life therefore really lived is literature] (III, 895). Who touches this book touches a man. According to Rimbaud's formula, "je est un autre," I am an other. The goal of Proust's Socratic narrator is to project himself as object of his own consciousness.

During the course of thousands of pages, we never learn the surname of the major figure in the novel, and only three times – all within the same short note from Albertine (III, 157) – is the name "Marcel" applied directly to him. In Marcel Muller's apt remark, "As for his name, it seems protected by an interdiction as severe as the one which stamps the name of Jehovah."[10] Michihiko Suzuki[11] and Harold A. Waters,[12] after studying early versions of Proust's published manuscripts, each advance the plausible argument that the attribution of the name "Marcel" to the protagonist should not be accepted uncritically. They point to elaborate circumlocutions employed throughout precisely to avoid naming the hero, as well as to manuscript passages in which the name "Marcel" was suppressed by Proust in his revisions for publications. As for the passage in *La Prisonnière* in which "Marcel" did reach print, Suzuki questions whether this finally establishes the narrator's name.

> No, for it is necessary to take into account the fact that this passage occurs in the part which was not corrected by Proust. Death came to put an end to his

maniacal desire to perfect and revise without end. Otherwise, he would have modified the passage and would have inserted some sort of sentence to call attention to the appearance of the name. . . . [13]

Waters arrives at the conclusion that: "if Proust had had time to revise 'La Prisonnière' satisfactorily, the quotation in question would have no longer mentioned Marcel."[14]

According to Suzuki and Waters, Proust's main concern in suppressing the name was to avoid any possible confusion between himself and the character he created in a novel. This is compatible with his insistence in *Contre Sainte-Beuve* that a work of literature not be confounded with the life of its author. *A la recherche* remains, by circumstances and by design, a great unfinished cathedral. Yet for convenience critics will continue to refer to its protagonist and narrator as "Marcel," as if possession of a name did not suggest that character and creation were in fact finished.

Proust's Marcel becomes somewhat similar to Geoffrey Chaucer's narrator-protagonist Geoffrey, who is as infrequently mentioned by name in *The Canterbury Tales* and *The House of Fame*. Geoffrey is likewise a passive figure who is more sinned against than sinning, and his timorousness is exaggerated for comic effect. Yet, with both Marcel and Geoffrey, there is an implicit sense that their experiences and observations will be transformed into a work of art, the one in fact which we read. A denial of self ultimately leads to the assertion of a self integrated into an objectified world.

As the sections "Nom de pays: Le Nom" in *Du Côté de chez Swann* and "Nom de pays: Le Pays" in *A l'ombre des jeunes filles en fleurs* testify, names are as vital in the novel as they are in Genesis. Such names as Balbec and Venice or Guermantes and Bergotte are as infinitely suggestive to the young Marcel as the etymology of French names is to the Combray priest who visits Léonie. In effect never abandoning "the age at which one believes that he creates what he names" (I, 91), Marcel endows words with mystical properties. Passing through the Champs-Elysées, he overhears the name "Gilberte," which instantly furnishes nebulous impressions with substantial reality. "Ainsi passa près de moi ce nom de Gilberte, donné comme un talisman qui me permettrait peut-être de retrouver un jour celle dont il venait de faire une personne et qui, l'instant d'avant, n'était qu'une image incertaine" [Thus passed near me the name of Gilberte, provided like a talisman which would perhaps permit me someday to rediscover the one whom it had just brought into existence and who, just an instant earlier, was only a dim image] (I,142), Adam asserts his dominion over beast and fowl by naming them, and the narrator, beginning with Guermantes and Méséglise as the two categories under which everything is subsumed, proceeds to bring a complex world of titles, genealogies and place names under his control.

But artistic power derives from the *manipulation* of names, which sometimes requires their temporary suppression. "If God the Father created things by naming them, it is by removing their name or providing them with another that the artist recreates them." It is significant that the protagonist of *A la recherche* is anonymous throughout most, if not all, of the novel. Like the main character in Sand's *François le champi*, "Marcel" begins as a foundling of sorts who eventually "makes it" in the world precisely by making the world. Like any visionary or pilgrim, he begins with the conviction of his own unworthiness and of a chasm between the self and the external world. The foundling is gradually adopted into the more exclusive circles of society, until at the end he is welcomed at the Guermantes reception as if he possessed the most regal title. Like an epic hero, he must achieve a name for himself; like Odysseus, he must overcome his status as "Noman."

Similarly, the novelistic activity within *A la recherche* represents a search for the protagonist's identity, which is his name. To the extent that the fictional novelist succeeds in projecting a living figure who is inseparable from everything he has experienced, Marcel becomes onymous. The creation of the novel we read is a supreme act of naming, and *A la recherche* as a dynamic continuum becomes itself an ostensive definition – the only kind to keep label from libel – of its central figure. Given the thousands of pages in each of the infinite readings of the novel, "Marcel" is a pardonable abbreviation for the begotten self.

IV   THE MIRROR AND THE MAGIC LANTERN

Marcel attempts to seize both the day and eternity, *le jour* and *toujours*, in his novelist's way. He undertakes the epic task of coming to terms with reality, whether reality be something within or beyond, a function of the self or of the external world. The structure of *A la recherche* suggests the novel is a search for the truth which it itself is. And such expressions as "en réalité," "certes," "il est vrai que," or "à vrai dire" recur frequently enough to reinforce the epistemological concerns implicit in the form of the fiction.

One of the most pervasive notions in *A la recherche* is that of something beyond, "au-delà." A propos of his investigations after the fugitive Albertine, Marcel speaks of:

Mensonges, erreurs en deçà de la réalité profonde que nous n'apercevions pas, vérité au-delà, vérité de nos caractères dont les lois essentielles nous échappaient et demandent le Temps pour se révéler, vérité de nos destins aussi (III, 507).

[Falsehoods, errors on this side of the profound reality which we were not aware of, the transcendent truth, truth about our characters whose essential laws have been escaping us and require Time to reveal themselves, truth also of our fates]

He thus posits a transcendent truth in opposition to an immanent falsehood, as when he elsewhere declares, "It seems that certain transcendent realities emit radiations to which the masses are sensitive" (I, 450).

Likewise, it follows that a book of value, of truth even, must lead us beyond, must constitute an original departure from accepted tradition. Although fiction, it ". . . might open for us perspectives on the new, on the unknown, might open sleeping senses in us for the contemplation of universes which we would never have known" (III, 216). Such a doctrine approaches Charles Baudelaire's compulsion to plumb the unknown in guest of novelty to journey "au fond de l'Inconnu pour trouver du *nouveau!*" It is, in fact, possible to view the several trips Marcel makes to Balbec, Doncières or Venice as an attempt to transcend *l'en deçà* and arrive *au delà*, the locus of the unknown and the new, of the mystical source of the Combray Vivonne. What matters and what is real are beyond, and Marcel's life is an accelerated reaching out, a progressive exhaustion of novelty.

Love, like travel or entry into different social milieux, is a catapult for transcendence. To the extent that a woman remains recalcitrant to him, she interests Marcel. He loves her, just as the child loved what surrounded but was independent of him – "en ce temps-là tout ce qui n'était pas moi, la terre et les êtres, me paraissait plus précieux, plus important, doué d'une existence plus réelle que cela ne paraît aux hommes faits" [at that time everything that was not myself, the earth and its beings, seemed to me more precious, more important, endowed with an existence more real than it appears to grown men] (I, 157). But as soon as a woman relinquishes her sovereignty and becomes his prisoner, moving from "beyond" to "within" he is apathetic. This paradigm of love pervades the novel, notably in the cases of Gilberte, the Duchesse de Guermantes, Albertine, Odette, and Rachel. Love, nothing other than "space and time made perceptible to the heart" (III,385), is thus the protagonist's analogue of the narrator's activity in moving outward, toward the external world, to discover the unknown for his novel.

However, truth is also seen as a hidden treasure waiting to be excavated. For example, Marcel speaks of "that truth which I had not known how to extract from the performance of la Berma" (I, 456), as well as of "some precious and true element hidden in the heart of each thing then extracted from it by this great writer thanks to his genius" (I, 550).With truth internal rather than external now, it becomes a question "de la profondeur, la seule direction qui ne nous soit pas fermée, où nous puissions progresser, avec plus de peine il est vrai, pour un résultat de vérité" [of depth, the only direction which is not blocked to us, where we could proceed, with admittedly more trouble, toward a truthful result] (I, 907). Even love becomes a projection of internal states out onto an external object.

These two provisional conceptions of truth are as arbitrary a polarization as are the Guermantes and Méséglise ways. Each becomes as cruel and implacable a mistress to Marcel as is Odette to Swann. Truth, whether internal or external, demands all of his powers in an unremitting effort. One pause and everything, time included, is lost. Self-effacing servitude to this supreme reality is the only course; "il faut sacrifier son amour du moment, ne pas penser à son goût, mais à une vérité qui ne vous demande pas vos préférences et vous défend d'y songer" [it is necessary to sacrifice one's love of the moment, not think of one's taste but of a truth which does not ask you your preferences and forbids you to think of them] (III, 1044). This truth is universally accessible, but, like the ultimate love object, eternally independent.

> D'ailleurs que nous occupions une place sans cesse accrue dans le Temps, tout le monde le sent, et cette universalité ne pouvait que me réjouir puisque c'est la vérité, la vérité soupçonnée par chacun, que je devais chercher à élucider (III, 1046).

> [Moreover, we occupied a place endlessly growing in Time; everyone feels it, and this universality could only delight me, since it is the truth, the truth each of us suspects, which I had to attempt to bring to light]

Agents of Youdi's organization and of obscure but imperious voices, the narrators of Beckett's novels, fashioned no less thoroughly by an epistemological dialectic, will likewise act in selfless obedience to a sense of duty as austere as tat of a Biblical Patriarch.

The artist emerges as an intermediary agent of revelation, an interpreter of the absolute. The writer, in bondage to a reality greater than himself, can only express it, however imperfectly, in his work. The image of the artist as glass, of the work as, in Stendhal's phrase, "a mirror conveyed along a roadway," emerges here. It is after an admiration, at times misdirected, for Bergotte lasting seven volumes that Marcel reflects: "Si j'avais compris jadis que ce n' est pas le plus spirituel, le plus instruit, le mieux relationné des hommes, mais celui qui sait devenir miroir et refléter ainsi sa vie, fût-elle médiocre, qui devient un Bergotte" [If I had only understood before that it is not the smartest, the most informed, the best placed of men, but rather the one who knows how to become a mirror and thus reflect his life, however mediocre, who becomes a Bergotte] (III, 722). This mirror, insignificant in itself, is important only as means for transmitting a vaster reality. Writing becomes a process of self-extinction, consistent with Marcel's near-anonymity and his "negative capability" reminiscent of Golo's ability to assume the shape of whatever object in the room the magic lantern focuses on. A translator has no business being flamboyant.

> Je m'apercevais que ce livre essentiel, le seul livre vrai, un grand écrivain n'a pas, dans le sens courant, à l'inventer, puisqu'il existe déjà en chacun de nous, mais à le traduire. Le devoir et la tâche d'un écrivain sont ceux d'un traducteur (III, 890).

> [I was becoming aware that for this essential book, the only real book, a great writer does not, in the current sense, have to invent, since it already exists in each of us, but rather to translate it. The duty and the task of a writer are those of a translator]

The task is immense and exhausting, and the more of a cipher the laborer is the better, since he can then surrender himself fully to the work.

> De même ceux qui produisent des œuvres géniales ne sont pas ceux qui vivent dans le milieu le plus délicat, qui ont la conversation la plus brillante, la culture la plus étendue, mais ceux qui ont eu le pouvoir, cessant brusquement de vivre pour eux-mêmes, de rendre leur personnalité pareille à un miroir, de telle sorte que leur vie, si médiocre d' ailleurs qu'elle pouvait être mondainement et même dans un certain sens, intéllectuellement parlant, s'y reflète . . . . (I, 554 – 5).

> [Likewise those who produce works of genius are not those who live in the most refined setting, who have the most brilliant conversation, who are the most extensively cultivated, but those who have the ability, abruptly ceasing to live for themselves, to render their personality identical to a mirror, so that their life, however mediocre it might otherwise be in worldly and even, in a certain sense, in intellectual terms, is reflected there]

A mirror possesses no identity outside of that which it must reflect.

But in the very sentence in which he describes artists as "abruptly ceasing to live for themselves," Marcel shifts his emphasis and adds: "genius consisting of reflecting power and not of the intrinsic quality of the reflected phenomenon" (I, 555). He seems now to stress the subject, the writer, although still a mirror, and not the object. Furthermore, the narrator appears to reverse his other notions of the effacement of the artist when, in the *madeleine* scene, he ponders the role of the mind.

> C'est à lui de trouver la vérité. Mais comment? Grave incertitude, toutes les fois que l'esprit se sent dépassé par lui-même; quand lui, le chercheur, est tout ensemble le pays obscur où il doit chercher et où tout son bagage ne lui sera de rien. Chercher? pas seulement: créer. Il est en face de quelque chose qui n'est pas encore et que seul il peut réaliser, puis faire entrer dans la lumière (I, 45).

[It is up to it to discover the truth. But how? Grave uncertainty every time the mind feels surpassed by itself - when it, the seeker, is simultaneously the dark country where it must seek and where all its baggage is useless. Seek? Not just that but: create. It confronts something which as yet is not and which it alone can realize and then bring into the light]

Rather than the pre-existent and independent noumenon which one can only attempt to illuminate, reality according to this becomes the creation of the artist. What matters is the searcher and not what he seeks, since it is the quest which creates its own goal.

From one end of *A la recherche* to the other, these two conceptions contend. One insists on the object and the pilgrim's need to sacrifice himself, while the other emphasizes the creative function of actualizing what previously did not exist. Even Marcel's aesthetic theories do not escape this ostensible contradiction. At one point, he declares:

Ce livre, le plus pénible de tous à déchiffrer, est aussi le seul que nous ait dicté la réalité, le seul dont "l'impression" ait été faite en nous par la réalité même. De quelque idée laissée en nous par la vie qu'il s'agisse, sa figure matérielle, tracé de l'impression qu'elle nous a faite, est encore le gage de sa vérité nécessaire (III, 880).

[This book, the most difficult of all to decipher, is also the only one which reality has dictated to us, the only one "impressed" on us by reality itself. No matter what idea life has left in us, its material form, traced out of the imprint it made in us, is still the proof of its necessary truth]

This idea of the dictation of impressions suggests a mimetic theory: art consists of an imitation of primary reality. At the same time, it brings to mind the figure of the impressionist painter Elstir, who neutralizes his extraordinary mental equipment in order to appear before nature as a *tabula rasa*. The relationship between the artist and the universe is that between a reader and a book. Yet the narrator also declares that "no one could help me with any rule; this reading consisted of an act of creation in which no one could fill in for us or even collaborate with us" (III, 879). And art once again becomes a unique creation and not an imitation.

A la recherche is thus a vast suspension of polarities. Aside from Méséglise and Guermantes and the self and the world, even more structurally and epistemologically basic are those of immanence and transcendence and creation and reflection. Clearly, presentation of conflicting approaches to literature and reality is appropriate in a work which discloses and dramatizes its own conception and construction. The entire impetus of *A la recherche* is toward the achievement of a supreme unity in which all apparent contradictions are resolved. To the extent that it is the account of a process, of the life of a self which has not yet found itself, these dualities are vividly present. To the extent that *A la recherche* is a product, objective demonstration of journey's end, the harmony of self and world and of the varying points of view which have contributed to the novel we read is emphasized. For those who are not yet initiated into the truth of this unity, it is necessary to begin with conflict. The categories of Méséglise and Guermantes are heuristic devices without which we would be oblivious to the capital significance of the marriage between Gilberte and Saint-Loup. In the Cave of *The Republic*, the Sun must be apprehended by means of shadows. But the contradictions – concomitants of the world of flux – dissolve once time is redeemed and Marcel finds his vocation.

In the world at the mercy of time, all is *mensonge*, sham, since no formulation can keep pace with the kaleidoscopic flow. Yet we can declare, with Marcel and with truth, "D'ailleurs, dans ces mensonges, nous sentons bien qu'il y a de la vérité" [Besides, in these falsehoods we rightly sense that there is some truth] (III, 352). *A la recherche* is large enough to contain its multitudes. "Time passes, and little by little everything said in falsehood becomes true" (III, 461). In time everything becomes truth. But this occurs because the truth is everything. And the truth can lift us out of time. Partial truths both precede and compose the final unity that is *A la recherche*, a fact which those of us who return to Combray know.

V   FIN AGAIN

Germaine Brée declares that: "No other novelist has, like Proust, linked within a single book the story of the spiritual genesis of a vocation, the story of the genesis of a work, and the very embodiment of that work."[15] And her former student George Stambolian affirms:

> *A la recherche* is not simply the biography of a novelist who resembles Proust, it is the description of the very experiences by means of which the hero becomes a novelist who shares Proust's own conception of art and of the creative process. It is because of this emphasis on the creative "becoming" of its hero that Proust's novel can be seen as the fictionalized description of its own genesis.[16]

Yet Brée elsewhere rejects *A la recherche* as a genuinely self-begetting novel. According to that view, the narrative does not circle back into itself because *A la recherche* is not the novel that Marcel the novelist will write. "It is not the production of the narrator's book which interests Proust, but how, humanly, it becomes possible."[17]

One argument Brée invokes against the acceptance of *A la recherche* as a continuum from Combray to authorship to Combray is that of plausibility.

Actually, the point at which the narrator leaves off at the end of the novel can in no way in the world be superimposed on his starting point. The contrary would have presented a considerable aesthetic problem. The title of the novel indicates that it is a matter of a "quest," and what would this quest be if the narrator himself knew its outcome? What would be the "revelation" of the end if not a specious revelation which would destroy the value of the narrator's account and of the long discouragement which it cancels?[18]

When discussing the *madeleine* episode, Germaine Brée properly notices "a double perspective and an ambivalence which are fundamental."[19] There is certainly a disparity between the perspective of the narrator and that of Marcel the protagonist in the narrative. It might at first seem offensive to twentieth-century sensibilities to accept this narrator as an omniscient graduate of an earlier reading of *A la recherche* and therefore capable of foreseeing and manipulating everything as dextrously as Thackeray. All difficulties can of course dissolve on the assumption that Marcel the novelist trouvé creates a narrator persona who is as distinct from him as he is from Marcel Proust. But, in any case, the element of *la recherche*, of the novel as unresolved process, need not be sacrificed. It is even reinforced by the possibility of an infinite progression of novels spawning novels, each in turn an account and a demonstration of its own genesis.

Marcel never really succeeds in rediscovering lost time and in integrating his authentic self into the world until he actually objectifies time and the self in a novel available for public scrutiny. The quest cannot terminate simply with a statement of aspirations, since "excuses do not figure in art, intentions are not counted in it" (III, 879 – 80). Just as we witness the protagonist in his *recherche* of the self, we observe his alter ego fictive novelist in the *process* of objectifying that self, creating a novel which in turn creates its offspring. . . . At the end of each cycle, Marcel joins an expanding pedigree of fictive novelists, while a new protagonist, with all of his struggles still before him, is born.

Examination of the narrative perspective *A la recherche* employs is extremely complex and touches on the question of whether Proust truly "finished" his work. Marcel Muller, while denying that he is calculating "how many persons can dance on the point of the needle of the I,"[20] actually distinguishes seven discrete narrative voices based on differing temporal relationships between speaker and event. Within the larger design of the novel, they can all be considered a creation of the fictive novelist. But Germaine Brée points to a shift in temporal perspective as further support for her refusal to accept a pattern of self-begetting:

This entire account, in which the imperfect of elapsed time dominates, is retrospective. On the other hand, from the first lines of Chapter III of *Le Temps retrouvé* the relation of tenses changes. We pass to a dramatic account, propelled by a series of verbs in the past definite tense, where the play of tenses is completely characteristic of the literary narration of events in the process of becoming. There is in the narrator an abrupt change of orientation toward time, a change which is essential and strongly dramatic. . . . It is around this change in orientation that, in a deliberate asymmetry and not in a circle, the entire world is arranged.[21]

While there is certainly a remarkable change in orientation during the course of the novel, it need not bar the novel's self-propagation. Clearly, the protagonist Marcel undergoes a conversion, and narrator and hero approach identity asymptotically. But at any point in the novel, it is difficult to deny that the narrator might not be lapsing into "represented discourse" in order to portray the attitudes of his former self at the time; he freely moves in and out of simultaneous and retrospective points of view.

And consistency in tense is very difficult to pin down throughout *A la recherche*. At every point in the narrative, reference is made to the creation of a novel, from the narrator's early aside about "quand je commençai de composer un livre" [when I began to compose a book] (I, 116) to the narrator's very late retrospection not simply on his life but on his Life – "on a vu que divers épisodes de ce récit me l'avaient prouvé" [it was seen that diverse episodes of this account had proven it to me] (III, 1045). If the novel we read is not the novel which the aging Marcel will compose, time permitting, his expressed intentions make it quite plain that the two will be extremely similar in theme, content and form. To attempt to differentiate between them would serve no purpose. Instead, the novel we re-read is the continuing, tentative goal of its progenitor's quest. It is also the embodiment of *une tentative*, Marcel's effort within the ravages of time to overcome temporality; "je découvrais cette action destructrice du Temps au moment même où je voulais entreprendre de rendre claires, d'intéllectualiser dans une œuvre d'art des réalités extratem-porelles" [I was discovering this destructive action of Time at the very moment in which I wished to undertake to clarify, to intellectualize in a work of art some extratemporal realities] (III, 930). *A la recherche* is the world, and "The creation of the world did not take place in the beginning; it takes place every day."

Georges Poulet, appropriating an image from Proust's own *Pastiches et mélanges*, declares of *A la recherche* that "the book is an immense 'echo chamber' [caisse de résonance]."[22] It is a resounding success. Like Oriental boxes enclosing boxes, *A la recherche* is rooted in the restricted world of Combray and in the physical limitations of a few volumes, but it reaches outward without end. "Une heure n'est pas qu'une heure, c'est un vase rempli de parfums, de sons, de projects et de climats" [An hour is not just an hour; it is a vase filled with perfumes, with sounds, with projects, and with climates] (III, 889). A chrismatory of eras, events, and characters, *A la recherche* through its form can trigger Baudelaire's "expansion des choses infinies," the expansion of infinite things promised in the poem "Correspondances." Its action is reinforced by the typically dazzling leaps of metaphorical construction and by the device of involuntary memory capable of moving from *madeleines* and paving stones to a whole world. It proceeds through the liberation of huge reality from closed containers: "le geste, l'acte le plus simple reste enfermé comme dans mille vases clos dont chacun serait rempli de choses d'une couleur, d'une odeur, d'une température absolument différentes" [the simplest gesture, act remains enclosed as within a thousand sealed vases each filled with things of a color, an odor, a temperature absolutely different] (III, 870). *A la recherche* extracts and unifies these essences through its pattern of propagation, yielding an infinite sequence of vases as well as the inexhaustible novelty that is Proust's criterion for aesthetic progress.

A la recherche is Proust's unfinished symphony, not simply because the author died before seeing it all into print. Its open form never ceases to extend itself, and it is itself one of those great books the narrator discusses:

> Et dans ces grands livres-là, il y a des parties qui n'ont eu le temps que d'être esquissées, et qui ne seront sans doute jamais finies, à cause de l'ampleur même du plan de l'architecte. Combien de grandes cathédrales restent inachevées! (III, 1033).

> [And in those great books, there are parts which have only had time to be sketched and which will doubtless never be finished, because of the very scope of the architect's plan. How many great cathedrals remain unfinished!]

Aside from occasional lapses of chronological consistency, *A la recherche* is a very tightly constructed work, but it is also open-ended. It is a detailed account, within the nineteenth-century Naturalist tradition, of all the factors contributing to the development of an individual. But chance, *le hasard*, is critical during each significant, privileged moment, and the protagonist, determined by his environment even in the choice of vocation, transcends it ultimately by stepping out of the novel to become its author.

An exalted notion of art and the possibilities of freedom is the result of this structure. Yet Robert Brasillach detected ambivalence in the novel's sense of its own achievement.

> But is it sure of having found the truth? And in its acceptance, in its apparent joy, in the artificial exaltation of its last book, is there not still a shudder of uneasiness? "Yes or no," it seems to say to itself, "have I been deceived? But it is too late; I have chosen."[23]

Uncertainty and suffering, inevitable for anyone rooted in time, certainly plague Marcel every step of the way. But "c'est le chagrin qui développe les forces de l'esprit" [it is sorrow which develops the powers of the mind] (III, 906), and "on peut presque dire que les œuvres, comme dans les puits artésiens, montent d'autant plus haut que la souffrance a plus profondement creusé le cœur" [it can almost be said that works of art, as in artesian wells, climb higher as suffering digs more deeply into the heart] (III, 908). Anxiety and conflict, as with each of the polarities in the novel's rich dialectic, are necessary stages in the movement toward final unity, a movement, however, which in *A la recherche* can never fully end.

Confident in his *méthode* of substantiating self and world, Descartes, at least in light of Beckett, was no skeptic. Recent novelists, adapting the Proustian paradigm to their own visions, will begin the process of reduction emphasizing the self-doubts inherent in the reflexive form. But *A la recherche* still posits a Romantic faith in the sublime affirmation of artistic creation. The only irony in the Bergotte funeral scene resides in the disparity between the pettiness of the author's life and the grandeur of his immortal works:

> On l'enterra, mais toute la nuit funèbre, aux vitrines éclairées, ses livres disposés trois par trois, veillaient comme des anges aux ailes éployées et semblaient, pour celui qui n'était plus, le symbole de la résurrection (III, 188).

> [They buried him, but throughout the mournful night, in the bright windows his books arranged three by three kept watch like angels with wings unfurled and seemed, for the one who no longer was, the symbol of resurrection]

A la recherche is immortal not because its author has been dead fifty-seven years and it has since been assimilated as a "classic" and not simply because it is the semblance of a life in time lifted out of time. "Perpétuel devenir," perpetual becoming, is an oxymoron emblematic of the many dualities through which the novel's unity is achieved. The work projects an image of constant renewal through its plot and, more significantly, through its own example. As long as it is re-read it does not die.

3 La Nausée

Pour obtenir cet effet, suivez-moi, j'invente un personnage
de romancier, que je pose en figure centrale; et le sujet du
livre, si vous voulez, c'est précisément la lutte entre ce que
lui offre la réalité et ce que, lui, prétend en faire.
André Gide, *Les Faux-Monnayeurs*, p.233

I THE BEGETTING OF A *ROQUET*

If there were no Antoine Roquentin in modern literature, he would have
to be invented. This is precisely what occurs in *La Nausée* (1938),
Jean-Paul Sartre's first and most important novel. At the opening of this
first-person narrative, Roquentin has been existing for three years in the
drab town of Bouville, self-effacingly pursuing historical reseach on the
Marquis de Rollebon. Despite present oblivion, Roquentin has apparently led a colorful life. He has traveled extensively throughout Europe,
Northern Africa, and the Orient and has engaged in a somewhat
turbulent love affair with a woman named Anny. His "adventures" have
included the theft of Rollebon papers from the Soviet archives in 1923
(p.139)[1] and a narrowly averted death at the hands of a knife-wielding
Moroccan (p.57). Roquentin, like the hero of *La Divina Commedia*, is
midway in his life's journey. Thirty years old (p.242), poised between
past and future, this *roquentin* – a dotard who thinks himself young –
awaits rebirth.

The Bouville Museum apparently contains nothing but portraits of
individuals. The painting hanging at the entrance, *La Mort du Célibataire*,
is distinctive and has special significance for Roquentin, but all of these
works of art, like Joyce's *Bildungsroman* and like *La Nausée* itself, are
re-creations of individuals and not landscapes or crowd scenes. Sartre
appropriately chooses as his epigraph Louis-Ferdinand Céline's statement "C'est un garçon sans importance collective, c'est tout juste un
individu" [He is a fellow without collective importance; he is just barely
an individual] (p.5). *La Nausée* is a portrait of Roquentin, and the
creation of one entails the creation of the other.

Withdrawn into a monologue, Roquentin is a supremely solitary
individual. Like des Esseintes or Marcel, he is a confirmed bachelor. He
lives alone, and his contacts with others are reduced to a minimum – the

necessities of renting a room, obtaining a meal, and engaging in occasional passionless but cathartic sex with an obliging café proprietress. Unlike the bourgeois "salauds" [scum] surrounding him in Bouville, Roquentin apparently has no family ties. Aside from a casual reference to an aunt (p.243), he makes no mention of any forebears and certainly none of any offspring. Instead, he is merely responsible for himself and is free to act as he pleases and go where he chooses. Furthermore, Roquentin is not even a victim of the economic forces which determine the bourgeois world of Bouville and provide life there with a necessary structure, endowing Sunday, the day of rest, with peculiar significance. He obscurely hints at a source of modest but regular income which frees him of any economic bondage and enables him to choose his situation. Roquentin is as effectively a bastard as are Gide's Lafcadio and Bernard or Sand's François; and for those who lack a father, it is a psychological, if not logical, necessity to beget themselves.

Like Descartes or des Esseintes, Roquentin begins his activity reductively. To begin anew, he must provisionally discard the old he has taken for granted. From the vast international stage on which he had been operating, Roquentin has withdrawn to the insignificant municipality of Bouville – *ville de boue*, city of mud. He has given up his relationship with Anny and now lives alone, devoid of personal desires or ambitions. In fact, Roquentin's entire existence in Bouville becomes dedicated to the resurrection of the obscure nineteenth-century Marquis de Rollebon. To the extent that Roquentin sacrifices his own reality, that of Rollebon is affirmed. As he comes to recognize later, "il avait besoin de moi pour être et j'avais besoin de lui pour ne pas sentir mon être" [he needed me in order to be, and I needed him in order not to feel my being] (p.140). Distant kin to the Antony who, "a triple pillar of the world," gladly relinquishes global power for the tranquillity of Egypt, Antoine Roquentin is content to lose himself in the process of finding the Marquis de Rollebon. His austere existence in Bouville might also recall the solitary trials of a saintly namesake. Roquentin begins by mortifying the ego, a procedure which Claude-Edmonde Magny in fact relates to the classical quest for salvation:

> Like the ascesis which moral and religious systems have always prescribed, this depersonalization and stripping away of all social elements are not undertaken for their own sake. They are justified only because they serve as preparatory to something else. They permit us a contact with certain aspects of reality which we might otherwise never know.[2]

So far, Roquentin appears to be adhering to the Cartesian pattern of systematic hyperbolic doubt as a means of arriving at indubitable truth or to the Proustian formula of withdrawing from the world in order to re-discover it in the self.

But Roquentin's contraction must proceed even further, as, at the beginning of the novel, he begins even to doubt the validity and the value of his historical research. After three years of patient labor among diverse source materials, of living by proxy through the resurrection of the Marquis de Rollebon, Roquentin begins to question the reality of history. He does not doubt the isolated pieces of data he amasses, but he cannot discover any coherence in the motley threads of Rollebon's life.

Ce ne sont pas les documents qui font défaut: lettres, fragments de mémoires, rapports secrets, archives de police. J'en ai presque trop, au contraire. Ce qui manque dans tous ces témoignages, c'est la fermeté, la consistence. Ils ne se contredisent pas, mais ils ne s'accordent pas non plus: ils n'ont pas l'air de concerner la même personne (p.25).

[It is not the documents which are at fault: letters, fragments of memoirs, secret reports, police archives. On the contrary, I almost have too much of them. What is missing in all this testimony is stability, consistency. They do not contradict each other, but they do not agree either; they do not seem to be about the same person]

A comprehensive pattern imposed on past existence can only be delusion, a result of what, in Sartrean theology, is the cardinal sin, *mauvaise foi* (bad faith), impatience with the gratuitousness of existence. Rollebon was a contingent and fundamentally superfluous being, and hence there is no necessary structure to his reality. Any attempt to characterize him or any other phenomenon in terms of a static formula is as deceptive and inadequate as Doctor Rogé's attempt to subsume the fluid reality of M. Achille under a frozen but convenient stereotype: "A présent, rien de ce que fera M. Achille ne saurait nous surprendre: *puisque* c'est un vieux toqué!" [At present, nothing which M. Achille does would be able to surprise us, *since* he is an old loony!] (p.101).

The self-doubting Roquentin now begins to turn his skepticism against the myth of history as well. He decides to abandon his project on Rollebon. It is an impossible task. "Comment, donc, moi qui n'ai pas eu la force de retenir mon propre passé, puis-je espérer que je sauverai celui d'un autre?" [How then, can I, who have not had the strength to hold on to my own past, hope to save that of someone else?] (p.136). Roquentin has at least temporarily failed in his quest for *le temps perdu*. Occasional random recollections of his own experiences serve to convince him that the past is fragmented and dead; even the photographs that l'Autodidacte insists on being shown are treated with the cold scorn of an impotent old man: "these aphrodisiacs scarcely have any effect on my memory any longer" (p.53).

Existence, like a walnut tree, a stone, or a piece of wet newspaper, is a dense reality which remains impervious to human formalization; "the world of explanations and reasons is not that of existence" (p.183). Roquentin can write again, but "pas un livre d'histoire, ça parle de ce qui a existé – jamais un existant ne peut justifier l'existence d'un autre existant. Mon erreur c'était de vouloir ressusciter M. de Rollebon" [not a book of history; that tells of what has existed – never can an existant justify the existence of another existant. My error was in wanting to resuscitate M. de Rollebon] (p.248). After recognizing that Rollebon is as contingent as the other "salauds" of Bouville, Roquentin is still able to visualize him. However, it is no longer as an historian, as he hints at the novelist either still to be born or to be stillborn. "Je pouvais former ses traits à volonté, peut-être avec plus de facilité qu'auparavant. Seulement ce n'était plus qu'une image en moi, une fiction" [I could form his traits at will, perhaps with greater ease than previously. Only it was no longer anything but an image within me, a fiction] (p.139).

At this point, Roquentin is left to his own devices. He has lost the prop of teleology, and everything, including himself, is now palpably *de trop*. As this proto-Existentialist wittily phrases it, "L'essential c'est la contingence" [The essential is contingency] (p.185). An orphan without any social ties, he has now denied even the possibility of family and society as anything but inauthentic and arbitrary. All he can do now is create.

In an extended passage central to *La Nausée*, Roquentin, who earlier, in a rare remembrance, confesses "Quand j'avais vingt ans, je me soûlais et, ensuite, j'expliquais que j'étais un type dans le genre de Descartes" [When I was twenty years old, I used to get soused, and afterwards I would explain that I was a fellow in the class of Descartes] (p.84), undergoes a Cartesian birth. After experiencing nausea and reflecting on the futility of writing a book on Rollebon, Roquentin is finally able to make the simple but triumphal assertion: "I exist" (p.141). This marks the beginning of his enlightenment and his salvation. While for Descartes it is thought which provides the assurance that there is a subject who is thinking, nausea becomes the prime mover in the Sartrean universe. As soon as he is able to see beyond the delusions of custom, Roquentin faces the world *en-soi* in all of its unmanageable density and viscosity. Nausea, symptomatic of his resulting vertigo, is, like the Cartesian *cogito*, the result of a fresh, creative awareness; and its physical manifestations align him with the slimy reality which has motivated it.

After the epiphany of "j'existe," the language Roquentin employs to convey the refinements of his initial inspiration manifestly echoes that of Descartes, so much so that there is some validity in the claim that: "The Sartrean *cogito* appears rather like a sort of tragic caricature of the *cogito* of Descartes. Sartre, moreover, certainly realizes it, and it is deliberately that he has conceived his novel as a parody of the *Discours de la méthode*."[3] In a formulation which certainly casts a backward glance at Descartes's

"I think, therefore I am" and anticipates the paradoxically life-affirming death-wish of Beckett's The Unnamable, Roquentin declares:

> Ma pensée, c'est moi: voilà pourquoi je ne peux pas m'arrêter. J'existe par ce que je pense . . . et je ne peux pas m'empêcher de penser. En ce moment même – c'est affreux – si j'existe, *c'est parce que* j'ai horreur d'exister (p.143).

> [My thought is me – that's why I cannot stop. I exist by means of what I think . . . and I cannot prevent myself from thinking. At this very moment – it is frightful – if I exist, *it is because* I have a horror of existing]

A kind of negative Cartesianism, it is Roquentin's horror of existing, even more so his horror of thinking which, itself a thought, causes him to exist.

> Je suis, j'existe, je pense donc je suis, je suis parce que je pense, pourquoi est-ce que je pense? je ne veux plus penser, je suis parce que je pense que je ne veux pas être, je pense que je . . . parce que . . . pouah! (p.144).

> [I am, I exist, I think therefore I am, I am because I think, why do I think? I no longer want to think, I am because I think that I do not want to be, I think that I . . . because . . . ugh!]

The Cartesian faith in method and in his ability to construct a network of indubitable truth, including that of God's pre-eminence, is absent. And Sartre finds the Cartesian mind–body duality unacceptable. But Roquentin, like Descartes, is thrown back on his own individual epistemological resources and is unable to elude the primacy of his own existence.

Sartre presumably would have little quarrel with the Biblical myth that portrays man as created out of the slimy matter of clay. Yet in *La Nausée* creation is emphatically self-creation and is continually being renewed. L'Autodidacte, whose project is to make himself into a universal man by reading from beginning to end every single book placed in the library by others, is a comic portrait of shoddy self-begetting. Roquentin comes to recognize that, much as he might long for airy nothingness, it is that very longing which endows him with a local habitation and a name.

> C'est moi, *c'est moi* qui me tire du néant auquel j'aspire: la haine, le dégoût d'exister, ce sont autant de manières de *me faire* exister, de m'enfoncer dans l'existence. Les pensées naissent par-derrière moi comme un vertige, je les sens naître derrière ma tête . . . si je cede, elles vont venir là devant, entre mes yeux – et je cede toujours, la pensée grossit, grossit et la voilà, l'immense, qui me remplit tout entier et renouvelle mon existence (p.143).

> [It is me, *it is me* who pulls myself out of the nothingness to which I aspire; the hatred, the disgust for existing, these are so many means of making me exist, of

immersing me in existence. Thoughts are born behind me like a dizziness, I feel them being born behind my head . . . if I give in, they are going to come in front there, between my eyes – and I always give in, the thought grows, grows, and there it is, immense, completely filling me and renewing my existence]

Slime – whether clay, mud, or vomit – makes Roquentin confront his own existence *en soi* and initiate an endless chain of self-begetting.

With the collapse of the Rollebon enterprise, Anny, Roquentin's former mistress, represents the last possibility of external justification for his existence. Yet his meeting with her vividly confirms the rule that "never can an existant justify the existence of another existant." Since their last meeting, Anny too has undergone many changes. Her faith in "perfect moments" emblematized by the engravings in her copy of Michelet's *L'Histoire de France*, has been as effectively shattered as has Roquentin's confidence in his own historical research. However, despite Roquentin's belief that "we have lost the same illusions, we have followed the same paths" (p.210), communion even between the two of them is an illusion, and each must go his separate way.

Only two external obligations remain for Roquentin – to return his library books and to pay his back rent. Once these are taken care of, he prepares to leave Bouville for Paris, once again rejecting the past and the specious net of determinism it attempts to spread over the future. Roquentin pays a last visit to the café *Rendez-Vous des Cheminots* and insists that the jazz record "Some of These Days" be played and replayed on the phonograph. He is curiously moved by this song. He especially admires its refrain, a recurring means of confronting flux by establishing a sense of absolute appropriateness. Although the song also expresses a sense of anguish over the contingency of existence, the power of its expression lies in its ability to overcome this superfluousness, as if to say to the listener, "Il faut faire comme nous, souffrir *en mesure*" [You must do as we do, suffer *in measure*] (p.243). Roquentin envisions a distinction between being and existing, and the song is able to create the illusion of being. "Elle n'est pas, puisqu'elle n'a rien de trop; c'est tout le reste qui est trop par rapport à elle. Elle *est*" [It does not exist, since it has nothing superfluous; it is everything else which is superfluous in relation to it. It *is*] (p.244).

However, of capital importance to Roquentin as self-begetter are his reflections on the singer and composer of "Some of These Days." He imagines the singer as a Negress who is perhaps dead and the composer as an impoverished Jew sweltering on the twenty-first floor of a New York tenement. If, as Eugenia Noik Zimmerman claims, singer and composer of "Some of These Days" can be identified as Sophie Tucker and Shelton Brooks, respectively, and hence "Sartre's Jewish composer is a Negro composer and Sartre's Negro singer is, in all probability, a Jewish singer,"[4] the two jazz artists are nonetheless as much social outcasts as Roquentin. But he realizes that they have succeeded in overcoming their utter gratuitousness by transcending their superfluous and temporal realities and creating necessary selves. They have learned to impose a rhythm on their sufferings. Leaden life has transmuted itself again into golden art. Even if dead, they have been born into new lives outside of time.

> En voilà deux qui sont sauvés: le juif et la Négresse. Sauvés. Ils se sont peut-être crus perdus jusqu'au bout, noyés dans l'existence. Et pourtant personne ne pourrait penser à moi comme je pense à eux, avec cette douceur. Personne, pas même Anny. Ils sont un peu pour moi comme des morts, un peu comme des héros de roman; ils se sont lavés du péché d'exister (pp. 247–8).

> [There are two who may be saved: the Jew and the Negress. Saved. They might have believed themselves lost until the end, drowned in existence. And yet no one could think of me the way I think of them, with this fondness. No one, not even Anny. They are for me a bit like dead people, a bit like heroes of a novel; they have been cleansed of the sin of existing]

This is not merely salvation through art, but rebirth. Each time Roquentin listens to the record he speculates on the lives of its composer and singer and the extent to which, out of whatever motivations and misery, they have succeeded in creating more enduring lives through the music.

> Voilà, je suppose que ça ne lui ferait ni chaud ni foid, à ce type, si on lui disait qu'il y a, dans la septième ville de France, aux abords de la gare, quelqu'un qui pense à lui. Mais moi je serais heureux, si j'étais à sa place, je l'envie (p.247).

> [There, I suppose that this guy would not care one way or the other if he were told that there is, in the seventh city of France, in the area of the station, someone who thinks about him. I, though, I would be happy, if I were in his place; I envy him]

At the end of the novel *La Nausée*, boarding his train and escaping from Bouville, Roquentin resolves to create a novel.

> Un livre. Un roman, Et il y aurait des gens qui liraient ce roman et qui diraient: "C'est Antoine Roquentin qui l'a écrit, c'était un type roux qui traînait dans les cafés," et ils penseraient à ma vie comme je pense à celle de cette Négresse: comme à quelque chose de précieux et d'à moitié légendaire (p.249).

> [A book. A novel. And there would be people who would read this novel and who would say: "It's Antoine Roquentin who wrote it. He was a red-headed fellow who used to hang around cafés." And they would think about my life the way I think about that Negress's: as if about something precious and half legendary]

As in fact does occur when we read *La Nausée*, Roquentin hopes that his novel, unlike a book of history, will succeed in projecting a Roquentin who will live as the Negress lives through the song. Although it is not explicitly to be autobiographical and *La Nausée*, while a portrait of Roquentin, lacks the broad *Bildungsroman* sweep of *A la recherche*, his expectations are not radically different from those of Marcel:

> Mais il viendrait bien un moment où le livre serait écrit, serait derrière moi et je pense qu'un peu de clarté tomberait sur mon passé. Alors peut-être que je pourrais, à travers lui, me rappeler ma vie sans répugnance (p.249).

> [But there would surely come a moment when the book would be written, would be behind me, and I think a little light would be shed on my past. Perhaps then I would be able, through it, to recall my life without disgust]

To accomplish this will be to create a self of his own with satisfactory beginning, middle and end. As Georges Poulet points out, this task, if not godly, is at least superhuman: 'Sartrean Existentialism can only conclude with an ethic whose object would be to prove that *le bien*, the good, can be drawn from *le rien*, nothingness. It is almost the position of a God who has to create himself.'[5]

At one point in his journal, Roquentin remarks that it is necessary to choose between living and narrating: "il faut choisir: vivre ou raconter" (p.60). The characters of Samuel Richardson seem to spend almost all of their waking hours writing letters which must often necessarily be reflexive, and Samuel Beckett's yearn to be through with both living and narrating. If *La Nausée* is indeed the novel Roquentin will write, the fact that it is presented to us in a rough version by anonymous editors who claim to have found it among the papers of Antoine Roquentin suggests that he might have chosen between *vivre* and *raconter*. The new life he has been born into is also an ending: "cette liberté ressemble un peu à la mort" [this freedom is somewhat like death] (p.220).

Germaine Brée and Margaret Guiton, who do not accept a cyclical pattern in *La Nausée* and do not see it as the novel Roquentin wants to write, conjecture that the real conclusion to the novel is insanity and possibly suicide.[6] The figure of Roquentin created is something of a *roquet*, a peevish but petty man, and his pathological obsession with slimy substances might suggest coprophilia. Noticing soiled bits of paper on the ground, he declares: "pour un peu je les porterais à ma bouche, comme font les enfants" [I would just as soon bring them up to my mouth, the way children do] (p.21). Roquentin certainly is not, like Gustave Impétraz, who is preserved as a civic statue, a paradigm of social adjustment, but his alienation, even more than that of Camus's Meursault, is potentially creative. It leads to awareness of a reality to which the self-confident Bouville *salauds* are insensitive. If Roquentin does die at the conclusion of *La Nausée*, he suffers a sea change. We have only to turn to the beginning of the resulting work of art to find something rich and strange.

Just as Roquentin listens to "Some of These Days" and imagines its composer and singer, we read *La Nausée* and envision its fictive author, even if he is dead. And, as numerous biographical studies attest, some of us are also led to think about its real author. Sartre has since soundly attacked his own early work and renounced the ethic of salvation through art.[7] But, in a statement paralleling Flaubert's "Madame Bovary c'est moi" and confirming *La Nausée* as a self-begetting novel which becomes a self, Sartre has more recently declared, "*J'étais* Roquentin, je montrais en lui, sans complaisance, la trame de ma vie." [I *was* Roquentin; I portrayed in him, with misgivings, the web of my life][8]

As the painting *La Mort du Célibataire* foreshadows, the bachelor Roquentin dies, but only to be reborn as a work of art. At the end of the novel, he has found a way to extricate himself from Bouville, the city of mud, and from the viscosity of being *de trop*. To do this is – according to the Sartre of *Qu'est-ce que la littérature?* – to create himself. "Une issue, ça s'invente. Et chacun, en inventant sa propre issue, s'invente soi-même. L'homme est à inventer chaque jour." [An outcome has to be invented. And each of us, in inventing his own outcome, invents himself. Man must be invented each day][9]

II   BRINGING A NOVEL INTO BEING

Studies relating Sartre to Proust, treating Sartre as both literary critic and novelist, abound.[10] As a critic, Sartre has on several occasions presented forceful views on Proust's novel. In *L'Etre et le Néant* (1943) he attacks what he considers to be the traditionalist notion of causality and motivation promulgated in *A la recherche*. And in the famous introductory manifesto "Présentation des *Temps modernes*" in the first issue of his journal *Les Temps modernes*, Sartre uses the occasion to launch an assault against Proust on several fronts.[11] He portrays Proust as symptomatic of the analytic and bourgeois tradition which he, Sartre, seeks to overthrow. He finds untenable what he takes to be the Proustian view that love is an innate, discrete constituent of human nature. In addition, Sartre has severe misgivings about what he considers Proust's attempts to extrapolate universal rules of human behaviour from limited, homosexual experience. And Sartre chides Proust for an alleged indifference to the proletariat and a preoccupation with a degenerate aristocracy. Yet *Qu'est-ce que la littérature?* does contain brief incidental praise for the richness and range of Proust's fictional world.[12] The indictment by the author of *La Nausée* against *A la recherche du temps perdu*, while suggesting the disillusionment of a headstrong disciple, is often perverse and willfully polemical. At least as harsh an invective could be leveled against *La Nausée* by anyone so inclined.[13]

Of more enduring interest, at least within this context, are the similarities between Proust's and Sartre's first-person narratives of men who eventually decide to write their own novels. *La Nausée* is, of course, a much sparer work, almost ascetic in comparison to Proust's opulent and sprawling *summa*. Sartre's novel, unlike his novella *L'Enfance d'un chef*, lacks the equivalent of a Combray. In fact, aside from some of Anny's random recollections and the tableau of the Sunday promenade in Bouville in which family life is treated with a scorn more appropriate to W. C. Fields than Proust, childhood is notably absent from *La Nausée*, except when a pervert attempts to molest a child. Instead, Roquentin is most often in the position of Marcel at the beginning of *Le Temps retrouvé*, a solitary grown man for whom the past seems inert and irretrievable. Yet both works culminate in a decision which renders meaningful everything that has gone before. Although one may loosely be identified with "symbolism" and one with "realism," both *A la recherche* and *La Nausée* feature novelists as their central protagonists, and Reinhard Kuhn appears justified in locating them both within an identical novelistic tradition:

> It is perfectly obvious that both of these works are Künstlerromanen, novels of the novelist, a genre which we tend to identify with the Romantic movement. . . . So it might be said that while superficially Sartre and Proust belong to the two different traditions previously mentioned, basically their roots are to be found in another tradition, anterior to the English or American one, and which in France began with Chateaubriand's *René*, Senancourt's *Obermann* and Constant's *Adolphe*, in Germany with Goethe's *Werther*, Hölderlin's *Hyperion* and Novalis's *Heinrich von Ofterdingen* and which later produced Gottfried Keller's *Der Grüne Heinrich*.[14]

Music plays a major role in both *A la recherche* and *La Nausée*. Roquentin's favorite piece of music, the jazz song "Some of These Days," is analogous to the *petite phrase* of Vinteuil's violin sonata. The latter is "high art" and the former is merely "popular music." But both works-of-art-within-a-work-of-art reappear at important points within their novels and exert a crucial influence on their respective protagonists, ultimately contributing to their determinations to become artists. Both "Some of These Days" and the Vinteuil composition, to which Roquentin and Marcel, respectively, listen with rapt attention, embody the possibility of an extratemporal reality more alluring than the mire of existence in which the potential artists are temporarily trapped.

There is an undeniable difference in tone between Proust's highly wrought, fugal opus and Sartre's reductive, frugal novel, and so a café jazz record is perhaps a suitable translation of Vinteuil's repeated phrase for *La Nausée*. It seems closer in spirit, but not function, to the song which Sam plays again – and again – and which evokes a pre-war romance in the film *Casablanca*. Henry A. Grubbs, after considering a few of the similarities between the nature and role of the two musical creations, can thus conclude with the following generalization about the novels in which they appear:

> I think rather that Sartre was familiar with Proust's work, that he found interesting and significant at least two elements in it: the theme of the effect of a work of music, and the conclusions involving the relation of artistic creation to the discovery of hidden reality and the recovery of lost time. May I suggest that Sartre was taking a wry pleasure in making *La Nausée* an ironic counterpart of *A la recherche du temps perdu*; a reduced model, ironic, modern, realistic, a little sordid – in a word, a poor man's Proust.[15]

A poor man's Proust. If, as he proclaims in contrast to Proust, Sartre's allegiance is to the proletariat, then this epithet might not be so glib. In any case, it does emphasize a vital continuity between *A la recherche* and *La Nausée*.

But more needs to be said about the similarities between Proust and Sartre in regard to the specific form of the self-begetting novel. It is the *refrain* of "Some of These Days" which most impresses Roquentin. Like the recurrent *petite phrase* in Proust, it suggests the continuous form of the work of art whose conclusion rejoins its beginning. "Some of these days/You'll miss me honey" goes the song. Like Ronsard in "Quand vous serez bien vieille," the poet is apparently celebrating a lover, but also reminding her of the ravages of time and that eventually she will come to view him with the tenderness of retrospection. The doctrine of the immortalizing power of art, that, according to Shakespeare, "in black ink my love may still shine bright," is not explicitly advanced, but the song does serve as a model of art's capacity to lift a suffering individual out of the temporal contingency of "some of these days."

It is aptly enough a café waitress named Madeleine who plays and replays the record for Roquentin, just as it is the *madeleine* cake which provides Marcel with an early intimation of the possibility of redeeming time. And for Roquentin, as for Marcel, the piece of music leads to reflections on the petty and even sordid reality from which art emanates and over which it triumphs. When Roquentin listens to "Some of These Days," it leads him to speculate on the tormented lives of its creators, two social outcasts, a Negress and a Jew. Similarly, Marcel, who is struck by how so mediocre a personality as Bergotte could have produced such magnificent writing, is painfully aware of the fact that behind Vinteuil's consummate music lies the pathos of his daughter's lesbianism. Like the saxophone in *La Nausée*, Bergotte and Vinteuil seem to say, "You must do as we do, suffer *in measure*." In the Bouville Museum, where portraits of the town's social giants hang "larger than life" (the painting of Olivier Blévigne almost succeeds in camouflaging his height, a mere 1.53 meters), Roquentin becomes aware of art's power to transform mean, mortal lives into timeless exemplars.

> Admirable puissance de l'art. De ce petit homme à la voix suraiguë, rien ne passerait à la postérité, qu'une face menaçante, qu'un geste superbe et des yeux sanglants de taureau. L'étudiant terrorisé par la Commune, le député minuscule et rageur; voilà ce que la mort avait pris. Mais, grâce à Bordurin, le président du club de l'Ordre, l'orateur des Forces Morales était immortel (p.134).

> [Admirable power of art. From this little man with the high-pitched voice, all that would pass on to posterity would be a menacing face, a superb gesture, and the brutal eyes of a bull. The student terrorized by the Commune, the tiny, irascible deputy – death has purged these. But thanks to Bordurin, the President of the Club de l'Ordre, the orator of "Moral Forces" was immortal]

The tone here is one of derision toward the bad faith of the society's bogus standards. Yet the novel Roquentin is to write will succeed in immortalizing a *roquentin*.

Marcel receives random visitations from involuntary memory, and the feeling of "adventure" seizes Roquentin briefly from time to time, intensifying and unifying his experience within a meaningful framework.

> Je me disais: "Ce sentiment d'aventure, il n'y a peut-être rien au monde à quoi je tienne tant. Mais il vient quand il veut; il repart si vite et comme je suis sec quand il est reparti! Me fait-il ces courtes visites ironiques pour me montrer que j'ai manqué ma vie?" (p.83).

> [I used to say to myself: "This feeling of adventure – there is perhaps nothing in the world I care as much about. But it comes when it will; it leaves again so quickly, and how empty I am when it has gone again! Does it make these short, ironic visits to me to show me I have blown my life?"]

Anny, the sometime believer in privileged situations and perfect moments, is most closely associated with the possibility of adventure. She is a figure out of Roquentin's past, and the past is a key element in adventures. "J'ai voulu que les moments de ma vie se suivent et s'ordonnent comme ceux d'une vie qu'on se rappelle" [I wanted the moments of my life to follow each other and be arranged like those of a life that is recollected] (p.62), says Roquentin. The owl of Minerva only spreads its wings at dusk, and adventures, each with a beginning, middle and end, are a function of retrospection. Roquentin never feels as if he is undergoing an adventure while it is occurring, and the past, the proper repository of adventures, remains, aside from occasional epiphanies, inaccessible to him. His memory, like the magic lantern in Marcel's Combray bedroom, has the creative potential of imposing the form of adventures on random occurrences.

> Un soleil torride, dans ma tête, glisse roidement, comme une plaque de lanterne magique. Il est suivi d'un morceau de ciel bleu; après quelques secousses il s'immobilise, j'en suis tout doré en dedans. De quelle journée marocaine (ou algérienne? ou syrienne?) cet éclat s'est-il soudain détaché? Je me laisse couler dans le passé (p.51).

> [A torrid sun, in my head, shifts stiffly, like a magic lantern slide. It is followed by a patch of blue sky; after a few shakes, it comes to a stop, and I am all radiant inside from it. From what Moroccan (or Algerian? or Syrian?) day has this splendor suddenly broken away? I let myself sink into the past]

For the most part, Roquentin fails to recover his past through memory, and Anny, emblematic of his past and of the possibility of a life of adventure (because of her ideas and because of the promise of a romantic encounter with her), proves as elusive as Marcel's Albertine *disparue*; "je cesse de rechercher une Anny disparue" [I have given up seeking a missing Anny] (p.202). "Adventures are in books," (p.58), complains Roquentin. And in that lament is a forecast of the manner in which his anguished existence will in truth be projected as an adventure.

On a smaller scale than *A la recherche*, with its panoply of fictional sonatas, paintings, plays and poems, *La Nausée* likewise features elements which remind the reader that he is reading a work of art concerned with the relationship between art and life. Most prominent of these devices is, of course, the jazz song "Some of These Days," to which Roquentin listens early in the novel (p.36), as well as at its conclusion. At one point, immediately following the abandonment of the Rollebon enterprise (as historian despairing of voluntary memory), Roquentin also describes the experience of listening to a song with the words "When the low moon begins to beam/Every night I dream a little dream" in the *Bar de la Marine* (p.147). The portraits hanging in the Bouville Museum represent a bourgeois exploitation of the creative potential of art.

Furthermore, images of literature appear at various points before Roquentin's climactic decision to create his own work of literature. During one of his working days in the Bouville Library, Roquentin discovers a copy of Balzac's *Eugénie Grandet* lying open on a table. Simply to relieve the boredom of his own activities, he begins reading the novel from the page at which it happens to be open, page twenty-seven (p.47). Later, he carries the book with him into the Vézelize restaurant, where, surrounded by the chatter of old men playing cards and the gossip of a middle-aged couple, he begins reading, for want of anything better to do. "It's not that I derive much pleasure from it; but it is quite necessary to do something" (p.72). At this point, the text of *La Nausée* alternates between the dreary contemporary reality and the scene in *Eugénie Grandet* in which mother and daughter discuss the latter's burgeoning love for her cousin.

Later, Roquentin encounters a copy of *La Chartreuse de Parme* in the Bouville Library and unsuccessfully attempts to find refuge in Stendhal's novel from the burden of his existence. "J'essayais de m'absorber dans ma lecture, de trouver un refuge dans la claire Italie de Stendhal. J'y parvenais par à-coups, par courtes hallucinations, puis je retombais dans cette journée menaçante . . ." [I was trying to become absorbed in my reading, to find a refuge in Stendhal's bright Italy. I was succeeding at it sporadically, through brief hallucinations, and then I would fall back again into this dreadful day] (p.116). Anny, who has been an actress in London, hangs a reproduction of the portrait of Emily Bronte by the novelist's brother in every room in which she stays. Moreover, it is in leafing through the *Satirique Bouvillois*, whose compiler was accused of treason, that Roquentin begins to question the authority of the town's exemplars (p.119). *Roquentin* originally referred to a medieval satirical singer, and not the least of the purposes of Roquentin's own novel will be subversion.

As will be the case in Butor's *La Modification*, where the main protagonist carries an unopened novel with him throughout, the various allusions to writers and books in *La Nausée* prepare the way for Roquentin's determination to construct his own novel. And they also pose the question of the relationship between art and life. Roquentin must come to terms with the question before the end of this novel.

The reader, or re-reader, of *La Nausée* detects clues all along to what Roquentin's final choice of vocation will be, a choice which is perhaps responsible for the presence of *La Nausée*. While still working on his historical study of the Marquis de Rollebon, Roquentin finds his random data recalcitrant to any unity and observes that a figure in a novel might be more satisfactory. "Encore suis-je bien sûr que des personnages de roman auraient l'air plus vrais, seraient, en tout cas, plus plaisants" [I am still quite sure that the characters of a novel would seem more real, would in any case be more pleasant] (p.26). Later, after speculating on an hypothesis which would subsume all of the contradictory information he has assembled on the elusive Rollebon, Roquentin concludes a diary entry with the remark: "Seulement, si c'était pour en venir là, il fallait plutôt que j'écrive un roman sur le marquis de Rollebon" [But if it was in order to arrive at that, I should instead have written a novel about the Marquis de Rollebon] (p.87). From history to historical novel to novel, Roquentin gradually abandons the world of existence for something beyond it. He will write a book, but not a work of history, since that would once again enmire him in existence. And he is incapable of providing the necessity for someone else's existence. He will, instead, compose:

Une autre espèce de livre. Je ne sais pas très bien laquelle – mais il faudrait qu'on devine, derrière les mots imprimés, derrière les pages, quelque chose qui n'existerait pas, qui serait au-dessus de l'existence. Une histoire, par exemple, comme il ne peut en arriver, une aventure (p.248).

[Another kind of book. I do not especially know which – but it would be necessary to guess, behind the printed words, behind the pages, something which would not exist, which would be above existence. A story, for example, which could never happen, an adventure]

La Nausée is presented to us in the form of a private journal kept by Roquentin. Like *Werther*, *René*, and *Adolphe*, it is introduced by editors as if it were a posthumous work. Instead of the assortment of perfect and imperfect past tenses employed in *A la recherche* to convey a sense of emotion recollected in tranquillity, *La Nausée* relies on present, conditional, and future tenses. Its device of diary entries recorded almost daily and directly following the events they depict creates a feeling of immediacy and reinforces the notion of oppressive contingency. As Roquentin comes to realize, it is only in the retrospect of narration that phenomena become adventures – "pour que l'événement le plus banal devienne une aventure, il faut et il suffit qu'on se mette à le *raconter*" [in order for the most banal event to become an adventure, it is necessary and sufficient that you begin *narrating* it] (p.60). Through its journal form and the impression of narrative contemporaneity, *La Nausée* vividly emphasizes the fragmented, slippery reality that nauseates Roquentin and propels him toward transcendence.

At the end of his prefatory, undated notes, Roquentin writes: "Dans un cas seulement il pourrait être intéressant de tenir un journal: ce serait si" [In only one case could it be interesting to keep a diary; that would be if] (p.12). As the editors of the journal scrupulously observe, this sentence remains unfinished. Roquentin's journal itself is, to some extent, a completion of this statement, a solution to the urgent riddle: why write?

Although he eventually decides to write a novel, Roquentin is skeptical of literature when it is, like the Bouville paintings, an objectification of *bad faith*. Writing is for him a pragmatic and cognitive activity, certainly not an ornamental exercise in style. "Je n'ai pas besoin de faire des phrases. J'écris pour tirer au clair certaines circonstances. Se méfier de la littérature. Il faut écrire au courant de la plume; sans chercher les mots" [I have no need to make phrases. I write in order to clarify certain circumstances. Beware of literature. It is necessary to write with the flow of the pen: without searching for words] (p.84). The paradox, is, of course, that the very act of scorning literature produces it. And Roquentin as novelist aims to produce a work which will project the illusion of primordial existence undistorted by art. With its semblance of documentary realism, arising from attention to the sordid areas of life and fidelity to the illegibility and the dating of the supposed source manuscript, *La Nausée* portrays the birth of Venus out of slime. By concentrating on the "certaines circonstances" of existence, the novel seems to deny itself at the same time as it depicts the basis for its own genesis.

Roquentin expresses contempt for art exploited as solace for maimed spirits.

Dire qu'il y a des imbéciles pour puiser des consolations dans les beaux-arts. Comme ma tante Bigeois: "Les *Préludes* de Chopin m'ont été d'un tel secours à la mort de ton pauvre oncle." Et les salles de concert regorgent d'humiliés, d'offensés qui, les yeux clos, cherchent à transformer leurs pâles visages en antennes réceptrices. Ils se figurent que les sons captés coulent en eux, doux et nourrissants et que leurs souffrances deviennent musique, comme celles du jeune Werther; ils croient que la beauté leur est compatissante. Les cons (p.243).

[Admit that there are imbeciles who draw consolation from the fine arts. Like my Aunt Bigeois: "Chopin's *Preludes* were such an aid to me after the death of your poor uncle." And concert halls are bloated with the humble, with the injured who, eyes closed, seek to transform their pallid faces into receiving antennas. They imagine that the sounds they pick up pass through them, sweet and nourishing, and that their sufferings become music, like those of young Werther. They believe that beauty is compassionate toward them. The assholes]

Significantly, Roquentin's only reference to a member of his family appears here in his derision of the bourgeois Aunt Bigeois. Although he himself discovers consolation in art from the burden of existence, it is of a higher order, and it is an illusion he accepts with no illusions. "Some of These Days," the vulgar jazz song which is Roquentin's choice for aesthetic anthem, is not the soothing, soporific kind of concert piece designed to ease the sufferings of lonely hearts. Instead, it appears more precisely to fulfill the criterion which Roquentin establishes for his own projected creation: "Il faudrait qu'elle soit belle et dure comme de l'acier et qu'elle fasse honte aux gens de leur existence" [It would have to be beautiful and firm as steel and make people ashamed of their existence] (p.249).

This art must disturb rather than appease. Like Théophile Gautier's "art robuste" which "seul a l'éternité," it must be an adamantine contrast to the viscosity which has served throughout as the metaphor for existence. Such art will reflect and communicate Roquentin's initial unmediated vision of the horror of existence *en-soi*; the consequence, that it "make people ashamed of their existence," is somewhat similar to Sartre's later *engagé* injunction that "the writer give society a bad conscience."[16] Roquentin begins his spiritual progress with a sense of shame for his existence and is eventually inspired to transcend existence through art. Perhaps his novel, far from being a reassuring crutch for dotards like Aunt Bigeois, will open onto still further works by likewise shocking and inciting others. Murdoch's *Under the Net* suggests that it has. *Et tout le reste est littérature.*

As befits a work which has attempted to embody raw existence but which has also consistently been pointing beyond itself, *La Nausée* concludes somewhat provisionally in the future tense: "Tomorrow it will rain on Bouville" (p.249). The tone is one of expectation, as we look forward to Roquentin's departure from Bouville to Paris and to the first page of the novel he will write, a perfectly ordered form which will embody an awareness of the very existence it is transcending. However, also suggested is a traditional kind of novel-ending: a tentative opening outward after certain complications are resolved and characters in a work like *Germinal* can begin to look to the future.

"Demain il pleuvra sur Bouville." On the one hand, this statement suggests a sort of baptismal cleansing promised in a non-empiricist certainty about what will occur in the future. However, on the other hand, rain in Bouville will bring nothing more than mud, the emblem of dirty superfluousness in that city of mud.

La Nausée is thus open to the future, and Roquentin has the freedom which Sartre regrets is missing in the case of François Mauriac's characters.[17] Although the presence of editors suggests his disappearance or death, Roquentin has been born again. And, although the novel has come to an end, a new one is being born. Furthermore, if, as Roquentin insists, art's value is instrumental, then its life only begins with its death, the final page.

The question of whether *La Nausée* is itself the novel that Roquentin will write is probably unresolvable. It certainly successfully illustrates the criteria that Roquentin establishes. In addition, it does permit us to understand something of Roquentin's development, consistent with his vision of "the moment when the book would be completed and his life would take on some clarity" (p.249). To that extent, as with *A la recherche*, the conclusion of *La Nausée* propels us back to the beginning. Yet the work we return to remains open and lacks the finished form of a conventional novel. Cast in the mode of a journal, it might suggest scattered notes toward a novel rather than a novel which its author lived to complete. However, Roquentin's program calls for a fundamentally disquieting sort of creation, and this novel *La Nausée*, with its vivid present tense perspective on an unmasked reality, is certainly that. Whether the cunning required to devise *La Nausée* in its given form is ascribed to Jean-Paul Sartre or to his fictive author Antoine Roquentin, *La Nausée* self-consciously extends the tradition of the self-begetting novel. Time spent with it is not time lost.

4 *La Modification* and Beyond

Moi je serais devenu fou s'il avait fallu que la femme que
j'aimais habitât Paris pendant que j'étais retenu à Rome.
Marcel Proust, *A la recherche* (I, 563)

Ce que je voudrais, disait Lucien, c'est raconter l'histoire,
non point d'un personnage, mais d'un endroit, – tiens, par
exemple, d'une allée de jardin, comme celle-ci, raconter,
ce qui s'y passe – depuis le matin jusqu'au soir.
André Gide, *Les Faux-Monnayeurs* (p.13)

I A NOVEL WITH A *VOUS*

Michel Butor's *La Modification* (1957) belongs squarely within that
paradoxical French tradition exemplified by the novels of Proust and
Sartre. Recognizing and rejecting its parentage, and hence its tradition,
it begets itself. Like *A la recherche*, *La Modification* fashions its own poetic
diction, involving verse paragraphs and sentences of Faulknerian length,
in an effort to suggest a transcendental reality available in dreams and
works of art. Like *La Nausée*, *La Modification* focuses unremittingly on the
unexceptional lives of contemporary characters suffering the oppression
of space and time. It is both ambitious *summa* and well-wrought *récit*.
Restricted to a third-class railroad compartment on a trip from Paris to
Rome, the novel adheres to the unities of the French classical theater.
Yet memories, anticipations, projections, and fantasies expand the
narrative and implicate the reader in a drama as portentious as is the
continuity of Western civilization. The oxymoron devised by Michel
Leiris to describe, *La Modification*, "Le Réalisme mythologique de
Michel Butor,"[1] is an appropriate formulation of this fusion of Proustian
and Sartrean elements. In any case, *La Modification*, like its predecessors,
depicts the growth in self-awareness on the part of a central protagonist
and culminates in his decision to write his own novel.

  La Modification follows the activities and thoughts of a man from the
time he enters the third-class compartment of a train in Paris at 8:10

a.m., Friday to the time he prepares to walk out into Rome on Saturday at 5:45 a.m. He is the director of French operations for the Rome-based Scabelli typewriter company, and his wife Henrietta lives in Paris, while his lover Cécile lives in Rome. His trip from Paris to Rome is begun with the intention of leaving his family and bringing Cécile back to Paris to live with him.

We are told that his valise, a birthday gift from his family, is inscribed with the initials "L. D." (p.12).[2] Much later there is a recollection of the time when Cécile, returning from a trip to Paris, sees him on the train and shouts: "Léon!" (p.210). And, at another point, a clergyman also traveling in the compartment is portrayed as a teacher, and he is thought of as assigning the following topic: "Imagine that you are M. Léon Delmont and that you are writing to your mistress Cécile Darcella to tell her that you have found a job for her in Paris" (p.118). These constitute the only three references, indirect as they are, to the name of the principal character of the novel. Like Proust's Marcel, Durrell's Darley or Beckett's The Unnamable, Léon Delmont emerges as yet another anonymous or semi-onymous protagonist. Once again, the novel which portrays him provides him with a sort of begetting and christening. The modification in *La Modification* occurs in and through the identity of Léon Delmont. His identity is inseparable from that of the novel in which he appears, and until it is complete neither is he.

The most remarkable technical feature of Butor's novel is its use throughout of the formal second-person pronoun.[3] Instead of the conventional device of first-person or third-person narration, the central protagonist of *La Modification*, this typewriter bureaucrat named Léon Delmont pulled between Paris and Rome and between Henrietta and Cécile, is consistently, except for brief excursions into dreams, referred to as "vous." Numerous critics, including Butor himself, have called attention to the intermediary status of the second person as a provisional attempt to fuse objective and subjective perspectives.[4] *Vous* stands between *je* and *il* on more than a grammatical chart.

In addition, the second person introduces accusatory, hortatory, and interrogatory elements into the discourse. More so than *je* or *il*, *vous* suggests the paradigms of a courtroom and a schoolroom, and both dream sequences and fictional projections within the novel reinforce this. The rhetorical stance of *La Modification* serves insistently to question, admonish, and advise the main character about the very nature of his existence. This is certainly the case, for example, in the recurring image of the huntsman in the Fontainebleau forest, *le grand veneur*, whose challenges are later assembled and reasserted by a phantom police interrogator: "Qui êtes-vous? Où allez-vous? Que cherchez-vous? Qui aimez-vous? Que voulez-vous? Qu'attendez-vous? Que sentez-vous? Me voyez-vous? M'entendez-vous?" [Who are you? Where are you going? What are you looking for? Whom do you love? What do you want? What are you waiting for? What are you feeling? Do you see me? Do you hear me?] (p.252). Like the conventional epic and like *L'Innommable,* which begin with questions, or like Robert Pinget's *L'Inquisitoire, La Modification* proceeds as an inquiry, an inquest, if not a quest. Henriette is characterized by "that perpetual air of accusation" (p.109), and even "the King of Judgment" puts in a spectral appearance (p.259). The stern, direct address of *vous* satisfies Roquentin's dictum that a novel "make people ashamed of their existence" and thereby assists in the realization of the modification that occurs.

Furthermore, the prolonged apostrophe to a "vous" whom we may conditionally label "Léon Delmont" serves to create the novel's hero right before our eyes and while the work is in progress. It is as if a disembodied voice is generating the world in the act of naming it, miraculously endowing Léon Delmont with certain attributes as soon as it tells him what they are. One of the dreams in the text is of a Charon-like ferryman who, waiting to row Léon to the opposite shore, states: "I see clearly that you are dead" (p.219). The novel serves to guide Léon across that symbolic river and restore hm to life. In an essay contrasting Alain Robbe-Grillet's *chosisme* with Butor's humanism, Roland Barthes draws attention to the manner in which the narrative begets its protagonist, in which "a new man is ceaselessly being born":

> Now *La Modification* is not merely a symbolic novel; it is also a *creative* novel in the fully active sense of the term. I, for one, do not at all believe that the second-person pronoun employed by Butor in *La Modification* is a formal artifice, a clever variation on the novelistic third person for which we must give credit to "the avant-garde." This use of the second person appears literal to me; it is that of the creator to his creature, named, formed, created in all his actions by a judge and producer. This form of address is crucial, for it establishes the hero's consciousness. It is by hearing himself described from without that the hero's personality is modified and he abandons his initially firm plan to consecrate the adultery.[5]

Like the "tu" begotten in Apollinaire's "Zone," Butor's "vous" receives its identity from the expanding fictional universe in which it is implicated.

But the second-person *vous* also marks a direct address to us, the readers. We are thrust into the center-stage of the novel and are forced to assume full responsibility for what occurs. Beginning with the necessary "willing suspension of disbelief," we are asked to assume the identity of Léon Delmont for the length of the novel. However, it is not a question of what is called "identifying with" a ready-made character who happens to appeal to us as we find him in a work of literature. Instead, we are impelled to participate in the birth of a novel which entails the begetting of its hero. As we read further and are provided with more information, our outlook changes. This modification signals the growth in self-awareness, which is nothing less than the growth in self, comprising the novel. Ultimately, both reader and principal personage – if there is a distinction – grow to so lucid an awareness of the circumstances in which they find themselves that they are prepared to write the novel which will formalize this enlightenment.

The second-person point of view in *La Modification* thus functions as a means of projecting a self-begetting novel. In Albert Camus's *La Chute* (1956), we are forced to become something like defendant-confessor to complement Jean-Baptiste Clemence, the "judge-penitent." And in Robert Pinget's *Quelqu'un* (1965), "quelqu'un" refers both to the main character, an Everyman, and hence an emblem for us, and to the Someone he is seeking, a reader, "someone who would read over my shoulder."[6] Butor's *La Modification* insists even more emphatically than do these examples on the active, creative participation of the reader in the fate and genesis of hero and novel. Without the reader's complicity, the work is sterile. But with it, we once again share in the twin births of a novel and its major protagonist.

This insistence on reader collusion is not entirely absent from earlier French examples of the self-begetting novel. Proust emphasizes the fact that learning to read a novel is tantamount to learning to read oneself when, in the final volume of his self-begetting novel, the narrator affirms:

> En réalité chaque lecteur est, quand il lit, le propre lecteur de soi-même. L'ouvrage de l'écrivain n'est qu'une espèce d'instrument optique qu'il offre au lecteur afin de lui permettre de discerner ce que sans ce livre, il n'eût peut-être pas vu en soi-même (*Le Temps retrouvé*, III, 911).

> [In reality each reader is, when he reads, reading himself. The writer's work is only a kind of optical instrument he offers the reader in order to allow him to perceive what, without that book, he might never have seen in himself]

Carried to its logical conclusion, as in *La Modification*, the novel becomes an incarnation of the reader. Since the novel is inseparable from the consciousness of its main character, the reader must thereby assume the shifting identity of this character.

Similarly, in his *Le Journal des Faux-Monnayeurs*, André Gide self-consciously comments on the paramount role which the reader must play in the creation of his novel *Les Faux-Monnayeurs*:

> Puis, mon livre achevé, je tire la barre, et laisse au lecteur le soin de l'opération; addition, soustraction, peu importe: j'estime que ce n'est pas à moi de la faire. Tant pis pour le lecteur paresseux: j'en veux d'autres (pp.116–17).

> [Then, my book completed, I draw the line and leave the responsibility of operation to the reader; addition, subtraction do not matter much – I do not think it is up to me to do it. Too bad about the lazy reader; I want others]

Gide anticipates the active contribution of the reader in creating *La Modification*, as well as Marc Saporta's *Composition no. 1* (1962) – a novel whose pages are printed only on recto and where "Le lecteur est prié de battre ces pages comme un jeu de cartes. De couper, s'il le désire, de la main gauche, comme chez une cartomancienne. L'ordre dans lequel les feuillets sortiront du jeu orientera le destin de X." [The reader is requested to shuffle these pages as in a game of cards. To cut, if he wishes, with his left hand, as at a fortune teller's. The order in which the sheets emerge from the game will determine the fate of X][7] He further declares:

> Je voudrais que, dans le récit qu'ils en feront, ces événements apparaissent légèrement déformés; une sorte d'intérêt vient, pour le lecteur, de ce seul fait qu'il ait à rétablir. L'histoire requiert sa collaboration pour se bien dessiner (p.35).

> [In the narrative that they will constitute, I would like these events to appear slightly distorted; there is a kind of interest for the reader in the mere fact that he has to reconstruct. The story requires his collaboration in order to be set up properly]

Sartre's Garcin, who discovers that Hell is other people, remarks at the end of *Huis clos* that: "l'enfer, c'est les Autres." And Sartre himself has often stressed the importance of others in giving life to the heavens and hells of literary fiction. Even Antoine Roquentin, Sartre's consummate misanthrope, admits that: "Quand on vit seul, on ne sait même plus ce que c'est que raconter" [When you live alone, you no longer even know what it is to tell a story] (*La Nausée*, pp.17–18). Narration remains merely potential without both narrator and audience, a fact which the theoretician of *Qu'est-ce que la littérature?* reaffirms: "There is art only for and through another" (*Situations II*, p.93). More recently, in an exchange – published as *Que peut la littérature?* – with several of the younger French critics who concentrate on the text as autonomous system of signification, Sartre stresses the importance of the reader in creating this system. Recognizing that "There is creation in reading,"[8] the sometime novelist goes on to assert:

> J'essaie de m'imaginer que je suis mon propre lecteur – tous les auteurs font cela; travailler consiste à se couler idéalement et critiquement dans la peau d'un autre, le lecteur, qui est au fond celui qui saisira complètement l'objet, celui qui sera le créateur.[9]

> [I try to imagine to myself that I am my own reader – all authors do that. Our work consists of slipping ideally and critically into the skin of another, the reader, who is basically the one who will grasp the object completely, the one who will be the creator]

Such proclamations do not render inevitable Butor's extension of the tradition of the self-begetting novel through a second-person narrative. But they at least support his view, especially apparent in such later noncontinuous productions as *Mobile* (1962), *6 810 000 litres d'eau par seconde* (1965), and, particularly, *Votre Faust* (1962), an opera written in collaboration with Henri Pousseur in which the audience votes on how the plot is to unfold, that the reader, or at least the notion of a reader, is a vital element in creating a novel which is forever in the act of being created. Discussing *La Modification* in an interview, Butor, with a reminder that reflexive fiction did not begin with the twentieth century, states:

> I have lately been studying the works of Diderot a bit. In *Ceci n'est pas un conte*, he tells us that when you tell a story you always tell it to an interlocutor who answers. He likewise introduces into his text someone to play the role of interlocutor. By playing the role of interlocutor he also plays the role of reader. When you write something there is always a reader present.[10]

In this implicit and – through the device of *vous* – explicit interlocutory drama, the novel is continuously being born.

II   DETERMINED LIBERATION

The very first sentence of *La Modification* introduces the theme of determinism, central to French Naturalism as well as to the explorations by Proust, Gide and Sartre of the possibilities art offers of overcoming the dictates of circumstance. "Vous avez mis le pied gauche sur la rainure de cuivre, et de votre épaule droite vous essayez en vain de pousser un peu plus le panneau coulissant" [You have put your left foot on the copper grid, and with your right shoulder you try unsuccessfully to push the sliding panel a little more] (p.9). Léon Delmont, successful but aging businessman, is shown, like Don Quixote, doing battle against external forces with only partial success. Léon has celebrated his forty-fifth birthday a few days earlier, on November thirteenth.[11] Winter is approaching, and he is at a turning point in his life; but Léon resists the recognition, reinforced by the demands of a wife and four growing children, that space and time inevitably impose limitations. The opposition of a physical object like the door panel is symptomatic of his loss of youthful freedom, or at least the illusion of that freedom.

> Non, ce n'est pas seulement l'heure, à peine matinale, qui est responsable de cette faiblesse habituelle, c'est déjà l'âge qui cherche à vous convaincre de sa domination sur votre corps, et pourtant, vous venez seulement d'atteindre les quarante-cinq ans (p.9).

[No, it is not the hour, barely morning, that is responsible for this habitual weakness, it is already age which seeks to convince you of its domination over your body, and yet you have only just reached forty-five years]

La Modification and *the modification* – "this great labor which is going on inside you, little by little destroying your character, this change of lighting and perspective" (p.236) – consist, to a large extent, of a growing awareness of the nature of this tyranny of time and space, an awareness which permits a creative transcendence of the tyranny.

Léon's life in the novel is restricted to a crowded bench in a third-class compartment on a train following the tracks from Paris to Rome according to a very tightly controlled schedule. Since, unlike his regular monthly trips to the Scabelli directors' meeting in Rome, this unorthodox journey solely to see Cécile is not covered by company funds, he feels the pressures of economy now. Léon therefore must buy a third-class ticket instead of the first-class to which he is accustomed. A placard with the chiding inscription "Il est dangereux de se pencher au-dehors – E pericoloso sporgersi" (p.16) stares at him throughout. And each time he leaves the crowded compartment, for the dining car, the lavatory, or simply to smoke one of his rapidly disappearing cigarettes in the corridor, the chapter ends, and he effectively ceases to exist.

Yet he initially conceives the project of abandoning his wife and fetching the much younger Cécile as an act of liberation and rejuvenation. "Ce voyage devrait être une libération, un rajeunissement, un grand nettoyage de votre corps et de votre tête" [This trip should be a liberation, a rejuvenation, a great cleansing of your body and of your head] (p.26), he/we is told to think at the beginning. The routines of bourgeois family life and the intimations of mortality, telescoped in the birthday party given for him, have conspired to incarcerate Léon. He envisions Rome and Cécile as being somehow beyond his prison walls.

... vous avez eu l'impression qu'ils s'étaient tous entendus pour vous tendre un piège, que ces cadeaux sur votre assiette étaient un appât, que tout ce repas avait été soigneusement composé pour vous séduire (comment n'aurait-elle pas appris à les connaître, vos goûts, depuis près de vingt ans que vous vivez ensemble), tout combiné pour vous persuader que vous étiez désormais un homme âgé, rangé, dompté, alors qu'il y avait si peu de temps que s'était ouverte à vous cette vie tout autre, cette vie que vous ne meniez encore que quelques jours à Rome, cette autre vie dont celle-ci, celle de l'appartement parisien, n'était que l'ombre ... (p.38).

[... you have had the impression that they had all gotten together to set a trap for you, that those gifts on your plate were bait, that this entire meal was carefully arranged to seduce you (how could she have not learned to know your tastes during the twenty years you have been living together), all combined to persuade you that henceforth you were an aged, orderly, beaten

man, while there was so little time to become available to you this entirely
other, this life that you have as yet only led for a few days in Rome, this other
life of which this one, of the Parisian apartment, was only a shadow]

Léon's life with Henrietta is seen as confinement, asphyxiation – in
fact death; the only way in which he can be reborn is to embrace Cécile.
Married life in the Parisian apartment is seen as "that menacing
asphyxia" (p.38), while his thirty-year-old mistress in Rome represents
at the outset "that mouthful of air" (p.42). Léon has been the uncon-
scious victim of forces which have been shaping his life without his active
consent. When even an inchoate degree of awareness convinces him of
his slavery to custom, Léon's first reaction is rebellion and a naïve
assertion of what he considers his freedom, "your liberty who is named
Cécile" (p.55). In his first exuberant moments on the train, as Paris and
Henriette – but his hairline as well – recede, Léon's reaction is temporary
exhilaration. "But now that's it, it's done, you're free" (p.85). But
qualifications on this illusory sovereignty immediately begin to make
themselves felt.

Léon's life has been devoted to selling typewriters, *machines à écrire*, and
mechanistic metaphors play an important part in the novel in depicting
the tension between free will and a rigid chain of causality. There is, of
course, the railroad car, which is presumably Léon's celestial eagle
propelling him toward "this salvation, Cécile" (p.42), but it is also an
inexorable machine pushing him through space and time according to a
rigorously preordained scheme. Cécile's reprimand, based on her horror
of the Christian, rather than pagan, elements in Léon, contains a truth
which she does not recognize: "the humblest Roman cook has a freer
mind than you" (p.168). It is precisely Léon's melodramatic attempt to
deny his background, to abandon the values of Catholic Paris in favor of
imperial Rome that demonstrates his bondage to it.

His very decision to reject Henriette and undertake an heroic voyage
of liberation is thus very early in the novel placed within the context of
mechanistic inevitability. At the end of the first chapter, we are told: "it
is the mechanism which you have yourself set in motion which is
beginning to unwind almost without your knowing." The impersonal
clockwork is still scarcely perceived at this point, but later, when vexing
thoughts begin to subvert his original intentions, they are likened to the
relentlessly efficient gears on the train:

Mais il n'est plus temps maintenant, leurs chaines solidement affermies par ce
voyage se déroulent avec le sûr mouvement même du train, et malgré tous vos
efforts pour vous en dégager, pour tourner votre attention ailleurs, vers cette
décision que vous sentez vous échapper, les voici qui vous entraînent dans
leurs engrenages (p.163).

[But there is no longer any time now, their chains solidly strengthened by this trip unroll with the sure movement even of the train, and despite all your efforts to disengage yourself, to turn your attention elsewhere, toward that decision that you feel escaping you, here they are dragging you into their gears]

Ironically, if the decision to join Cécile is the necessary result of a sequence of events, if his journey of escape to Rome occurs on a swift, impersonal machine, and if, in fact, as flashbacks suggest, Léon's relationship with Cécile in the first place is the consequence merely of loneliness and passivity away from home, his own misgivings and eventual modification of the original plan are likewise seen in a deterministic context. After the project of casting his fate with Cécile is definitely abandoned, this abandonment itself is visualized as the product of a "mental machine."

Vous vous dites: s'il n'y avait pas eu ces gens, s'il n'y avait pas eu ces objets et ces images auxquels se sont accrochées mes pensées de telle sorte qu'une machine mentale s'est constituée, faisant glisser l'une sur l'autre les régions de mon existence au cours de ce voyage different des autres, détaché de la séquence habituelle de mes journées et de mes actes, me déchiquetant

s'il n'y avait pas eu cet ensemble de circonstances, cette donne du jeu, peut-être cette fissure béante en ma personne ne se serait-elle pas produite cette nuit, mes illusions auraient-elles pu tenir encore quelque temps (p.274).

[You tell yourself: if there had not been those people, if there had not been those objects and those images on which my thoughts have been hung in such a way that a mental machine was formed, making the regions of my existence slide over each other during this trip which is different from others, detached from the usual pattern of my days and my acts, shredding me

If there had not been this combination of circumstances, this deal of cards, perhaps this benign fissure in my personality would not have occurred tonight, my illusions could still have remained intact for some time]

In his paranoia – and in this novel where credence is creative, to believe in oppressive, impersonal forces is to endow them with reality – Léon sees Henriette and Cécile merging into the common identity of universal shrew. "Seriez-vous donc maintenant ballotté entre ces deux reproches, ces deux rancunes, ces deux accusations de lâcheté?" [Would you therefore now be tossed between these two reproaches, these two grudges, these two accusations of cowardice?] (p.109). During the cordial meeting of the two in Paris, "vous avez assisté à ce prodige: Cécile, votre secours, vous trahissait, passait du côté Henriette; à travers de leur jalousie quelque chose comme un mépris commun se faisait jour" [you were present at this wonder: Cécile, your support, was betraying you, deserting to Henriette's camp; through their jealousy something like a common scorn was developing] (p.186). Léon becomes convinced that both his illusion of "a marvelous life of adventure" (p.55) with Cécile and his painful recognition that it is merely illusion, "you can only love Cécile truly to the extent that she is for you the face of Rome" (pp.237–8), are conditioned reactions. Both his desperate grasp at liberation and his rejection of this naïve course of action are intertwined with the onerous world of the machine. Is there any escape when even leaning out the window is prohibited, and when even escape – and rejection of escape – is illusory?

Although Léon is restricted to a third-class compartment aboard a train speeding from Paris to Rome, he becomes the centrifuge of a much vaster universe. Past and future, memory and anticipation emanate from him as he sits quietly on the train. As he temporarily loses contact with his immediate surroundings, dreams provide him access to a super-natural realm populated by demons and huntsmen. Due to the move-ment of Léon's mind, a more thorough modification than the simple linear trajectory of the train from Paris to Rome, evocations of trips between the two capitals in both directions multiply. In addition to the Friday morning journey depicted in the present tense, there are, for example, Léon's wintry vacation trip with Henriette to Rome, his journey several days earlier to the monthly Scabelli meeting, his trips in both directions with Cécile when she decided to visit Paris, as well as Léon's steadily changing projection of what his return to Paris will be like when his current stay in Rome is concluded. Furthermore, we are increasingly assaulted with Léon's recollections of his activities in Paris and Rome, as well as with expectations of his future course of action at both ends of the line.

Moreover, the drama of the novel is not confined to the romantic tribulations of one undistinguished businessman. Instead, Léon – and his identification with *vous* is once again thematically functional – comes to attest to a crisis in Western civilization. The world in which he moves is saturated with traditional significations, and we are presented with the spectacle not merely of private memeory but of history. Léon's walks through Rome with Cécile, who is nothing less than "the face of Rome" (p.238), invariably bring him to the site of ancient ruins, an historical monument, or a gallery of time-honored paintings. The Delmont Parisian apartment is appropriately located on the place du Panthéon, within close proximity to the temple of French culture. Henriette is no less an incarnation of Paris, and each of Léon's attempts to transpose one of his two local goddesses into the domain of the other proves disastrous.

Henriette's greatest satisfaction in Italy comes when she visits the Vatican and sees the Pope, but Cécile, whose allegiance is to the spirit of pre-Christian Rome, has an utter aversion to entering the Vatican. Her harshest words for Léon come in the accusation: "Tu es pourri de christianisme jusqu'aux moelles, malgré toutes tes protestations, de dévotion la plus sotte" [You are rotten to the marrow with Christianity, despite all your disclaimers, of the stupidest kind of devotion] (p.168). Yet Léon's affair with Cécile represents an attempt to enter into the spirit of pagan Rome, of the ancient emperors and gods who visit him in a vision (p.268). This typewriter salesman somewhat incongruously begins building a collection of Latin authors in his Paris apartment. Included are the letters of the apostate Emperor Julian. As much as anything else, his actions throughout the novel constitute an effort to balance the two worlds with each other and to establish a continuity between both traditions and the future, which is not simply the unfolding of his personal fortunes. In a dream, he is told that he, like Aeneas, is "à la recherche de ton père afin qu'il t'enseigne l'avenir de la race" [in search of your father so he can teach you the history of the race] (p.214). His venture has a much larger significance than that of determining whether he will end up with a new mate, and its failure threatens "an immense historical fissure" (p.274).

The wealth of meaningful detail which radiates from Léon's fertile confinement in the railroad car thus conjures up allusions to classical and Christian European civilization. In so doing, it tentatively suggests a way out of the machine. Léon is walking through the Louvre or sipping tea on the via Monte della Farina at the moment he is supposed to be imprisoned in a train.

Yet, however liberating these other worlds potentially are, they prove to be but deception and *déception*. The polarization of Paris and Rome is as much an operational fiction as is Marcel's diametrical opposition of Guermantes and Méséglise ways. In Paris, Léon works for a Roman firm, goes into a Roman bar, looks at Italian paintings, and passes the baths of the apostate Emperor Julian. And the Vatican, associated with Henriette and Paris, is in Rome, as is the French embassy, where, ironically, Cécile works. Most destructive of the notion that this is a tale of two cities is the fact that the guardian angels of Paris and Rome, Henriette and Cécile, come increasingly to resemble one another, despite a difference in age. During their meeting in Paris, they hit it off well and even seem to be conspiring against Léon. There is no escape for him from Paris, which incorporates both pagan and Christian worlds. Every one of his journeys to Rome entails a return to Paris.

Eventually, of course, Léon determines to abandon his naïve original scheme. He will not even inform Cécile of his arrival in Rome. Instead, he will head for a hotel room where, like Marcel and Roquentin before him, he will begin to write a novel. In it, history will not be the nightmare from which both Léon, with his recurring dreams of an inquisitor, and Stephen Dedalus are trying to awake. All of the circumstances and allusions leading up to his decision to write a novel will be presented lucidly, and the past, rather than controlling the future through the pressure of its unexamined myths, will be re-created in this "future and necessary book" (p.283). If it is necessary, the novel would seem to possess the Augustinian necessity of free will exercised in making the only right choice and the Aristotelian necessity which makes literature more meaningful than history. Left behind is the imprisoning necessity of the machine. Léon tells himself:

il me faut écrire un livre; ce serait pour moi le moyen de combler le vide qui s'est creusé, n'ayant plus d'autre liberté, emporté dans ce train jusqu'à la gare, de toute façon lié, obligé de suivre ces rails (p.272).

[I must write a book; this would be for me the way to fill the vacuum which has been created, no longer having any other freedom, carried in this train until the terminal, in any event linked, forced to follow these rails]

Léon will remain in Rome until Monday evening to begin writing his novel. For the first time in his life, he will be absolutely free. No one in the world – not Henriette, not Cécile, not Signor Scabelli – will know where he is or how to get in touch to continue demands on him. Instead, like the traditional solitary novelist figure and unlike a corporation executive, he will remain in creative confinement in his Roman hotel room composing his *roman*. He does recognize: "I cannot hope to save myself alone" (p.274); but the novel, a product of solitude, will be a means both of reaching toward "that future liberty out of our reach" (p.274) and of re-composing a sundered community. It will implicate *vous* in every stage of its enlightenment.

Léon recognizes that he will continue to live with his family at 15 place du Panthéon, will continue in "this false, damaging work at Scabelli's" (p.272), and will even continue to see Cécile during monthly visits to Rome. The modification which occurs in the novel and by means of a novel is more momentous than a mere change in plans. The truth has set Léon free. He learns to view his illusions and actions with total clarity by means of a novel, and the novel becomes an assertion of his freedom. The final sentence of *La Modification*, which is only the beginning of another novel, reveals an emancipation: "You leave the compartment" (p.283). Whether in Paris or Rome, it is invigorating to stretch our legs.

III   VARIATIONS ON A THEME BY PANNINI

As Butor demonstrates in his essay "Les Oeuvres d'art imaginaires chez Proust,"[12] he has carefully studied the manner in which *A la recherche* incorporates the work of such fictive artists as Elstir, Vinteuil or Bergotte into its total design. His own discussions of painters, including Claude Monet, Jacques Hérold and Mark Rothko, place him in the tradition of such Frenchmen as Baudelaire, Apollinaire and Malraux.[13] Not surprisingly, *La Modification*, which is the account of the birth of a novel, is replete with references to achievements in all the major arts.

Léon's travels take him to Saint Peter's and Notre Dame, but, simply sitting in his easy chair within view of the Pantheon, he listens to portions of Monteverdi's *Orfeo*, gazes at two Piranesi etchings hanging on his wall, and opens his copy of the *Aeneid*. He walks through the Louvre, but his main interest takes him past the abundance of works by Guardi, Magnasco, Watteau, Chardin, Fragonard, Goya and David; the Louvre has a more impressive collection than the Bouville museum. If Proust's novel can rely on fictional works of art, "imaginary gardens with real toads in them," Butor takes his work one step further. He has his imaginary Léon halt his tour of the Louvre in front of two "real" paintings by the minor Italian artist Pannini.[14] But these works themselves in turn depict galleries of fictive paintings:

> Ce que vous avez amoureusement détaillé, ce vers quoi vos pas vous avaient mené, ce sont deux grands tableaux d'un peintre de troisième ordre, Pannini, représentant deux collections imaginaires exposées dans de très hautes salles largement ouvertes où des personnages de qualité, ecclésiastiques ou gentilshommes, se promènent parmi les sculptures entre les murs couverts de paysages, en faisant des gestes d'admiration, d'intérêt, de surprise, de perplexité, comme les visiteurs dans la Sixtine . . . (p.66).

> [What you have lovingly detailed, what your steps had led you toward, are two large pictures by a third-rate painter, Pannini, representing two imaginary collections exhibited in very high, spacious rooms where figures of quality, clergy or gentlemen, walk among the sculptures between the walls covered with landscapes, while making gestures of admiration, of interest, of surprise, of perplexity, like visitors in the Sistine . . .]

We are confronted with a Chinese box puzzle of a work of art within a work of art within a work of art; and there is the added complication that the second in the series is an "authentic" invention, whereas its two frames are merely contrivances devised by Butor.

However, the Pannini paintings are even more extraordinary in the relationship they posit between their imaginary works of art and what they represent as the reality actually surrounding them within the paintings. They manifest:

> . . . ceci de remarquable qu'il n'y a aucune différence de matière sensible entre les objets représentés comme réels et ceux représentés comme peints, comme s'il avait voulu figurer sur ses toiles la réussite de ce projet commun à tant d'artistes de son temps: donner un équivalent absolu de la réalité, le chapiteau peint devenant indiscernable du chapiteau réel, à part le cadre qui l'entoure, de même que les grands architectes illusionnistes du baroque romain peignant

dans l'espace et donnent à imaginer, grace à leurs merveilleux systèmes de signes, leurs agrégations de pilastres, et leurs voluptueuses courbes, des monuments rivilisant enfin dans l'effet et le prestige avec les énormes masses réeles des ruines antiques qu'ils avaient perpétuellement sous les yeux et qui les humiliaient, intégrant méthodiquement les détails de leur ornementation comme base même de leur langage (pp.66–7).

[. . . the remarkable feature that there is no perceptible difference between the objects represented as real and those represented as painted, as if he had wanted his canvases to portray the success of that ambition common to so many artists of his time: to provide an absolute equivalent of reality, the painted capital becoming indistinguishable from the real capital, aside from the frame surrounding it, in the same way as the great illusionist architects of the Roman Baroque paint in space and lead you to imagine, thanks to their marvelous systems of signs, their collections of pilasters, and their voluptuous curves, monuments ultimately rivaling in effect and prestige the enormous real masses of ancient ruins which they had forever under their eyes and which humbled them, methodically assimilating the details of the ornamentation as the very foundation of their language]

As in the Pannini paintings, and in *A la recherche* and *La Nausée*, the numerous references to artistic creations within *La Modification* produce a reflexive effect. The novel self-consciously calls attention to its own problematic ontological status. Nevertheless, the second-person technique of reader involvement tends to collapse the outer frame, as the "reality" in which we readers bathe interacts with the "artificial" world of the novel. In addition, works of art are so pervasive and function so prominently and vitally in *La Modification* that, as with Pannini's painted column and real column, everything becomes meaningful and potentially creative for Léon and tends to merge into a new continuum. Like the Baroque Roman illusionists referred to, *La Modification* learns to live with the oppressive mass of lingering works of Western art by fashioning them all into a fresh reality. There will be no opposition of art and life in Léon's new stance.

The reflexiveness of *La Modification* even reaches as far as ironic self-criticism. Léon fantasizes about the clergyman sitting across from him and sees him as a teacher grading writing assignments. He imagines that the comments the teacher would make about Léon's own attempt to compose on topics such as "Imagine that you are the representative in Paris of an Italian typewriter company, you are writing your Roman director to explain to him that you have decided to take four days off" or "Imagine that you want to separate from your wife; you are writing her to explain the situation to her" (pp.117–18). These themes are of course variations on the plot of *La Modification* itself. Léon envisions the comments the clergyman would make about his writing attempts, such judgments as "The sentences you make are too long," "Off the subject," or "You obviously have never been in love" (p.118). These attacks could presumably be leveled against the novel *La Modification* itself. Its sentences at times extend over several pages, it consistently "digresses" from the immediate situation of the train compartment, and, as a treatment of the eternal romantic triangle, it is curiously lacking in love. These invented writing topics and points of criticism of course represent stages in Léon's automotion toward awareness. They already cast him in the role of a novelist increasingly sensitive to his material and to the refinements of his art.

In fact, Léon assimilates the bare reality in which he moves via a fictionalizing process no different in kind from that of the novelist. This is obviously the case when he strays into the dream world of huntsmen, gods and inquisitors, as well as when he mythologizes Paris and Rome and personifies them through Henriette and Cécile. However, Léon also tends in his own mind to invent a name and a story for each of the varied passengers who share the compartment with him during sections of his journey from Paris to Rome. He never has a conversation with any of them. Relying simply on visual impressions, he assigns hypothetical occupations and nationalities to each of his fellow strangers on a train. In addition to the clergyman whom he envisions as a teacher, one becomes a professor of law, another a traveling salesman, still another a manual worker. A man in a raincoat is allotted the identity of an Englishman somewhat inept in a Continental setting and ignorant that, for example, use of the toilet is prohibited while the train is in a station. A young man and woman sitting opposite Léon are cast as newlyweds named Pierre and Agnès. In what is in effect the mental novel he composes for them, he imagines them taking this train on their honeymoon and projects elements of his own early days with Henriette onto them. Léon guesses that one of his fellow passengers is Italian and christens him Signor Lorenzo, only to discern later on an opened passport the name Ettore Carli (p.160).

Almost everyone on the train comes equipped with some reading material. "Agnès" has a guide book and a woman's magazine, the clergyman is absorbed in a breviary, the "Englishman" has a copy of the *Manchester Guardian*, the "salesman" has a movie magazine, and the "professor" is busy with a legal text of some sort. All these representations of the act of reading once again remind us that we are reading a novel exploring the powers of literature. Like Léon's home library, the image of the train passing Lamartine's famed lake (p.70), and the dream of "the shower of scraps of pages" (p.224), they create a context of literary reflexiveness and look forward to the pages Léon will write.

Along with a train schedule, Léon himself carries a novel with him on his trip. It is a volume he has selected at random, "without reading either the title or the name of the author" (pp.13–14), from the book shop in the Paris station. Léon never begins to read the novel during his entire journey, and he never even learns who wrote it or what it is called. He does speculate on its contents, as he does on the identities of his fellow passengers, once again fantasizing and extrapolating elements from his own difficult situation:

> il faudrait qu'il soit question par exemple d'un homme perdu dans une forêt qui se referme derrière lui sans qu'il arrive, même pour décider de quel côté il lui convient d'aller maintenant, à retrouver quel est le chemin qui l'a conduit là, parce que ses pas ne laissent nulle trace sur les feuilles mortes accumulées dans lesquelles il enfonce (p.202).

> [it would have to deal, for example, with a man lost in a forest which closes in behind him without his succeeding, even in order to decide which direction he should take now, in finding again which path took him there, because his steps do not leave any trace in the mass of dead leaves into which he sinks]

Léon's companion book functions as a place-holder for him; at the ends of chapters, he abandons the compartment for brief periods and leaves the novel on his seat to indicate someone will be back. Ironically ignored and even mistreated – Léon is shown sitting on it and later letting it slip onto the floor – throughout the journey, this anonymous novel-within-a-novel serves as a surrogate for the gradually onymous hero.

> Enfoncé dans la rainure où se rejoignent la banquette et le dossier, il y a ce livre que vous aviez acheté au départ, non lu mais conservé tout au long du voyage comme une marque de vous-même, que vous aviez oublié en quittant le compartiment tout à l'heure, que vous aviez lâché en dormant et qui s'était glissé peu à peu sous votre corps (p.272).

> [Wedged into that groove between the seat and the back is that book that you had bought on leaving, not read but saved throughout the trip as a marker for yourself, which you had forgotten on leaving the compartment earlier, which you had let go of while sleeping, and which had gradually slipped under your body.]

Une marque de vous-même, the book Léon holds is also a temporary proxy for the novel he will write at the end of his trip, "that future and necessary book whose form you hold in your hand" (p.283). In effect a blank slate silently recording all that occurs during the momentous train journey, the book is both an image of Léon's future novel and a stimulus for its conception:

> vous retournez entre vos doigts ce livre que vous n'avez pas lu, mais par la présence duquel commence à s'imposer si fortement à vous un autre livre que vous imaginez, ce livre dont vous désireriez tant qu'il fût pour vous, dans les circonstances présentes, ce guide bleu des égarés . . . (p.231).

[you turn over between your fingers that book you have not read, but by whose presence another book which you are imagining, that book which you wish so much could be, in the present circumstances, that blue guide to the perplexed, begins to assert itself so forcefully]

Léon will learn to use words in a manner for which Scabelli's machines only suggest the potential. Similarly, the book which he holds and which is in effect empty will come to be filled with his identity. Who touches that book touches Léon Delmont, and not simply because it marks his presence on the train.

Ultimately, just as the novel on the train serves as a double for the novel Léon will write, his gradual development as a writer will be the basis for the novel in which he appears, *La Modification*. The protagonist becomes the book he carries, and the novel he writes becomes the life of its principal character. *La Modification* again, it is the begetting of a *vous*. Recognizing "it would be necessary to show in this book the role which Rome can play in the life of a man in Paris" (p.277), Léon outlines the program of his projected novel:

> Le mieux, sans doute, serait de conserver à deux villes leurs relations géographiques réeles,
>
> et de tenter de faire revivre sur le mode de la lecture cet épisode crucial de votre aventure, le mouvement qui s'est produit dans votre esprit accompagnant le déplacement de votre corps d'une gare à l'autre à travers tous les paysages intermédiaires (p.283).

> [It would doubtless be best for these two cities to retain their real geographical relations,
>
> and to attempt to revive in the method of reading that crucial episode of your adventure, the movement produced in your mind accompanying your body's journey from one station to the other through all the landscapes along the way]

The descriptions apply quite well to the novel we have just concluded reading, and an anonymous novel has finally found a name, *La Modification*. Once again we have witnessed – or rather participated in – the begetting of a novel. *La Modification* is no exception to Jean Roudaut's assertion: "No work of Butor's ever concludes."[15] To read Léon's – and our – novel, we must turn back to the first page to begin the account of a change in outlook whose manifestation is a work of literature. After their disappointing vacation in Rome, Léon promises Henriette: "As soon as we can, we will come back" (p.282), Léon will return to his family and job after his trip, and *La Modification* arches back to its origins. The novel does not conclude with the exit from the compartment. Instead, as soon as we are able we must return to read the novel Léon writes.

But the return here is no more a repetition than it is in *A la recherche*. A modification has occurred in Léon and, more importantly, in ourselves. "Il faut changer la vie" [life must be changed], declares the essayist Butor, echoing Rimbaud.

> Any literature which does not assist us in this plan, even if despite its author, is at a more or less crucial deadline (and the press of events creates such urgency, the disorder of the world is so acute that I tend more and more to believe that it is a very imminent deadline) inevitably condemned.[16]

La Modification, which demands the active participation of *vous* in the construction of a subtle network of tropisms, is not the static performance its author deplores. "A book must be a mobile stimulating the mobility of other books, a flame igniting their fire,"[17] affirms Butor; he answers with *Mobile*, a collage attempt at representing the United States by juxtaposing varied details of it, and *6 810 000 litres d'eau par sedonde*, an attempt through sight and sound to duplicate the rush of Niagara Falls. *La Modification*, too, is a moving experience.

IV   OTHER FRENCH NOVELTIES

In an essay whose very title, "Le Roman comme recherche," reveals a debt to the Proustian form, Butor presents a manifesto for the self-begetting novel. Contending that "the novel is the laboratory of narrative,"[18] he elevates the highly sophisticated, self-conscious characteristics of works like *A la recherche*, *La Nausée* and *La Modification* into a prescription for the novel in general. For him, as for the Roquentin who declares, "a man is always a storyteller; he lives surrounded by his stories and the stories of others" (*La Nausée*, p.60): "Until we die and from the time we begin to understand words, we are perpetually surrounded by stories, in our family first of all, then at school, then through encounters and readings."[19] The duty of the writer is to seize these stories, which are merely raw material, and to help shape them into novel forms. Each of his efforts, like those of Butor himself, must represent a fresh departure, a *roman expérimental* more thorough than any of Zola's in its exploration of the technical possibilities of the genre. Alain Robbe-Grillet concurs in the view that "the modern novel is a quest, but a quest which itself creates its own meanings gradually."[20]

In "Intervention à Royaumont," Butor's personal poetic testament, the work of fiction is seen as an organism capable of independent reproduction, and the novelist becomes a mere midwife, "the instrument for its entry into the world, its obstetrician." As in *La Modification* and similar works in which protagonist and novel are cast in maieutic roles, the novel begets itself, and its historical author is important simply as delivery boy. Furthermore, through this kind of immaculate conception, the novel is able to pursue that formal exploration which Butor sees as its proper activity.

> If it is true that there exists an intimate connection between form and content, as they used to say in our schools, I believe it is right to insist on the fact that in reflecting on form the novelist finds a privileged means of attack, a means of forcing the real to reveal itself, to conduct its own activity.[21]

Fictional possibilities are not restricted to the narrative which culminates in the decision of its hero to write a novel. But reflection on its own techniques and goals must be explicit in the work. "The novel is naturally and inevitably drawn toward its own elucidation."[22]

Yet Butor admits that there exist novels which cannot be considered *recherche*, which are blatantly devoid of the self-consciousness upon which he insists:

> We are well aware that situations exist which are characterized by an incapacity to reflect upon themselves, which endure only through the illusion they maintain toward their subject; and it is to them that those works within which that unity cannot appear correspond, those novelistic attitudes which refuse to be interrogated on the nature of their work and the validity of the forms they employ, of those forms which could not be reflexive without immediately exposing their inadequacy, their falsehood, of those forms which give us an image of reality in flagrant contradiction with that reality which gave birth to them and which they are trying to conceal.[23]

Judgment of these deviants must be unequivocal and severe. It becomes the responsibility of criticism to ferret out such offenders against the reflexive imperative.

> There are some impostures which criticism is obliged to denounce, for such works, despite their charms and their merits, support and deepen the darkness, maintain the consciousness in its contradictions, in its blindness risking to lead it toward more fatal disorders.[24]

As critic, Butor has devoted articles to such admirably sophisticated writers as Joyce, Proust, Pound, Mallarmé and Diderot. However, in "Balzac et la réalité,"[25] he attempts to defend the prolific nineteenth-century author in terms of the standards of the reflexive novel. Balzac has in effect been hanged in effigy by Robbe-Grillet, who, in *Pour un nouveau roman* (1963), portrayed *La Comédie humaine* as an embodiment of the obsolete values which the "new novel" must discard if it is to renew itself. Yet Butor calls attention to the figure of d'Arthez in *Un Grand homme de province à Paris*, a novelist-within-a-novel who is determined to revolutionize the genre beyond Scott. In addition, there are the *Etudes philosophiques, Etudes analytiques,* and the foreword of 1842, which incorporate some degree of self-awareness. Butor can thus graciously exempt Balzac from a stern proscription imposed against those who have sinned against the light of the self-begetting novel.

Butor's activities do not neatly divide into the categories of creative and critical. His novels certainly project a consciousness of their own aims as well as those inherent in the genre, while his essays are *recherches* with the same preoccupations, and their goal is modification of the reader. This combination is by no means unique in contemporary French letters, as such varied examples as Alain Robbe-Grillet, Claude Mauriac and Philippe Sollers testify.

Jean-Paul Sartre, a novelist who has abjured his former bourgeois magic in favor of criticism, notes: "We have today, since Mallarmé, entered into the period in which art criticizes itself. . . . Subsequently, most of the arts and even literature have been criticizing themselves."[26] This view is shared by Butor, who maintains that reflexiveness, far from being the idiosyncrasy of a few specialized *Künstlerromanen,* ". . . is one of the fundamental characteristics of contemporary art: novel of the novel, theater of the theater, cinema of the cinema. . . ."[27] Still another influential observer in and of the French scene, Roland Barthes, nods to the creator of Roquentin and suggests that reflexiveness is so characteristic of contemporary literature that this might very well be known as the century of *Qu'est-ce que la littérature?*[28] Barthes formulates his historical overview thus:

> Over the centuries, our writers did not imagine that it was possible to consider literature (the word itself is recent) as a language, subject, like any other language, to logical distinction. Literature never reflected on itself (sometimes on its figures, but never on its being); it never divided itself into an object at once observing and being observed. In short, it spoke but did not speak to itself. But then, probably with the first tremors of the proper bourgeois conscience, literature began to feel double – simultaneously object and view of that object, speech and speech about that speech, literary object and meta-literature.[29]

This sketch of creative evolution would seem to ignore pre-modern writers like Diderot or Fielding, as well as the extremely sophisticated use of doubles, mirrors, and plays-within-plays during the Renaissance to produce "meta-literature," a means of examining the literature itself. Claude Mauriac even contends, in *L'Alittérature contemporaine* (1958, new edition 1969), that the history of literature is congruent with the history of what he calls *alittérature.* In any case, though, Barthe's reading of history would commend the self-begetting novel to a central position in post-World War II French thought. The sense of progress implicit in his statement – note the iconoclastic delight in "les premiers ébranlements de la bonne conscience bourgeoise"[the first tremors of the proper bourgeois conscience] – suggests that Barthes, like Butor, prescribes, rather than merely describes, reflexive fiction.

Furthermore, if the novel must beget itself, so too must criticism. Many of the elements incorporated into the self-begetting novel can in fact be found among the contemporary writers to whom the term *structuralist* is more or less loosely applied and who echo Barthes's call for criticism that is "*connaissance* of the other and *co-naissance* of oneself into the world." In their essays in *Tel quel* and its stepchild *Change*, they adopt an approach to the literary text as an autonomous system of signs, contending with Barthes that "for the writer, *write* is an intransitive verb."[30] A novel thus comes to define itself through its own internal resonances. In "L'Histoire dans l'histoire,"[31] therefore, Jean Ricardou picks up Gide's notion of *mise en abîme* and examines the manner in which stories-within-stories function to develop and refine fictional themes. And Jean Thibaudeau regards "Le roman comme autobiographie," as if every novel were a reflexive *Bildungsroman*. As in works which beget themselves and their creators, "it is a matter not of constructing a 'self,' in its relations to another, but of inventing a non-subjective "I," simply producer of the text."[32] Philippe Sollers, director of the *Tel quel* series and novelist, declares in the cover-note to his *Drame*: "nous sommes donc, au présent, sur la scène de la parole." [We are therefore, at present, on the stage of speech][33] With their linguistic orientation, the Structuralists as critics and novelists invite us to witness in each work the birth of language even prior to the birth of literature. As Ricardou points out, in "Naissance d'une déesse,"[34] it was in fact a mistaken etymology of the name Aphrodite which was responsible for concocting the myth of a goddess born from the sea: hence his belief that the birth of linguistic forms precedes the birth of fiction. With these developments in French writing, we are in the anteroom even of the *anti-roman*.

Amid the bustle of self-begetting in art and criticism over the past twenty-five years, the terms "New novel" and, to a lesser extent, "anti-novel" have emerged as rallying points. Robbe-Grillet and Butor have been the two novelists most sensationally associated with the label *nouveau roman*. However, a number of others, chiefly under the patronage of the publishing, house *Les Editions de minuit*, such as Claude Simon, Robert Pinget, Nathalie Sarraute and Samuel Beckett, are also usually considered "new novelists." Their approaches differ so substantially that it is difficult to isolate qualities common to them all, and some critics have even doubted that the epithet *nouveau roman* is anything but a creature of public relations. Nevertheless, an Anglo-Saxon, John Sturrock, has hazarded a generalization, arriving at the conclusion that "the property common to all *nouveaux romans* is that they embody the creative activity of the novelist – they display the novelist at work."[35] Such a definition could as aptly be applied to the self-begetting novel.

Epistolary elements in Pinget's *Baga* (1958) stress the theme of writing, and his *Quelqu'un* (1965) does, like *La Modification,* insist on reader participation in its creation, as we become the "someone" capable of overcoming the narrator's isolation. Similarly, Robbe-Grillet's novels typically involve fragments of a crime which the reader, in imitation of the novelist's activity, must reconstruct for himself. And he appropriately stresses the active and conscious role of the reader in contemporary fiction.

> For, far from neglecting it, the author today proclaims the absolute need he has for his cooperation, a cooperation which is active, conscious, and creative. What he asks of him is no longer to receive ready-made a world that is completed, full, self-contained; it is, rather, to participate in a creation, to take his turn in inventing the work.[36]

Nathalie Sarraute's *Entre la vie et la mort* (1968) is an account of the genesis of a novel, its hovering between life and death, and her *Les Fruits d'or* (1963) presents the differing critical reaction after the publication of a novel entitled *Les Fruits d'or.* Of Samuel Beckett's contribution to French fiction and the self-begetting tradition, much more later.

Nathalie Sarraute's *Tropismes* first appeared in 1939, and the most prominent "new novelists" continue to publish today. However, the *nouveau roman* first began to attract widespread attention about 1953, the year of *Les Gommes* and *L'Innommable,* and by the mid-sixties, as scholarly studies and histories proliferated, it had lapsed into respectability. In the nineteen-seventies, the "new novel" is no longer new, an observation which is itself no longer a novelty.

The works of the "new novelists" are generally highly self-conscious, employing, as does Simon, unusual styles that call attention to themselves or deliberately frustrating readers interested in the anecdotal element of fiction. But they certainly do not all explicitly concentrate on a novelist figure who constructs the work in which he appears. Butor, continuously compared to Robbe-Grillet, once gave his opinion of the distinction between himself and the other principal "new novelist:" "In the novels of Robbe-Grillet, there is no effort to reflect on the very work of the novelist within the novel; there seems to be no trace of the problem which I pose of the relations between people and works of art. That is to my mind an enormous difference."[37] Is there a proud hint of "vive la différence énorme!" here? Butor appears to be portraying himself as a more thoroughgoing practitioner of the self-begetting novel than his rival. According to Butor's assertions elsewhere about the obligations of the novel, *La Modification* would be a "purer" contribution to the genre than, for example, *Le Voyeur.* Robbe-Grillet's work certainly keeps the reader constantly mindful of the fact that he is constructing a fiction; but this literary self-consciousness is more intricately articulated in the account of the genesis of a novel. If, as Butor and Barthes suggest, reflexiveness is a supreme virtue in literature, the self-begetting narrative is the *aqua pura* of the "new novel."

Vivian Mercier, in a study of the *nouveau roman*,[38] devotes a chapter to Claude Mauriac, although the latter began writing novels somewhat later than the others; and, not a protégé of *Les Editions de minuit*, he could not be lumped with those whom *Yale French Studies* designated "Midnight Novelists."[39] The eldest son of Sartre's bugbear, Claude Mauriac produced several works of non-fiction, including studies of Proust – *Marcel Proust par lui-même* (1953) – and Gide – *Conversations avec André Gide* (1951) – before finding at least one of his vocations as novelist in the late fifties.

La Marquise sortit à cinq heures (1961) is the third of four works featuring the novelist Bertrand Carnéjoux. Like *La Modification*, *La Marquise sortit à cinq heures* adheres to a unity of time, place, and action, It restricts itself to one hour, from five to six p.m., at one specific intersection in Paris, the Carrefour de Buci. However, like Butor's novel, this novel's strict localization is merely the occasion for an ambitious mental leap through space and time. Claude Desprez, an autograph dealer, realizes: "J'ai sous le yeux, d'un même regard, cinq minutes et cinq siècles de la vie du carrefour" (p.11) [I have beneath my eyes, in the same glance, five minutes and five centuries in the life of the intersection].[40] And this simultaneity of historical moments in one neighborhood does not remain isolated from the rest of the globe, as in various ways we are reminded of America, Algeria and Vietnam. Mauriac's novel likewise expands into a thorough probe of the relationship between fiction and "reality," a probe which reflects on its own genesis.

As we are informed in the epigraph, as well as within the work by a character who is writing a novel with the same opening sentence (p.89), the title *La Marquise sortit à cinq heures* derives from a statement by Paul Valéry. According to André Breton, in *Premier manifeste du surréalisme*, Valéry once declared to him that he would never submit to the novelistic practice of padding works with such superfluous statements as "La marquise sortit à cinq heures" [The marquise went out at five o'clock]. The first words of Mauriac's novel are "La marquise sortit à cinq heures," but the final ones recant: "La marquise ne sortit pas à cinq heures" [The marquise did not go out at five o'clock]. Between these two sentences, conventional novelistic practice is questioned while another sort of novel begets itself.

The two principal figures of *La Marquise*, Bertrand Carnéjoux and Claude Desprez, inhabit separate apartments overlooking the lively Carrefour de Buci. One can look across the intersection and see the other on his balcony, but they remain strangers, their only ostensible point of contact a shared cleaning woman. Yet she, reflecting that both are solitary bachelors and more concerned with paperwork than her housework, states: "the two make a pair, though they do not know each other" (p.13). Carnéjoux is a novelist and Desprez a collector of historical documents. These doubles suggest the two vocations of historian and novelist embodied in Roquentin or, for that matter, Marcel. In fact, *La Marquise*, which is entirely an objectification of juxtaposed speeches and thoughts (Mauriac, doubling back on Dujardin and Joyce, calls his tetralogy *Le Dialogue intérieur*), probes the concept of documentary realism. Like *A la recherche*, but with radically different emphasis, it features excerpts from the Goncourt journal (p.270ff.), as well as from many other sources.

Even if solitary, Desprez, by means of his massive research, senses solidarity with his neighbors throughout the centuries, "my neighbors of old" (p.22); "ils me pressent, m'étouffent, m'appellent de toutes part, moi leur voisin, leur ami et leur frère" [they press in on me, strangle me, call me from all sides, me their neighbor, their friend, and their brother] (p.236). In search of lost time, the historian Desprez succeeds in resurrecting and harmonizing isolated moments so that he is able to "participer à la seule existence qui ait quelque durée, celle de la collectivité à laquelle nous appartenons" [participate in the only existence which has some duration, that of the collectivity to which we belong] (p.122). His impulse is toward comprehensiveness, to consolidate everything within a continuous present. The tools Desprez employs are documents related to the Carrefour de Buci ranging from chronicles and censuses to the testimony of figures like Racine, Voltaire, or Balzac. No one, not even the artist, escapes the historian's grasp.

The novelist Carnéjoux likewise seeks to exclude nothing from his work. He begins to discard the artificiality of his opening sentence "La marquise sortit à cinq heures" in favor of an approach not completely at odds with that of Desprez. "Car je tiens l'inauthenticité en abomination, même dans un roman, surtout dans un roman où je ne me résigne à inventer que le minimum dont on ne peut se dispenser: l'anecdote sans importance, si vraisemblable qu'elle en est presque vraie" [For I regard inauthenticity as an abomination, even in a novel, especially in a novel where I am resigned to inventing only the minimum that cannot be dispensed with: the unimportant anecdote that is so plausible it is almost untrue] (p.58). The image of a marquise seems frivolous in relation to daily life in Paris. Gazing from his balcony down at the busy streets below, Carnéjoux conceives the idea of capturing this neighborhood throughout the centuries in his novel, re-creating it by giving it unity. "To the extent that I give it unity, meaning, beauty, I create the world that I see from my balcony" (p.172).

Carnéjoux and Desprez thus each day play the game of framing the other in his own creation of the world, or at least of controlling the book in which they both appear. However, the two distinct characters move toward a common identity asymptotically. Desprez, noting his own superfluousness and realizing that history requires a novelistic vision, laments: "If I were an artist, this would be something else" (p.204), but he does recognize that he is an "artist in my way" (p.205). The artist Carnéjoux in turn regrets his own ignorance of history.

> Je n'ai malheureusement de l'histoire de ma ville (et de celle de mon pays) qu'une connaissance fragmentaire, surtout pittoresque, en somme assez peu sérieuse, romantique pour tout dire, et qui s'accommoderait mal de ma passion du détail vrai (p.58).

> [Of the history of my city (and that of my country) I unfortunately only have a fragmentary knowledge; it is for the most part picturesque, all in all not very serious, in fact romantic, and not very consistent with my passion for the true detail]

He will overcome this failing by inserting into his novel someone capable of providing the store of "non-literary" details he desires, someone who will in fact resemble Claude Desprez. "Il serait bon que dans mon prochain livre, je choisisse parmi mes héros quelque bonhomme passionné du vieux Paris et qui n'en ignorait rien" [It would be a good idea for my next book to choose among my heroes some fellow who is excited about Paris and knows everything about it] (p.58).

The resultant of these two converging forces is the novel we read. Toward its conclusion, in an extended soliloquy of several pages, earlier elements are recapitulated telegraphically in a final *feu d'artifice*, as details of Paris past and present are put on record. The novel seems to have returned to its pre-technological role as compendium of information, encyclopedic data bank. A gap in the recitation intrudes at this point, and a blank space yawns at us, suggesting the infinite possibility of references that could be inserted in the future book. In "Le Temps immobile," Mauriac refers to it as "a blank which I put there to mark the potential place of one or several – surely several, innumerable – forgotten citations."[41]

Yet it is the novelist Carnéjoux who is apparently in charge, although he has abjured the factitiousness of a craft which leads him to contrive a sentence like "La marquise sortit à cinq heures." Another highly self-conscious example of "a writer – hero in the works of writers" (p.78), Carnéjoux, like Léon Delmont, envisions the reactions which his novel, the one in which he in fact appears, will elicit. "Gageons qu'il se trouvera un critique (il ne m'aura pas lu jusqu'ici) pour dire que le meilleur, dans mon livre, ce sont les citations, en quoi il n'aura pas tort" [You can bet that there will be a critic (who will not have read this far) who will claim that the best thing about my book is its citations, and he will not be wrong] (p.293). He seems content that his novel will succeed to the extent that it no longer appears a fiction, and he frankly admits that the character of the dying Mathilde is in reality based on his own cousin Agnès.

However, *La Marquise* does not conclude with the reflections of this self-begetting novelist figure on his own emerging work. Another turn of the screw remains. In the last few pages of the novel, the voice of the "real" novelist intrudes, framing the framer Carnéjoux. Cousin Agnès is as spurious as Mathilde. The artistic convolutions multiply, but the final commitment appears to be against invention; it is seen as death-oriented and incapable of preserving and uniting the lives of all those who have inhabited the Parisian neighborhood on which *La Marquise* focuses. The omniscient author steps in front of the lights to editorialize:

> Donc, Bertrand Carnéjoux enregistre dans son roman, et j'enregistre dans le roman où j'ai donné la parole et la vie à Bertrand Carnéjoux, cette impossibilité de concevoir ce qui paraît si naturel chez les autres et que l'on a passé sa vie à craindre, s'en sachant inéluctablement menacé dans les êtres que l'on aime et en soi-même: la mort. De sa cousine Agnès, il a fait la Mathilde de son livre, et je sais bien, moi, que le vrai nom de cette agonisante n'était pas plus Agnès que Mathilde. Bertrand Carnéjoux, personnage triple, puisqu'il est supposé écrire les livres où il joue lui-même en tant que héros un rôle. Romancier animé par un romancier que romancier moi-même, j'ai mis dans un roman où rien pourtant ne fût inventé, un jeu de miroir y prenant à ses pièges, des sensations, des sentiments et des pensées vécues . . . (p.311).

> [Thus, Bertrand Carnéjoux records in his novel, and I record in the novel in which I have given speech and life to Bertrand Carnéjoux, that impossibility of conceiving what appears so natural with others and what a whole life has been passed in fearing, knowing that those you love and you yourself are unavoidably threatened by it – death. Out of his cousin Agnès, he has made the Mathilde of his book, and I myself know very well that the true name of this sufferer was no more Agnès than Mathilde. Bertrand Carnéjoux, triple character, since he is supposed to be writing the books in which he himself plays the part of hero. A novelist has been brought to life by a novelist, and I, myself a novelist, have put into a novel, in which nothing though has been invented, a mirror game which catches in its snares sensations, feelings, and thoughts which have been experienced]

Like *La Nausée* and *La Modification*, *La Marquise* moves toward a feeling of liberation. Yet this novelistic triumph comes precisely through the sense of having abandoned literature in favor of the contingent world which has so nauseated Roquentin. Our revels now are ended, and what remains is more exhilarating than the artistic stratagems scorned first by Carnéjoux and, scorning him, then by the voice of Claude Mauriac. In a complex self-begetting novel which denies itself in favor of "reality," we are told that novels are nothing but sound and fury, except presumably when they induce a lively realization of this fact.

> Le bruit éteint, la fureur morte, il reste la liberté. Ainsi le roman s'est-il dans ses avant-dernières pages peu à peu évanoui, et a-t-il disparu, sans feintes ni

masques, au profit du romancier qui, s'il s'est mis directement dans son livre, l'a purifié à la fin de ses dernières traces de fiction en le faisant accéder à une vérité où l'exactitude littérale fût préférée à la littérature. La marquise ne sortit pas à cinq heures . . . (p.313).

[When the noise dims and the fury dies, what remains is freedom. Little by little in its concluding pages the novel thus has faded and disappeared, without feints or masks, in favor of the novelist who, if he has put himself directly into his book, has finally purified it of its last traces of fiction by making it surrender to a truth in which literal exactitude is preferable to literature. The marquise did not go out at five o'clock . . .]

La Marquise, a novel which creates and denies itself, thus qualifies as anti-literary *alittérature*. *Alittérature*, as Mauriac sees it in *L'Alittérature contemporaine* in such writers as Beckett, Butor, Robbe-Grillet, and Sarraute, is not content with the artistic achievements of the past. Instead, it, like Marcel and Léon, uses previous monuments merely as a starting point in an innovating, questioning effort which even submits itself to critical scrutiny. It is constantly examining the very limits of literature. "Terminating in the silence of Rimbaud, in the white page of Mallarmé, in the unarticulated cry of Artaud, *alittérature* in alliterations concludes by dissolving itself in Joyce."[42]

In an introduction to Nathalie Sarraute's *Portrait d'un inconnu* (1948), Sartre injects the term *anti-roman*, classifying Sarraute's work, as well as "the works of Nabokov, those of Evelyn Waugh and, in a certain sense, *Les Faux-Monnayeurs*,"[43] in that category. Another symptom of the fact that we live in an age of reflection, anti-novels according to Sartre challenge what they do while doing it.

It is a matter of the novel contesting itself, of destroying it before our eyes while it is apparently being constructed, of writing the novel of a novel which does not come about, of creating a fiction which would be to the great works composed by Dostoevsky or by Meredith what that canvas by Miro entitled "Murder of Painting" was to the pictures of Rembrandt and Rubens. Those strange and nearly unclassifiable works do not demonstrate the weakness of the genre of the novel; they merely indicate that we live in an era of reflection and that the novel is in the process of reflecting on itself.[44]

In an article entitled "Surprise pour l'anti-roman,"[45] Jean Pierre Faye reminds us that back in 1633 Charles Sorel published a narrative which he called *L'Anti-Roman*. As the essay "Sartre entend-il Sartre?"[46] suggests, Faye sees himself as the *alittérateur* to the *littérateur* Sartre (according to Mauriac's evolutionary thesis, "one is always the *littérateur* to someone"[47]), and he obviously relishes pointing out that that the term *anti-roman* was in currency over three hundred years before the author of *La Nausée* seized on it. Works that subvert the genre to which they contribute form, according to Faye, a tradition more extensive than apparently dreamt of in the philosophy of "a courageous and famous philosopher" who "made himself the tutor of a lady as yet unknown."[48] Mauriac similarly stresses the antiquity of literature which contests its own right to exist.

> *Alittérature* (i.e., literature freed of the devices which have given that word a pejorative sense) is an extreme never reached, but it is in that direction that trustworthy authors have been moving ever since men began to write. Therefore, the history of literature and that of *alittérature* are parallel.[49]

The existence of works like *Don Quixote, Joseph Andrews* or *Jacques le fataliste* indicates that reflexive literature is not a monopoly of the current era. According to Northrop Frye's theory of fictional modes, in an ordinary historical sequence "each work is 'romantic' compared to its successors and 'realistic' compared to its predecessors."[50] This, like Harold Bloom's theory of anxious influence, supports Claude Mauriac's view that the work of "trustworthy authors" is *alittérature* in relation to the artifice it displaces but mere *littérature* in the eyes of young Turks who want to refine even it. Reflexiveness would emerge as a relative quality.

Yet, even within the comparatively brief span from *A la recherche* to the current period, the French novel has undergone a modification. Nathalie Sarraute argued in her book of the same name that we are in an incredulous age, *L'Ere du soupçon*. Novelists adopt a skeptical attitude toward the fictional characters with which they deal, and readers are suspicious of both novelist and novel. Inclined toward becoming simply a repository of information, *La Marquise sortit à cinq heures*, for one, exhibits embarrassment over mere "literature." In *A la recherche*, the Goncourt journal yields to the developing novelist's profound vision, but the same document functions in *La Marquise* as a triumph over creative flights of fancy. Proust's highly self-conscious *Künstlerroman* represented an affirmation of literature as consummate achievement, the rebirth of a transformed self; Roquentin did find salvation of some sort in art; and the novel was even a useful tool of enlightenment for Léon. But some recent novels project a scorn for art as a needless burden, and individuals in an influential school of criticism exhibit their revolutionist disdain for the notion of individual creation. If the novel places us in "the laboratory of narrative," the contents of the test tube are discarded with the experiment. After *Les Gommes*, the pencil's eraser is as important as its point, although the point of the reflexive novel is that we need the point to tell us this. It remains for an Irishman, Samuel Beckett, to contribute masterful French fiction in the very act of denying its possibility, to give birth to novels which depict their own quests for death. In his hands, the self-begetting novel will also become the self-aborting novel.

5 The Self-Begetting Novel and the English Tradition

> ... a satisfactory novel should be a self-evident sham to which the reader could regulate at will the degree of his credulity. The entire corpus of existing literature should be regarded as a limbo from which discerning authors could draw their characters as required, creating only when they failed to find a suitable existing puppet. The modern novel should be largely a work of reference. Most authors spend their time saying what has been said before – usually said much better. A wealth of references to existing works would acquaint the reader instantaneously with the nature of each character, would obviate tiresome explanations and would effectively preclude mountebanks, upstarts, thimble-riggers and persons of inferior education from an understanding of contemporary literature.
>
> Flann O'Brien, *At Swim-Two-Birds*, p.25

> But you're like every man who was ever born into this world, Martin. You'd like to pretend that you made yourself, that it was *you* who made you – and not the body of a woman and another man.
>
> John Osborne, *Luther*, I, iii

I LA DIFFÉRENCE

In the final sentences of *Tristram Shandy*, Mrs Shandy, referring to one of innumerable internal digressions, asks: "what is all this story about?" Yorick replies: "A Cock and a Bull . . . . And one of the best of its kind I ever heard." Clearly, this crowning witticism is meant to apply not merely to the immediate incident of Obadiah and his cow but to Sterne's novel as a whole. Similarly, in the concluding lines of *To the Lighthouse*, Lily Briscoe, who has been laboring over a canvas from the very beginning of Virginia Woolf's novel, finally completes her painting. "It was done; it was finished. Yes, she thought, laying down her brush in extreme fatigue, I have had my vision." With this, the novel, too, is finished, and we are invited to consider the entire work as an artistic vision which encompasses Lily's.

However, despite such illustrations of reflexivity, despite the fact that it was in analyzing *Tristram Shandy* that Viktor Shklovsky provided Russian Formalism with its principle of "laying bare the literary device," and despite meticulous exploration of the genre exhibited by Fielding's introductory chapters or James's prefaces, the English novel in general lacks the sense of being "in the laboratory of narrative." The reflexive, self-begetting tradition is not as central to Anglo-Saxon fiction as it is to French. Like Aldous Huxley's Philip Quarles, British novelists have been apprehensive about focusing their works on introspective eccentrics. "The chief defect of the novel of ideas is that you must write about people who have ideas to express – which excludes all but about .01 of the human race."[1] Fielding's Square and Sterne's Phutatorius are not flattering portraits of the thinker. British – and especially American – fiction has been deeply suspicious of those who bear what André Malraux terms "the complex mark of the intellectual."

Of modern novelists who employ the resources of the reflexive tradition, such writers as Joyce, Durrell, Murdoch and Beckett have served French apprenticeships. Each is of Irish background, thereby setting these outsiders somewhat apart from the factory and cathedral concerns of the English novel. Durrell's Pursewarden envisions hordes of London publishers "tall hawk-featured men perched on balconies and high places, scanning the city with heavy binoculars." Not especially interested in the likes of Sterne or Joyce, "*They are waiting for the new Trollope to be born!*"[2]

Distilling the essence of a "national character" is a frustratingly elusive task. *Mirage* is an optical illusion, an hallucination, and it is appropriately also the technical term for the manner in which one culture views another. French literature, or at least a major branch of it, has, in the eyes of an American, been characterized "by the self-knowledge of Montaigne and the introspection of Pascal, by the maxims of La Rochefoucauld and the memoirs of Saint-Simon."[3] It is an embodiment of what is, next to wine and cheese, the most versatile and revered of French national resources, *esprit*. The outstanding qualities of French prose thereby emerge as individualism and introspection, leading Harry Levin to generalize: "No land has been more self-critical or more individualistic than France, and no literature has spoken for all of Europe with more authority."[4] French literature has been either invigorated or sicklied o'er with the pale cast of thought, and, in a less buoyant tone than Levin's, Victor Brombert refers to "a tradition which, from Pascal to Sartre, is haunted by the mirror-disease of thought, the solipsistic awareness of 'others,' the walled-in quality of experience."[5]

In Conrad's *The Secret Agent*, it is the belief of Winnie Verloc, who "wasted no portion of this life in seeking for fundamental information,"[6] that things "did not stand looking into very much."[7] This is surely an extreme formulation, but it does express an orientation distinguishing French from English fiction, where the virtues of *esprit* are less often projected into the fictional universe itself. Certainly, Conrad wasted no portion of his life in seeking for fundamental information; he productively devoted all of it to that *recherche*. But his Winnie Verloc, her flaccid husband Adolf, and her idiot brother Stevie are a different story. Winnie's obscurantist declaration is inconceivable coming from Marcel or Roquentin. Unlike Philip Quarles, French reflexive novelists do not consider it a liability to stock their domains with artists and thinkers, a scant minority of the population at large. If, in John Cruickshank's formulation,[8] French novelists from Sartre to Beckett have been "philosophers," it has also been possible to conceive a relatively representative study of modern French fictional characters under the title *The Intellectual Hero*. Citing the striking, and now dated, statistic that "85 per cent of the protagonists in today's French novel have at least their *baccalauréat*,"[9] Victor Brombert asserted: "Particularly since the thirties, French literature has been dominated by the figure of the intellectual."[10] By contrast, the Anglo-Saxon protagonist is more often *l'homme moyen sensuel*.

Racine is the root of many French achievements of import – and export. The tradition of the neoclassical theater, with its dedication to economy of means and to lucidity and with its fastidious concern for form, is perpetuated in the novel of Laclos, Constant and Flaubert and especially in the French reflexive novel. At least such is the mirage in terms of which the English reader, slighting Balzac and Zola, tends to view "the French novel." A consequence of this distinction between fiction in French and English is John Rodker's *bon mot* that Ford's *The Good Soldier* is "the finest French novel in the English language."[11] Lacking the same tyranny of the neoclassical and somewhat impatient with introspectives, Britain will be less congenial soil for the self-begetting novel.

From Flaubert to Structuralism, France has served as a grand narrative laboratory. It has pioneered such vital literary movements as Naturalism, Symbolism, Surrealism and Existentialism, and its incessant manifestos and artistic coalitions cast it in the role of trial run for technical innovation subsequently assimilated in its own way by the rest of Europe. The term *avant-garde* did, after all, enter our language by swimming the Channel. Such a pioneering role endows virtually every French novel with the quality of *roman expérimental*. From the perspective of the English-speaking world, if French literature, that breeding ground of revolutionary forms and gestures, did not exist, it would have had to be invented, which is precisely what is constantly recurring within its own borders. Such a context is uniquely sympathetic to the self-begetting novel.

Old John of Gaunt's "fortress built by Nature for herself/Against infection and the hand of war" has proven notoriously vulnerable to French literary influences, as Chaucer, among many wrote in his mongrel tongue, can testify. Those who in recent history have introduced significant formalistic considerations into Anglo-Saxon poetry and prose, writers like T. S. Eliot and Henry James, have gone to school to the Symbolists and Flaubert. Even the technique of stream of consciousness, the pride of British modernism, has been traced back to Edouard Dujardin's *Les Lauriers sont coupés* (1887). Despite the infiltration of Goethe's *Wilhelm Meister* into English fiction and the example of Novalis's *Heinrich von Ofterdingen*, which, unfinished at its author's death in 1801, was to have concluded with an account of its own composition, it is to France that British Writers closest to the tradition of the self-begetting novel – Joyce, Huxley, Murdoch, Durrell and Lessing – have turned for inspiration. Samuel Beckett, in fact, did not return.

II   THE NOVEL AND ITS DUBLIN

Both *Bildungsroman* and *Künstlerroman*, elements of the self-begetting novel, occupy important positions in English literature – from Bede's account of the first onymous native poet, Caedmon, to Joyce's portraits of the artist and beyond. British fiction abounds in stories of a developing self and in portraits of the artist. However, it is rare that the two forms blend in the self-conscious fashion characteristic of Proust, Sartre and Butor. Dickens traces David Copperfield's life from birth to middle-aged success as a novelist; but he does not exploit his subject to examine the nature of literature and of the particular work in which David's story is told. Many British fictions begin, like Byron's *Don Juan*, wanting a hero, and some even overcome initial deficiencies by constructing a protagonist from scratch. Yet rarely does this construction itself incorporate an awareness of its own activity. The peevish heirs of Doctor Johnson find the rugged realities of plot and character the only fictional values worth kicking about. And even such outsiders as Iris Murdoch and Doris Lessing feel uneasy about the formalism of a Continental tradition each perpetuates in her own way. However, in James Joyce, the native streams of *Bildungsroman* and *Künstlerroman* converge to produce a fiction which, if not self-begetting, is at least highly self-conscious about its prospects for self-begetting.

One of the more memorable scenes in *A Portrait of the Artist as a Young Man* (1916) occurs when young Stephen Dedalus comes home for Christmas dinner. During the meal, the child witnesses a fierce argument over politics and religion between Mr Casey and Mrs Riordan. It is as if he is a passive observer storing up impressions for later use.

> – O, he'll remember all this when he grows up, said Dante hotly – the language he heard against God and religion and priests in his own home.

> – Let him remember too, cried Mr Casey to her from across the table, the language with which the priests and the priests' pawns broke Parnell's heart and hounded him into his grave. Let him remember that too when he grows up.[12]

Joyce's writings and the massive footnotes attached to them by friends and scholars alike have transformed the man and his work into a Shakespeare for our century, "the happy hunting-ground of all minds that have lost their balance."[13] Despite the evidence provided by *Stephen Hero* of how carefully Joyce reworked and transmuted his raw materials, the Olympian artist has become a cultural artifact, and personal letters and biographical data have joined the company of *Dubliners* and *Finnegans Wake*. Within this context, it is a rare critic who does not at some point treat *A Portrait of the Artist as a Young Man* as if it were Joyce's, or at least Stephen Dedalus's, remembrance of things past.

It is clear from the novel that Stephen does indeed remember the heated exchange between Mr Casey and Mrs Riordan and that the themes of politics and religion in Ireland, "the old sow that eats her farrow" (*A Portrait*, p.203), shape his life as it is shown unfolding. Diverse testimony indicates that James Joyce's development was similar to that of his fictional alter ego, and he did of course grow up to write two novels in which the aspiring artist Stephen appears. Joyce's novels, with their emphasis on the apprenticeship of an exceptional individual, their explicit discussion of theories of art, and their pervasive reflexivity, certainly exhibit elements of the self-begetting novel. But it must first be determined whether Stephen is closer to Marcel or to Swann – Proust's Casaubon-like artist *manqué* – before it can be conceded that these novels do indeed give birth to themselves.

In his biography of Proust, George Painter devotes three pages to the one brief meeting that occurred between Proust and Joyce. It was on 18 May 1922, not long before Proust's death or after Joyce had completed *Ulysses*. During this Olympian encounter, each claimed not to have read the work of the other. Yet Painter quotes from a letter Joyce wrote in October 1920, when he first arrived in Paris from Zurich: "I observe a furtive attempt to run a certain M. Marcel Proust of here against the signatory of this letter. I have read some pages of his. I cannot see any special talent but I am a bad critic."[14] In any case, despite scattered allusions to Proust in *Finnegans Wake*, the French novelist cannot be considered a significant influence on Joyce's fiction. However, the two major figures independently of each other created work which has much in common. In an unpublished letter to *The Times* (London), T. S. Eliot declared "*Ulysses* still seems the most considerable work of imagination in English in our time, comparable in importance (though in little else) with the work of Marcel Proust."[15] Proust and Joyce do occupy analogous positions of aloof dominion in their respective literatures. But they are comparable in more than "little else." Joyce exploited many of the same themes and techniques out of which Proust fashioned his self-begetting novel.

Stephen Dedalus, whose "destiny was to be elusive of social or religious orders" (*A Portrait*, p.162), struggles, like the Decadent des Esseintes or the bastard Lafcadio, "To discover the mode of life or of art whereby your spirit could express itself in unfettered freedom" (*A Portrait*, p.246). The most effective method of revolting against the claims of father and homeland is to reconstruct himself from the beginning as if those determinants had never existed. *A Portrait of the Artist as a Young Man* – as well as *Ulysses* and *Finnegans Wake* – is a celebration of the miracle of self-begetting. A child is to be father of the man. Through dedication to "silence, exile, and cunning" (*A Portrait*, p.247), the self-proclaimed artist attempts to create himself.

A Portrait begins in baby prattle and concludes with the hero's separation from his mother. Beckett noted that Mr Joyce does not take birth for granted, and birth is indeed as central an event in this *Geburtsroman* as it is in the maternity hospital in which Mrs Purefoy suffers her labor in *Ulysses*. Stephen's apprenticeship is depicted in terms of explicit birth imagery, and when he visits his father's old anatomy classroom, "On the desk he read the word *Foetus* cut several times in the dark stained wood" (*A Portrait*, p.89). A foetus throughout this novel of education, Stephen is struggling to be born.

According to Johnny Cashman "not his father's son," Stephen rejects Simon Dedalus as father. Seeking a new begetter, it is a *miglior fabbro*, the fabulous artificer Dedalus, whom he, as Icarus, invokes at the end of *A Portrait*: "Old father, old artificer, stand me now and ever in good stead" (p.253). In *Ulysses*, Stephen obviously finds a new father in Leopold Bloom, just as Leopold regards Stephen as a means of resurrecting his dead son Rudy. In the novel's mythological scaffolding, Telemachus seeks his father Odysseus. And Stephen's extended discussion of *Hamlet* in the National Library emphasizes the father-son relationship between the murdered King and his son, as well as the relationship between Shakespeare and his dead son Hamlet.

Yet Stephen's theory, which Buck Mulligan mockingly claims "proves by algebra that Hamlet's grandson is Shakespeare's grandfather and that he himself is the ghost of his own father" (*Ulysses*, p.18), contends that Shakespeare projected himself as both King Hamlet and Prince Hamlet. The willed quest for father and son reveals that both goals reside in the seeker. Literary creation, the pattern of such a quest, is also the creation of a new self as both father and son.

It is significant that, walking the Dublin streets, young Paddy Dignam is mistaken for his father who has just been buried. The patron saint of Joyce's fictions of self-begetting is Sabellius, and it is precisely the consubstantiality of Father and Son upon which the self-begetting novel insists when it depicts an individual authoring himself and a work of art serving as its own parent and offspring. The mystery of the Incarnation, "The Father contemplating from all eternity as in a mirror His Divine Perfections and thereby begetting eternally the Eternal Son" (*A Portrait*, p.149), makes a lasting impression on the devout young Dedalus, who eventually enters the holy calling of art rather than of religion. Rejecting the vocation of priesthood, Stephen reenacts the sins of both Lucifer and Sabellius in the arrogant belief that he can become a self-made man, both father and son.

It is out of the labyrinth of words and literature that Dedalus is to be born. Throughout his development, he is struck by such odd words as "suck," "tundish," and his own first and last names. As with Marcel and his "noms de pays," words function as talisman for the would-be artist. Both a human being and a literary creation await birth, and the two are interdependent. In his celebrated fingernail-paring simile (*A Portrait*, p.214), Stephen pairs the writer with the God of the Creation, later referring to Him in *Ulysses* as "The playwright who wrote the folio of this world and wrote it badly" (p.213). "In the virgin womb of the imagination the word was made flesh" (*A Portrait*, p.217).

Stephen Dedalus is *the* artist as a young man, the definite article serving both to undercut his grand pretensions and to emphasize the representative nature of the novel's hero. Extending the traditions of the *Bildungsroman* and *Künstlerroman*, Joyce is quite explicit in his treatment of the problem of the artist. Both *A Portrait* and *Ulysses* feature, in addition to detailed discussions of the role of art and the artist and allusions to Ovid, Byron, Homer, Shakespeare and many, many others, a character who wants to dedicate himself to the kind of activity which produces a work resembling the one in which he appears. *Finnegans Wake* has its Shem the Penman.

In *A Portrait*, Stephen lectures the less than totally sympathetic Lynch on his aesthetic theories. He defines the key terms *truth* and *beauty* thus:

> The first step in the direction of truth is to understand the frame and scope of the intellect itself, to comprehend the act itself of intellection. . . . The first step in the direction of beauty is to understand the frame and scope of the imagination, to comprehend the act itself of esthetic apprehension (p.208).

It is a defense of the reflexive novel. Truth and beauty are attained only in a self-conscious act which incorporates an awareness of the mechanism for attaining truth and beauty. Such a view is a justification for Joyce's own technique, which calls attention to itself in almost every sentence. It is a reflexivity characteristic of the self-begetting novel, which, through – and only through – an exploration of the possibilities of art, succeeds in becoming art. The ostentatious verbal density present in *A Portrait*, intensifying in *Ulysses* and reaching its limit in *Finnegans Wake*, foregrounds these highly sophisticated works of art. Joyce, supreme master of parody and pastiche, creates literature in the act of examining it.

But Joyce deliberately establishes considerable distance between himself and his protagonist Stephen Dedalus, who often poses more as an aesthete than an artist. Stephen is the victim of his author's Olympian irony, and, as critics have noted, he is "priggish, humourless"[16] and "sometimes laughable, sometimes pathetic, and nearly always what we should call 'difficult!'"[17] In *Ulysses*, Stephen's opening posturings soon pale beside the vital presence of Leopold and Molly Bloom.

A Portrait, then, is no self-portrait. If a self is begotten, a novel does not beget itself. William York Tindall has sharp scorn for the aspiring novelist Dedalus, believing: "whatever Stephen says, he is no Joyce. Talking about art is no substitute for art."[18] And Ellsworth Mason peremptorily dismisses "a confusion of the character Stephen with the writer Joyce (a booby trap which has led one commentator to the astounding conclusion that Stephen goes off at the end of *Ulysses* to write *Ulysses*)."[19] At the end of *Ulysses*, despite the benign influence of Bloom and the promise of rebirth, he is still Icarus, the headstrong, unsuccessful son. And toward the end of *A Portrait*, his 21 March diary entry proclaims: "Free. Soul free and fancy free" (p.248). This conclusion on a note of liberation is also found in the novels of Sartre, Butor and Mauriac. Its invocation here by an isolated figure whom we never do see succeed as artist is at least as ironic as in the French novels.

If reproduction is, as Temple reminds Stephen, the beginning of death, the moment of procreation marks the midpoint of an organism's parabolic career from birth to reproduction to death. But death is a necessary condition of rebirth, and reproduction, the beginning of death, is likewise the beginning of life. *Finnegans Wake*, whose subject is *Finnegans Wake*, begins in mid-sentence and stops at the start of the same sentence, so that we are propelled back to the first page, as in *A la recherche*. A recurrent ending, *fin* again, is also a beginning.

In a characteristically reflexive reference to the design of *Ulysses* itself, 16 June 1904, plucked from the crannied wall, Stephen declares:

> Every life is many days, day after day. We walk through ourselves, meeting robbers, ghosts, giants, old men, young men, wives, widows, brothers-in-love. But always meeting ourselves (*Ulysses*, p.213).

Joyce's work demonstrates that the creation of a self entails the creation of much more. As the artificer steps back from his handiwork, it continues to reverberate within itself autonomously. But the clock has already been wound. In *Tristram Shandy*, this fact would have prevented the interruption of procreation. Here it restricts the kind of textual self-begetting present in Proust. Stephen neither creates the novel in which he appears nor a self large enough to embody that novel.

III   THE JESTING PILOT

If the complexities of Joyce's ambitious achievement and his detailed study of a maturing novelist evoke comparison with Proust, Aldous Huxley's counterpart is Gide. *Point Counter Point*(1928) is Huxley's most thoroughly reflexive novel. With its cast of artist figures perpetually engaged in theoretical discussions and its inclusion of a novelist, Philip Quarles, who keeps a personal diary for the purpose of transmuting observed reality into fiction, *Point Counter Point* invites comparison with *Les Faux-Monnayeurs*. In fact, in a preface to the French translation of Huxley's book , André Maurois praises it for having introduced into the English novel the sound of Proust and Gide.

And the "sound" of *Point Counter Point* is self-consciously musical. "Counterpoint" is a musical term appropriated by Huxley to signify his narrative method of witty and pointed juxtapositions of characters and events. "In the human fugue there are eighteen hundred million parts" (p.26), and it is the novelist's task to create his own structure which will distinguish some of these parts. Yet another work of art which employs aesthetic terminology to draw attention to its own artifice, *Point Counter Point* is constructed according to the method which Philip Quarles labels "The musicalization of fiction" (p.301). Even more so than in E. M. Forster's *Howards End*, music is an important element in the plot of *Point Counter Point*, and its fictional network is conceived in terms of a correspondence with music. Bach's Suite in B minor is performed at the Tantamount House party early in the novel, and Beethoven's A minor Quartet figures prominently in Spandrell's suicide. In his reflections on novelistic technique, Philip Quarles invokes Beethoven's B flat major and C sharp minor Quartets and the Diabelli variations as analogies.

With Huxley's novel, we are in the elite company of a circle of unusually cutivated and articulate individuals, the ".01 per cent of the human race" which causes the novelist Quarles some qualms but which inspires Everard Webley, the Fascist artist of politics:

> It was not only property that was menaced, not only the material interests of a
> class; it was the English tradition, it was personal initiative, it was intelli-

gence, it was all natural distinction of any kind. The Freemen were banded to resist the dictatorship of the stupid; they were armed to protect individuality from the mass man, the mob; they were fighting for the recognition of natural superiority in every sphere (p.58).

Each of the uncommon principal characters is concerned with art in some way. In addition to Philip Quarles and Everard Webley, John Bidlake, Philip's father-in-law, is an exuberant old master painter recalling D. H. Lawrence. Sidney Quarles., Philip's father, is, like Casaubon or Swann, supposedly at work on a definitive treatise on political philosophy, which he never completes, despite frequent excursions to the British Museum. Denis Burlap, editor of and contributor to *Literary World*, is, like the novel in which he appears, "unceasingly and exclusively self-conscious" (p.63). Spandrell is portrayed as a connoisseur of the subtle art of debauchery, and even eccentric old Lord Edward Tantamount, a scientist who delights in severing the tails of newts, is dedicated to the art of creating new forms of animal life. His daughter, lovely but elusive Lucy, displays commanding artistry in her manipulation of human relationships. *Point Counter Point* exhibits the defect seen as shared by all novels of ideas that it must restrict itself to exceptional protagonists and avoid touching the full chromatic scale of the human comedy. But its writers, painters, musicians and aesthetes of other sorts permit it to deal directly with the familiar theme of art and life.

Like Gide's Edouard, Philip keeps a notebook in which he places observations and reflections to be absorbed into his next novel. Within the universe of *Point Counter Point*, a novel is shown drawing its sustenance from and curiously paralleling the "reality" in which the fictive Philip Quarles moves. He is struck by the Marjorie-Walter-Lucy triangle he observes, but all experience is an arch wherethrough his fictionalizing powers attempt to march in triumph, and fellow human beings are transformed into "My Walterish hero" and "his Lucyish siren" (p.300).

Like Marcel, Philip possesses a remarkable degree of negative capability, deriving his identity from his encounters with the contingent world.

> There was something amoeboid about Philip Quarles's mind. It was like a sea of spiritual protoplasm, capable of flowing in all directions, of engulfing every object in its path, of trickling into every crevice, of filling every mould, and, having engulfed, having filled, of flowing on toward other obstacles, other receptacles, leaving the first empty and dry (p.199).

However, like Edouard and unlike Marcel, Philip's amoebic self does not absorb the entire novel. *Point Counter Point*, like *Les Faux—Monnayeurs*, is narrated in the third person, and Philip is merely one of several characters it wryly contrasts. As young Philip's agonizing death, Sidney's romantic embarrassment, Webley's murder, and Spandrell's suicide indicate, jarring events outrace the novelist. Reality resists the imperialist artist's efforts to annex it. What remains is a sardonic portrait of the vapid posturings of members of English society during the twenties, but, although suggested, no new novel is born. Neither Philip Quarles nor his novel begets itself. Both are simply one element in Aldous Huxley's novel.

In *Eyeless in Gaza* (1936), one of Huxley's characters refers to Marcel Proust less than fondly as "for ever squatting in the tepid bath of his remembered past. . . a pale repellent invalid, taking up spongefuls of his own thick soup and squeezing it over his face." However, Huxley himself, reviewing *A l'ombre des jeunes filles en fleurs*, admired its "eighteenth-century methods" – its "exquisite frivolity of theme" and the manner in which Proust is "enlightened and very intellectual in all his ways."[20] In a much later study of the page proofs from *Ulysses and Finnegans Wake*, Huxley also paid tribute to "Joyce the Artificer."[21] A highly civilized and cerebral novelist, Huxley exults in his own artifice. The counterpoints in *Point Counter Point* are manifestly contrived, and the fiction is unmistakably a fiction. The effect is trenchant, reductive character analysis and art enlisted in the service of examining both art and life. But *A la recherche* much more than *Point Counter Point* creates the kind of effect likened by Philip Quarles to the Quaker Oats box. Nothing is bred here.

IV RAISING THE NET

The work of the philosophy don Iris Murdoch, born in Dublin and an unabashed francophile, is more plainly related to the French reflexive tradition. Her first published book was an examination of Jean-Paul Sartre, *Sartre: Romantic Rationalist* (1953).[22] As could be expected, it devotes a chapter to that French author's self-begetting novel, *La Nausée*.

Iris Murdoch's own first novel, *Under the Net*, was published in the following year. Dedicated to the contemporary French novelist Raymond Queneau, the text of *Under the Net* sparkles with an abundance of italicized French expressions – *par exemple, mêlée, frisson, tour de force, tête à tête, bien renseigné, dérèglement de tous les sens, je m'en fichais* and *au fond*. Some important scenes in the novel are set in Paris, and its narrator and central protagonist, Jake Donaghue, is English translator of the fictive French novelist Jean Pierre Breteuil. A discussion of Marcel Proust with Hugo Belfounder has significant consequences for Jake,[23] while Jake's description of "a suburb of southern London where contingency reaches the point of nausea" (p.150) recalls Sartre's distinctive terminology. On the very first page of Murdoch's very first novel, published soon after her study of Sartre, the narrator presents himself as, perhaps like his creator, arriving in England "with the smell of France still fresh in my nostrils" (p.3). His suitcases are heavy with French books.

Jake Donaghue never relinquishes the center of attention in this narrative, which is consistently related to us from his first-person perspective. Although he admits "I can't bear being alone for long" (p.19) and "I hate solitude" (p.30), Jake is in effect "a connoisseur of solitude" (p.204), as the moving scene of him alone in Paris during the mass celebration of Bastille Day indicates. A taciturn Irishman named Finn is Jake's constant companion, even valet, but Jake treats Finn more as a mirror for himself than as an independent human being. Finn's otherness, demonstrated by his removal to Dublin, eventually strikes Jake with the force of profound revelation. Meanwhile, though, Jake declares: "The substance of my life is a private conversation with myself and to turn it into a dialogue would be equivalent to self-destruction" (p.30). However, his introspective narrative will prove to be self-creative precisely through its recognition of the dense contingency of the external world.

Just the right age for a self-begetting hero, Jake introduces himself as "something over thirty, and talented, but lazy" (p.19). Jake is scarcely one of Sartre's bourgeois *salauds*. A confirmed bachelor ("It is not my nature to make myself responsible for other people" (p.9)), Jake is perpetually homeless and on the move. A recurrent element in the novel is his quest for a place to spend the night.

And Jake is as rootless in his thinking as he is in his housing. A Cartesian of sorts whose first reaction to any situation is: "That would need some thinking out" (p.6), Jake delights in "the sort of dreamy unlucrative reflection which is what I enjoy more than anything in the world" (6.6). His tendency to examine the self, the world, fiction, and the relationships among the three is one of the marks of the self-begetting novel.

Jake gets a job as an orderly in a hospital but remains an outsider in that rigid society. "I exuded an aroma which, although we got on so splendidly, in some way kept them off; perhaps some obscure instinct warned them that I was an intellectual" (p.223). Although he is a reader of James and Conrad (p.27), Jake most resembles Amis's Jim Dixon brand of roguish intellectualism. If he is a peripatetic philosopher, Jake is also a *picaro*. Throughout the novel, he demonstrates uncommon mastery of the art of picking locks, cracking safes, and pilfering money and property.

Like any self-respecting self-begetting novel, *Under the Net* has its own cast of artist figures. Anne Quentin is a singer, and her sister Sadie is an actress. Hugo Belfounder begins as the inventor of elaborate fireworks and later becomes a film producer; the scene at the Bounty Belfounder studio in which the cardboard movie set of ancient Rome collapses vividly demolishes at least one notion of art. With a gesture of Cartesian asceticism, Hugo concludes by divesting himself of his considerable fortune and devoting himself, as if at Ferney, to the humble but existentially pure occupation of watchmaker. Lefty Todd, editor of the *Independent Socialist,* is a political artist of sorts, and Dave Gellman is a philosopher, "a real one like Kant and Plato" (p.20). But the most important artist within this work of art is, of course, Jake Donaghue, who conceives of himself as sovereign of his narrative realm. At least in the beginning of the novel, everyone, especially Jake's submissive foil Finn, exists as an extension of his creative self. "I count Finn as an inhabitant of my universe, and cannot conceive that he has one containing me; and this arrangement seems restful for both of us" (p.5).

Like Marcel or Roquentin, Jake is a writer. He has composed an epic poem entitled "And Mr Oppenheim Shall Inherit the Earth," but he is able to earn money by translating best-selling but mediocre contemporary novels by Jean Pierre Breteuil. One of them, *Le Rossignol de bois* (in the Donaghue translation, *The Wooden Nightingale*), is itself about the relationship between reflection and creation. "It's about a young composer who is psychoanalyzed and then finds that his creative urge is gone" (p.18). Jake also transforms his coversations with Hugo Belfounder during a cold-cure experiment into a philosophical dialogue he publishes as *The Silencer.* In his book, which is poorly received, Jake becomes Tamarus and Hugo becomes Annandine, but reality does not submit so easily to the writer's colonizing efforts; "it *was* a travesty and falsification of our conversations" (p.65).

Jake's development as a novelist is inseparable from his growth as an individual. Both produce *Under the Net.* With his literary hack work as mere translator of second-rate fiction, Jake consciously restricts his originality. But his friendship with Hugo, who serves as a kind of Quietist prophet for him, makes him aware that: "The whole language is a machine for making falsehoods" (p.62). All literature, even his more serious efforts in *The Silencer,* thereby becomes fraud, if indeed "It is in silence that the human spirit touches the divine" (p.88).

However, despite his philosophical misgivings and his constitutional laziness, Jake throughout cherishes a dim ambition to write a novel. From the very beginning, in the midst of homelessness, poverty, and the forces of inertia, the possibility of his future novel suggests itself. "I had contrived, in fact, to stop myself just short of the point at which it would have become clear to me that the present age was not one in which it was possible to write a novel" (p.17). Much later, Jake, faithful to a still indistinct vision of his destiny as novelist, refuses a job as movie scriptwriter.

> The business of my life lay elsewhere. There was a path which awaited me and which, if I failed to take it, would lie untrodden forever. How much longer would I delay? (p.199).

One of the major factors in shaping Jake's new identity as novelist is the transformation of Jean Pierre Breteuil, the French author. With the publication of *Nous les vainqueurs*, Breteuil himself undergoes a reincarnation from mercenary to genuine artist. Jake, visiting Paris, sees Breteuil's new novel awarded the Prix Goncourt and receiving universal critical acclaim. He is dumbfounded. How can it be?

> Jean Pierre had no right to turn himself surreptitiously into a good writer. I felt that I had been the victim of an imposture, a swindle. For years I had worked for this man, using my knowledge and sensibility to turn his junk into the sweet English tongue; and now, without warning me, he sets up shop as a good writer. I pictured Jean Pierre, with his plump hands and his short grey hair. How could I introduce into this picture, which I had known so well for so long, the notion of a good novelist? It wrenched me, like the changing of a fundamental category. A man whom I had taken on as a business partner had turned out to be a rival in love (pp.185-6).

Breteuil's artistic birth forces Jake to question his own neatly formulated conceptions of reality. In the process, it inspires him to attempt to rival the Frenchman by producing his own novel. He resolves that he will never waste his time translating *Nous les vainqueurs* when he could be creating his own original work of art. Ironically, as long as Breteuil turned out worthless books, Jake was content to translate them and thereby commit himself to imitation of trash. However, as soon as Breteuil challenges Jake's notion of "a bad novelist" and actually writes something of value, the newly enlightened Jake can no longer settle for the role of mere translator.

Eventually, Jake also arrives at some understanding of the romantic rectangle – Hugo tells him: "I love Sadie, who's keen on you, and you love Anna, who's keen on me" (p.249) – involving himself, Anna, Hugo, and Sadie. But, with his novel awaiting birth, he is now a new man.

> It was the first day of the world. I was full of that strength which is better than happiness, better than the weak wish for happiness which women can awaken in a man to rot his fibres. It was the morning of the first day (p.276).

A self has been begotten by the narrator in imagery which consciously evokes the Creation. Jake is to be both father and artificer, as an earlier pun about his relationship to Madge forecasts. "After all, she had no father and I felt *in loco parentis*. It was about the only *locus* I had left" (p.11).

At the end of *Under the Net*, Jake returns to Mrs Tinckham's cat-congested newspaper shop, which he has visited in Chapter One. Now, in a scene remarkably parallel to the one in which Roquentin listens to a recording of the English song "Some of These Days" in the *Rendez-Vous des Cheminots* café, he hears Anna Quentin singing in French on the radio.

Like a sea wave curling over me came Anna's voice. She was singing an old French love song. The words came slowly, gilded by her utterance. They turned over in the air slowly and then fell; and the splendour of the husky gold filled the shop, transforming the cats into leopards and Mrs. Tinckham into an aged Circe (pp.276-7).

It is a stunning illustration of the potential power of art.

Yet one more image of birth is reserved for the concluding lines of the novel. Jake discovers that Maggie the cat, whose pregnancy has been noted in the first chapter, has borne a litter of four kittens. Unaccountably, two of the kittens are tabby and two are pure Siamese. Instead of attempting to impose the rational explanation of Mendelian genetic theory on this phenomenon, Jake is now content simply to accept it as one of the mysteries of life. His final comment, "It's just one of the wonders of the world" (p.279), is an indication of Jake's progress as human being and artist in embracing the untidy dappledness of the world. He is now ready to create the work which will embody this new self and this novel vision. Sensitive to pied beauty, his language will not be "a machine for making falsehoods" any more than *Under the Net*'s is.

The title of the novel, *Under the Net*, is alluded to within an excerpt from *The Silencer*. Annandine asserts:

. . . the movement away from theory and generality is the movement towards truth. All theorizing is flight. We must be ruled by the situation itself, and this is unutterably particular. Indeed it is something to which we can never get close enough, however hard we may try, as it were, to crawl under the net (p.87).

The sense of rebirth, rededication, and liberation at the conclusion of *Under the Net* derives from the promise of a work which will succeed in understanding the contingent world and thereby uttering what is "unutterably particular."

Early in the novel (it must be assumed that, despite consistency in his use of tenses, Jake's narrative perspective undergoes a change), the unredeemed Jake declares: "I hate contingency. I want everything in my life to have a sufficient reason" (p.22). Iris Murdoch the critic indicts Sartre for possessing what she considers the same heretical beliefs.

Sartre has an impatience, which is fatal to a novelist proper, with the *stuff* of human life. He has, on the one hand, a lively interest, often slightly morbid, in the details of contemporary living, and on the other a passionate desire to analyse, to build intellectually pleasing schemes and patterns. But the feature which might enable these two talents to fuse into the work of a great novelist is absent, namely an apprehension of the absurd irreducible uniqueness of people and their relations with each other.[24]

Murdoch's reading of Sartre suggests a view of French fiction as aseptic. She regards it as her British, and human, duty to introduce microorganisms, "the *stuff* of human life," into the Petri dish furnished by her teachers on the Continent.

Because of what she sees as this distaste for the contingent, individuated world, despite graphic images of the viscosity of existence, Murdoch considers Roquentin's a "rather dubious salvation."[25] Her own Jake Donaghue, on the other hand, is portrayed as overcoming that orientation "which is fatal to a novelist proper." His career in *Under the Net* is framed by his visits to Mrs Tinckham's, appropriately "a dusty, dirty, nasty-looking corner shop" (p.12). And, having developed an understanding of and fondness for this reality, Jake is presumably about to become "a novelist proper," if not a proper novelist, at the conclusion of *Under the Net*.

In *A Portrait of the Artist as a Young Man*, which likewise ends on a note of liberation, Stephen also employs the image of a net. He proclaims to the nationalist Davin:

> When the soul of a man is born in this country there are nets flung at it to hold it back from flight. You talk to me of nationality, language, religion. I shall try to fly by those nets (p.203).

However, the net trope functions differently in *A Portrait* than it does in *Under the Net*. For Stephen Dedalus, freedom is a matter of flight, of escape beyond the crippling power of nets. In Murdoch's novel, on the other hand, it is a question of trying "to crawl under the net." Her narrator commits himself to accepting life within the British Isles. Artistic rebirth paradoxically becomes a process of entering rather than departing, immersing yourself in the hair of the dog that bit you. Theorizing is the enemy, and "All theorizing is flight."

In her essay "Against Dryness," Murdoch contrasts imagination with fantasy. According to her view, imagination, which respects the contingency of the world, is a reflexive, provisional faculty, whereas fantasy naïvely distorts reality by hypostatizing it in inflexible myths. Fantasy, rather than an emancipator, is a servile attempt to flee messy ambiguities for a realm of complacent artifice. Imagination, by plunging us into the complex mire of human existence, is thereby an exercise in free will, which depends on an awareness that we are:

> . . . benighted creatures sunk in a reality whose nature we are constantly and overwhelmingly tempted to deform by fantasy. Our current picture of freedom encourages a dream-like facility; whereas what we require is a renewed sense of the difficulty and the complexity of the moral life and the opacity of persons.[26]

Literature, as evident in the example of Jake Donaghue, can be an effective means of accommodating the contingent world. Murdoch promises: "Through literature we can re-discover a sense of the density of our lives. Literature can arm us against consolation and fantasy and can help us to recover from the ailments of Romanticism."[27] And *Under the Net* is a striking portrait of its central protagonist's moral progress.

Although its narrator confesses, "I'm not telling you the story of my life" (p.19), *Under the Net* creates the illusion of an extended *Bildungsroman*. The narrative is defined by two visits to Mrs Tinckham's. When he returns to her shop at the end, Jake receives the following greeting: "'Hello, dearie,' said Mrs. Tinck. 'You've been a long time'" (p.269). In terms of clock-time, it has not been especially long – a matter of days rather than the years usually encompassed by novels about the making of a novelist. However, much has happened. Jake's life has undergone a transformation, one that, presented in a novel, is made possible by his commitment to the complexities of novel-writing. Begetting itself and a new self for Jake, *Under the Net* avoids flight. It returns for a candid assessment of itself and the world in which it is enmeshed.

V ONE QUARTET AND FOUR NOTEBOOKS

Among more recent fiction, *The Alexandria Quartet* (1961) and *The Golden Notebook* (1962) are further British variations on the self-begetting theme. Lawrence Durrell, an Irishman born in India, claims to feel at home in France. A constant traveler to Greece, Durrell impresses one Frenchman as "that unique phenomenon, a naturally Mediterranean Englishman."[28] If he is a Briton at all, Durrell, according to Gerald Sykes, "belongs to the great British tradition of imaginative travelers who realized their best talents by getting as far from Britain as they could."[29]

Durrell's *The Alexandria Quartet* is both *Bildungsroman* and *Künstlerroman*: "the whole business of the four books, apart from other things, shows the way an artist grows up."[30] As the musical term "quartet," like Huxley's "counterpoint," immediately warns us, we once again have to do with a highly self-conscious treatment of the relationship between art and life. Durrell's fictional tetralogy features no less than three novelists within the novel: Darley, narrator of three of the four volumes, *Justine, Balthazar* and *Clea*; Arnauti, Justine's first husband and the author of *Moeurs*, which contains valuable information about their marriage; and Pursewarden, eminent but eccentric English author whose works include *God Is a Humorist*. Another potential novelist is the hack journalist whimsically named John Keats, who is shown undergoing a conversion to art and discovering in the final volume: "I've become a writer at last!"

(*Clea*, p.172). And Clea is a painter. Her spiritual and aesthetic pilgrim's progress parallels that of the writer Darley. Looking forward to reunion with him, her concluding, triumphant words are: "I wait, quite serene and happy, a real human being, an artist at last" (*Clea*, p.275).

The novel's curious band of angels is quite well-read, among each other's manuscripts and in Literature in general, and they delight in the opportunity to parade their literary views. Even on a rugged expedition into the desert, Keats is as concerned about the copy of *The Pickwick Papers* he brings along, "a sodden, dog-eared little book with a bullet hole in the cover, smeared with oil" (*Clea*, p.171), as about anything else. When, after alluding to Petronius, the physician Balthazar exclaims: "The part that literature plays in our lives!" (*Clea*, p.61), it is an understatement.

The Alexandria Quartet is constructed in terms of the elaborate machinery of diaries, notebooks, epigraphs from the Marquis de Sade, prefaces, "Consequential Data," and "Workpoints." After Darley narrates his version of events in *Justine*, Balthazar, dissatisfied with the account, even furnishes his own critical commentary, referred to as the "Interlinear." All of these exposed structures, as well as the multiple presentations of the same incident in the manner of *The Ring and the Book* or *Rashomon*, serve to remind us that we are once again in the laboratory of the novel. Not exactly a finished product, Durrell's fiction gives at least one French critic "the impression of a novel not completely finished, but being made."[31]

The novel's characters are perpetually analyzing themselves and each other, and the work itself is certainly as thoroughly reflexive as any self-begetting novel. The style of *The Alexandria Quartet*, a consequence of employing self-conscious novelists to create its points of view, is mannered and ornate, what Pursewarden terms "touched with plum pudding" (*Balthazar*, p.241). It is difficult to forget that words are being massively deployed to create a baroque fiction about fiction.

Mirrors are prominent throughout this introspective quartet, and, while gazing at herself in her dressmaker's mirrors, Justine declares:

> Look! five different pictures of the same subject. Now if I wrote I would try for a multi-dimensional effect in character, a sort of prism-sightedness. Why should not people show more than one profile at a time? (*Justine*, p.18).

This is merely the first of several direct references to Durrell's multi-dimensional novel scattered within its own boundaries. Later, Balthazar, offering his Interlinear, tells Darley:

> . . . if you wished somehow to incorporate all I am telling you into your own *Justine* manuscript now, you would find yourself with a curious sort of book – the story would be told, so to speak, in layers. Unwittingly I may have

supplied you with a form, something out of the way! Not unlike Pursewarden's idea of a series of novels with "sliding panels" as he called them. Or else, perhaps, like some medieval palimpsest where different sorts of truth are thrown down one upon the other, the one obliterating or perhaps supplementing another (*Balthazar*, p.177).

The added significance of Balthazar's statement is, of course, evident. With its overlapping perspectives, *The Alexandria Quartet*, the "curious sort of book" in which he appears, is itself both sliding door and palimpsest. It also exemplifies the theories of space and time expressed by Pursewarden in his recommendation to Darley:

. . . you might try a four-card trick in the form of a novel; passing a common axis through four stories, say, and dedicating each to one of the four winds of heaven. A continuum, forsooth, embodying not a *temps retrouvé* but a *temps délivré*. The curvature of space itself would give you stereoscopic narrative, while human personality seen across a continuum would perhaps become prismatic? (*Clea*, p.126).

Such passages of explicit self-description within the novel are not unfamiliar to readers of Gide or Huxley.

In the tradition of Proust's Marcel or Butor's Vous, the name of the narrator and principal character of most of the tetralogy is not mentioned until nearly the end of the second volume (*Balthazar*, p.201). Even when he is identified, we never learn Darley's complete first name but simply the initials L. G. The novel is an account of Darley's sentimental education in the alembic of Alexandria. He gains something of a name in the process of increasing his awareness of others, himself, and his art. Darley realizes he is implicated in "simply the old story of an artist coming of age" (*Clea*, p.275). How old the story is we have some notion.

The work of art and the self are complementary. One cannot be begotten without the other. In another of his sententious declarations applicable to Durrell's creation as well as to his own, the novelist Pursewarden asserts: "The object of writing is to grow a personality which in the end enables man to transcend art" (*Balthazar*, p.133). This concept of growing a personality through and beyond art, common to the self-begetting tradition, is supported by Pursewarden's later evocation of the image of the snakeskin. "In my art, indeed, through my art, I want really to achieve myself shedding the work, which is of *no importance*, as a snake sheds its skin" (*Balthazar*, p.236).

The personality whose development is examined in greatest detail is, of course, Darley's. Darley even experiences the same despair as Proust's novelist when, revisiting Combray, Marcel becomes convinced he will never accomplish anything. "I have just realized that I am not an artist at all. There is not a shred of hope of my ever being one" (*Clea*, p.169), bemoans Darley. But, on the final page of *Clea*, Darley buoyantly announces that he has finally found himself and his calling. He has begun to write something that will succeed in capturing the inner reality of the self. And, once again, the metaphor of gestation is employed to depict the work of art toward whose conception the conclusion of *The Alexandria Quartet* points. According to Darley:

> It has been so long in forming inside me, this precious image, that I too was as unprepared as she had been. It came on a blue day, quite unpremeditated, quite unannounced, and with such *ease* I would not have believed it. I had been until then like some timid girl, scared of the birth of her first child (*Clea*, p.275).

Darley's projected novel will begin with the portentous words "Once upon a time. . ." (*Clea*, p.275). Such an opening sentence ensures that it will differ from *The Alexandria Quartet*, at the same time as it perpetuates this novel's concern with time. Durrell's fiction thereby does not circle back into itself. At the end of the volumes *Balthazar* and *Clea*, Durrell appends what he terms "Workpoints." These constitute suggestions for further developments in the plot, "a number of possible ways of continuing to deploy these characters and situations in further instalments" (*Clea*, "Author's Note"). The extrapolations of "Workpoints" and Darley's new novel suggest a movement outward, a transcendence of the given work of art, a shedding of the snakeskin.

Although he narrates three-quarters of it, *The Alexandria Quartet* is not Darley's novel. It is not an expression of the self in the same way *A la recherche* is of Marcel's. Darley is only one of several creative figures and, although he attempts to translate Alexandria into literature, his efforts are assisted and supplemented by others, so that *The Alexandria Quartet* we witness being born is something of a communal achievement. In the third volume, *Mountolive*, which is cast entirely in an objective, third-person form, Darley is, in fact, merely a peripheral figure. Durrell attempts "to turn the novel through both subjective and objective modes" (*Balthazar*, "Note"), but the final effect can only be to subsume the subjective beneath the objective. Joyce, as usual, anticipates something similar when he has Stephen discuss the evolution from lyric to dramatic modes, likening it to the pattern in *Turpin Hero*. "This progress you will see easily in that old English ballad *Turpin Hero* which begins in the first person and ends in the third person" (*A Portrait*. p.214). This is the reverse of what occurs in Camus's *La Peste*, where we belatedly discover that the entire account is the individual expression of Dr Rieux.

Despite Durrell's elaborate explanations of his Einsteinian rather than Bergsonian system, so that "This is not Proustian or Joycean method" (*Balthazar*, "Note"), *The Alexandria Quartet* is self-consciously a product of a self-conscious tradition. The tetralogy is a neo-Proustian demonstration of the proposition "life is really an artistic problem, all men being sleeping artists."[32] *The Alexandria Quartet* does not beget itself in the manner of *A la recherche*, but it does not assent to its characters or readers nodding.

Lessing's *The Golden Notebook* is yet another work whose major characters are artists who do not hesitate to discuss their craft and, in the process, the novel in which they appear. It is primarily the story of Anna Wulf's attempts to overcome a writer's block, to give birth to the novel which will endow her fragmented life with some degree of unity. She is a successful first novelist and, apart from much else, we are provided an account of the genesis of and reactions to her earlier creation, *Frontiers of War*. In one of her notebooks, Anna, despairing over both *The Golden Notebook* and the entire reflexive tradition of which it is a part, notes that the fictional theme of art and the artist, "the subject matter of art for this century, when it has become such a monster of a cliché," "has become so debased, the property of every sloppy-minded amateur."[33] *The Golden Notebook* will be a professional job.

Although she is able to live off the income from *Frontiers of War*, Anna goes to work reading manuscripts for the Communist Party, thereby adding to the stock of novelists within this novel. "I have not yet met one Party member, anywhere, who has not written, half-written, or is planning to write a novel, short stories, or a play" (p.168), the author Anna remarks. And she herself offers what appears to be a pastiche of the Henry Miller school of writing, in which a group of males is portrayed cultivating experiences so that one of their number will be able to transform them into literature:

> Dave scratched his crotch, slow, owl-scratching pure Dave. "Jeez, Mike," he said, "you'll write it someday, for us all." He stammered, inarticulate, not-winged-with-words, "You'll write it, hey feller? And how our souls were ruined here on the snow-white Manhattan pavement, the capitalist-money-mammon hound-of-hell hot on our heels?" (p.541).

Thus self-conscious even about its place in the tradition of self-conscious fiction, *The Golden Notebook*, like *Les Faux-Monnayeurs*, *Point Counter Point*, and *The Alexandria Quartet*, employs the device of a writer's notebook in order to examine its own design. In this case, there are actually four distinct notebooks: black, red, yellow, and blue. They ultimately yield to a fifth – the golden notebook. In her black notebook, Anna inserts material related to her experiences in Africa and to the novel *Frontiers of War*, which drew upon them. The red notebook is reserved for thoughts on her political life and her involvement with the Communist Party. The yellow notebook presents fictionalized versions of Anna's experience, as well as notes for projected writings. And the blue notebook represents an attempt at a diary, an objective record of Anna's daily existence. When asked why she keeps four separate notebooks, "as if Anna had, almost automatically, divided herself into four" (p.55), she replies: "Obviously because it's been necessary to split myself up" (p.598). The notebooks *are* Anna, and, in keeping four of them, she acknowledges that her identity is fragmented. However, the device of four notebooks will eventually enable her to arrive at a unified self-awareness and beget a single, golden notebook.

Within her yellow notebook, Anna creates an extensive narrative centering on the figure of Ella, who is manifestly a proxy for Anna herself. Like her creator, Ella is depicted as a novelist. Within this novella-within-a-novel, Ella publishes a novel on suicide, *The Shadow of the Third*, which clearly parallels material from her own life, as well as Anna's. This infinite regress of fictive novels demonstrates the Quaker Oats box effect that Philip Quarles merely suggests. As with all of her writing, Anna employs her surrogate novelist Ella as a means of distancing herself and thereby mastering self-awareness. The same procedure is evident in Anna's sessions with her psychoanalyst, Mrs Marks, whom she calls Mother Sugar.

However, despite Anna's numerous sophisticated strategies, she discovers that knowledge of the self, which entails knowledge of everything else as well, is frustratingly elusive. "I keep trying to write the truth and realising it's not true" (p.274). Like Beckett's unnamable narrator, whose identity is greater than the sum total of his creations Molloy, Moran, Malone and Macmann, Anna becomes painfully aware of the inadequacy of Ella as an expression of Anna Wulf.

> I see Ella, walking slowly about a big empty room, thinking, waiting. I, Anna, see Ella. Who is of course Anna. But that is the point, for she is not. The moment I, Anna, write: Ella rings up Julia to announce, etc., then Ella floats away from me and becomes someone else. I don't understand what happens at the moment Ella separates herself from me and becomes Ella (p.393).

Ego cogitans remains aloof from its own grasp, despite the subtle nets of fiction, which ironically succeed in conveying a portrait of this failure.

Anna's progress toward artistic expression and self-mastery is punctuated with all of the usual misgivings and feelings of unworthiness. The author of a well-received first novel, Anna imagines herself reviewing *Frontiers of War* as "A first novel which shows a genuine minor talent" (p.59). She is nevertheless dissatisfied with herself.

> Yet I am incapable of writing the only kind of novel which interests me: a book powered with an intellectual or moral passion strong enough to create order, to create a new way of looking at life. It is because I am too diffused. I have decided never to write another novel (p.61).'

This determination does falter, and order is ordained within a novel which exemplifies the criteria Anna establishes for a meaningful work.

The day will arrive when she is able to incarnate a new self in a novel book and declare: "I'll pack away the four notebooks. I'll start a new notebook, all of myself in one book" (p.607).

Playing what she privately calls "the game," Anna as a child imitates the creative powers of the novelist, who can bring the entire world into being simply by naming it. Her approach resembles that of Stephen Dedalus, who begins with the microcosm of the self in Clongowes and works outward to the macrocosm. Just as Stephen's inscription in the flyleaf of his geography begins with "Stephen Dedalus" and expands centrifugally to conclude with "The Universe" (*A Portrait*, p.16), Anna moves from her room to a Boethian vision of the entire earthly sphere.

> First I created the room I sat in, object by object, "naming" everything, bed, chair, curtains, till it was whole in my mind, then move out of the room, creating the street, then rise into the air, looking down on London, at the enormous sprawling wastes of London, but holding at the same time the room and the house and the street in my mind, and then England, the shape of England in Britain, then the little group of islands lying against the continent, then slowly, slowly, I would create the world, continent by continent, ocean by ocean (but the point of "the game" was to create this vastness while holding the bedroom, the house, the street in their littleness in my mind at the same time) until the point was reached where I moved out into space, and watched the world, a sunlit ball in the sky, turning and rolling beneath me (p.548).

The literary artist is a creator, and Anna will beget both herself and the rest of the universe through *The Golden Notebook*.

Excerpts from Anna's notebooks alternate with five objectively narrated sections entitled "Free Women." In addition to the theme of liberation through narration present in the tradition from Proust to Beckett, Lessing's novel is directly concerned with portraying women who challenge the roles society imposes on them. Hovering over the same incident from different perspectives, *The Golden Notebook* features an elaborate counterpoint of first and third-person presentations in an effort to examine contemporary feminist themes from every conceivable angle. At times the novel resembles a kind of *Congressional Record*, as newspaper reports of the fifties are inserted without commentary into the blue notebook. At other times, the novel is dominated by the bizarre fantasies of Anna Wulf, significantly née Freeman.

The Golden Notebook artfully alternates between subjective and objective approaches in a compound of strict diary reportage, stream of consciousness, deliberate fictionalization, and theoretical discourse. Yet Lessing's allegiance is not entirely to the French reflexive tradition, certainly not to its later ironic developments. She appears to share Murdoch's implicit assessment of the modern French novel as overly formalistic, lacking in the rich "human" concerns to which she attempts to adapt its devices. "If writers like Camus, Sartre, Genet, Beckett feel anything but a tired pity for human beings, then it is not evident from their work."[34] Refusing to accept the paradigm of the novelist as laboratory technician, Lessing exploits the resources of the self-begetting novel in order to be able to explore the problems of a "free" woman in a thorough manner worthy of the nineteenth-century realistic novel. "For me the highest point of literature was the novel of the nineteenth century, the work of Tolstoy, Stendhal, Dostoevsky, Balzac, Turgenev, Chekhov, the work of the great realists."[35]

Toward the conclusion of *The Golden Notebook* and of an intense, consuming relationship with the American Saul Green, Anna provides him with the first sentence of a novel – "On a dry hillside in Algeria, a soldier watched the moonlight glinting on his rifle" (p.642). We are told that he completed the novel, that it was published, and that it "did rather well" (p.643). At the same time, Saul devises a sentence to serve as the beginning for the novel Anna has had such difficulty writing – "The two women were alone in the London flat" (p.639). Returning to the first page of *The Golden Notebook*, we discover that this is precisely the same sentence which begins the book in which Anna herself, one of the two women in the London flat, appears. This account of Anna's fragmented personality is thus apparently also objective testimony to the fact that she has succeeded in reintegrating herself. Alchemy has been performed, and the leaden, discordant elements of a character's life are transmuted into *The Golden Notebook*.

6 The Self-Begetting Novel and American Literature

Self-existence is the attribute of the Supreme Cause, and it constitutes the measure of good by the degree in which it enters into all lower forms.
Ralph Waldo Emerson, "Self-Reliance"

... nobody, his presence stated, was his Pygmalion. He had sculpted himself.
Bernard Malamud, *The Tenants*, p.64

Fiction is one of the ways we have of creating ourselves and the lives we lead.
Ronald Sukenick[1]

I ART AMONG THE ARTLESS

If the reflexive tradition is less than central to the British novel, it might seem irrelevant to American fiction. After the writers, aesthetes and intellectuals who people French literature, the American novel appears as peculiarly the preserve of idiots, children, savages, miscreants, and other miscellaneous naifs. Characters like Natty Bumppo, Huckleberry Finn, Henry Fleming, Clyde Griffiths, Frederic Henry and Lena Grove are a vast ocean apart from the jaded, introverted likes of des Esseintes, Marcel, Edouard and Roquentin. More often a dramatization of unconsciousness, American literature has been almost synonymous with "the novel of violence" among Europeans. Whether in the manner of the pragmatist Hank Morgan challenging the fossilized conventions of the Arthurian court or of Lambert Strether bravely confronting Parisian worldliness, American literature is the drama of innocents abroad, the New World encountering the complexities of history. It is the story re-enacted, in varying forms, in the abandonment of America by Henry James, T. S. Eliot and the post-War "lost generation."

Richard Hofstadter cites an 1899 letter of William James as the first occurrence of the term *intellectual* in the United States.[2] Appropriately enough, though, *intellectual* is an import from France. The word was coined during the Dreyfus Affair, the phenomenon which had a major impact on both Marcel Proust and his novel. While French fiction is a gallery of "intellectual heroes," American literature, even when the product of highly cultivated intelligences, draws its sustenance from raw materials. And its audience of innocents has generally lacked the Gallic attention to subtleties of form.

"The Figure in the Carpet" is a story concerned directly with the public's insensitivity to elements pervading Hugh Vereker's novels. Discussing the work, Henry James, its author and brother of the pioneer Harvard *intellectual*, laments the fact that "no truce, in English-speaking air, had ever seemed to me really struck, or even approximately strikeable, with our so marked collective mistrust of anything like close or analytic appreciation."[3] Although an American expatriate living in Britain, Henry James viewed impatience with intellectual concerns as characteristic of the English-speaking world in general. Writing across the Atlantic to William Dean Howells, he complains: "*The faculty of attention* has utterly vanished from the general anglo-saxon mind, extinguished at its source by the big blatant *Bayadère* of Journalism, of the newspaper and the *picture* (above all) magazine."[4]

T. S. Eliot, who likewise deserted the New World for the Old, praised James precisely for those qualities which the two of them sensed missing from Anglo-Saxon letters. In the essay advancing the celebrated description of James as "a mind so fine that no idea could violate it," Eliot accepts the designation of France as "the Home of Ideas" and commends James's ability to maintain control over ideas.

> James's critical genius comes out most tellingly in his mastery over, his baffling escape from, Ideas; a mastery and an escape which are perhaps the last test of a superior intelligence.... James in his novels is like the best French critics in maintaining a point of view, a viewpoint untouched by the parasite idea. He is the most intelligent man of his generation.[5]

Both James and Eliot exchanged America for England. But their shared disdain for the crudity of English literature on both sides of the Atlantic suggests England as their Mount Nebo overlooking Calais. Eliot was a close student of French Symbolist poetry, and like Pound's Hugh Selwyn Mauberly, James's "true Penelope was Flaubert." If, like Mauberly and Pound, they regarded themselves as "born/ In a half savage country, out of date," France, where the nuances of form were taken seriously, was their true Ithaca.

More recently, Philip Rahv attempted to account for what he considered "the peculiar shallowness of a good deal of American literary expression."[6] Although he divides American literature into the opposing camps of "Paleface" and "Redskin," Rahv regards their respective standard bearers, James and Whitman, as both dedicated to what he terms "the cult of experience," the immersion into unfiltered life. As a result, he contends: "The intellectual is the only character missing in the American novel. . . . Everything is contained in the American novel except ideas."[7] Instead of Marcel's enlightened discourses on painting, music and literature, and his attention to nuances of form, American literature settles for Billy Budd's cherubic smile and Benjy Compson's pathetic brayings.

Such a context would appear uniquely forbidding to the self-begetting novel and its reflexive tradition so elaborately developed in France. American mistrust of the autonomy of art and the intellect would seem to offer stiff resistance to a novel whose central protagonist is himself a highly self-conscious novelist and who ultimately constructs the work in which he appears. Henry Adams, intensely aware of the victory of vibrant Philistines in the America of the Dynamo, admits: "He knew no tragedy so heartrending as introspection."[8]

Tragedy and introspection are certainly recurrent elements in French literature. Yet the symbiosis of the two does not seem nearly so inevitable as in American fiction – and life. The United States obviously has not lacked introspectives, notably a sequence of Henrys—Adams, Thoreau, James and Miller.[9] But if introspection has been the French national pastime, it has been an American mania. French thinkers, even *in extremis*, have been able to fish in the mainstream of society. Even when breaking with their culture, they have still managed, with the characteristic French talent for *liaison*, to group themselves into opposition parties.

In contrast, the energies of the New World were directed exclusively toward taming and settling a rugged continent. Under such circumstances, intellectual activity became at best an idle luxury. At worst, it was subversive of national priorities and conducive to the kind of self-doubt evident in the biographies of literary figures like Melville and Twain. When the clerisy itself was indoctrinated with a mistrust of its own role, it did not encourage the kind of unified affirmation of dissent found in the land of Voltaire and Zola. Emily Dickinson is almost a caricature of introspection forcing itself to skulk in attic corners. She sardonically envisions the consequences of defying consensus in the new positivistic democracy.

> 'T is the majority
> In this, as all, prevails.
> Assent, and you are sane;
> Demur, – you're straightway dangerous,
> And handled with a chain.[10]

However as James warns in an 1872 letter, being an American writer is a "complex fate." In the land of the Know-Nothing Party, the Scopes

Trial, Joseph McCarthy and George Wallace, American fiction has had to await the likes of Moses Herzog for a successful portrait of a European sort of intellectual. But it has not been totally devoid of the kind of reflexiveness conveyed through the figure of an intellectual in other literatures. In fact, defensiveness about the frivolousness of art and attention to formal subtleties has served to create rich tensions in American works. The result has often been a compelling awareness of the limitations, and possibilities, of literature incorporated into literature itself.

Henry Adams's thoughtful portrait of the thinker superannuated and aware of it endures. And Henry James, so critical of Anglo-Saxon doltishness, is almost himself sufficient refutation of the charge. Dramatizing the encounter of innocent Milly Theale or Maggie Verver with the complexities of Europe, James displays his own highly refined intelligence. Positioned strategically as "posts of consciousness," even his noble savages demonstrate dizzying powers of analysis. And James's own critical prefaces, written for the definitive New York edition of his works, function as stories-of-stories while exhibiting a sensitivity to the nuances of his art.

American literature, if not American society, has not been overpopulated by the figure of the intellectual, the character who considers himself heir to the wisdom of the ages. According to the formula of R. W. B. Lewis, much more representative has been the hero free of both history and the pale cast of thought, the "American Adam."[11] However, frequent appearance of the artist, if not the intellectual, has introduced an element of self-consciousness also found in French and British fiction. Henry James again, for example, composed a number of stories, notably "The Lesson of the Master," "The Real Thing," "The Death of the Lion," and "The Figure in the Carpet," in which the principal characters are novelists, painters, and critics. As in his prefaces, their actions and theoretical discussions enable James to examine the nature of his own art.

James's American master, Nathaniel Hawthorne, set the artists Miriam, Kenyon and Hilda against the background of Rome in *The Marble Faun*. In addition, Hawthorne's scientists and physicians, like Chillingworth in *The Scarlet Letter*, Aylmer in "The Birthmark," and Rappaccini in "Rappaccini's Daughter," are artists of sorts, obsessed with imposing their designs on the temporal human realm. Art thereby becomes cognizant of itself.

However, even more reflexive are the prefatory paragraphs of "Rappaccini's Daughter." The story that is to follow is there attributed to a foreign author, a M. de l'Aubépine. *Aubépine* is, of course, the French world for *hawthorne*. Aubépine's fictive editor mentions the title of some of his other works, among them *Contes deux fois racontées* and *Le Voyage Céleste à Chemin de Fer*. Hawthorne exploits this droll mask to summarize his own career and clarify the themes and techniques of his own work. In the process, Hawthorne is also able to acknowledge personal weaknesses and the reasons for limited popular success.

> His writings, to do them justice, are not altogether destitute of fancy and originality; they might have won him greater reputation but for an inveterate love of allegory, which is apt to invest his plots and characters with the aspect of scenery and people in the clouds and to steal away the human warmth out of his conceptions. . . . In any case, he generally contents himself with a very slight embroidery of outward manners, – the faintest possible counterfeit of real life, – and endeavors to create an interest by some less obvious peculiarity of the subject. . . . We will only add to this very cursory notice that M. de l'Aubépine's productions, if the reader chance to take them in precisely the proper point of view, may amuse a leisure hour as well as those of a brighter man; if otherwise, they can hardly fail to look excessively like nonsense.[12]

Furthermore, Hawthorne's introduction to *The Scarlet Letter*, his essay "The Custom-House," purports to be an autobiographical sketch. It is essentially an account of the genesis of the narrative we are about to read. We learn how Hawthorne, in his position as Surveyor of Revenue in Salem, comes upon an aged manuscript from which germinates *The Scarlet Letter*. Hawthorne utilizes his essay for observations on the workings of the imagination and for the famous assessment of his kind of romance as "a neutral territory, somewhere between the real world and fairy-land, where the Actual and the Imaginary may meet, and each imbue itself with the nature of the other."[13] Although an appendage to *The Scarlet Letter* and thus not an integral record of a narrative's begetting as in *A la recherche*, "The Custom-House" does at least anticipate Henry James's prefaces, with their anecdotes about the origins of certain plots, and Thomas Wolfe's *The Story of a Novel* (1936), a separate book on how *Look Homeward, Angel* (1929) was written.

American literature has produced some portraits of the artist incorporated into the fiction itself. When Melville's Pierre Glendinning departs the pastoral scenes of his youth in Saddle Meadows for the city, he is forced to become a literary hack. The depiction of the wretched life of Pierre and his fellow writers foreshadows Gissing's *The New Grub Street*. Ezra Pound's cycle *Hugh Selwyn Mauberly* (1920) is something of a self-portrait of the alienated figure who "strove to resuscitate the dead art/ Of poetry," although the aesthete Mauberly is probably as much a representation of Pound as Dedalus is of Joyce. In any case, this work, like most of Wallace Stevens's poetry, is art itself examining the nature of "the supreme fiction."

And in *Winesburg, Ohio* (1919), Sherwood Anderson presents the portrait of a nascent artist, the young George Willard. He is shown serving his literary apprenticeship as a sensitive observer of all the "grotesques" in his small midwestern town and as a reporter for the

Winesburg Eagle. Each of the town's inhabitants is a potential story, and it is assumed that someday George will be able to transform the isolated lives he has touched into a unified work, one which will synthesize the books each of them senses he contains. Doctor Parcival takes consolation from George's presence: "If something happens perhaps you will be able to write the book that I may never get written."[14] The final scene of *Winesburg, Ohio* portrays George on a train as Winesburg recedes in the distance. But *Winesburg, Ohio* perhaps looms ahead. Having faithfully accumulated impressions of the town, he is now ready to move on to a more creative role. Transporting George from Winesburg to the big city, the train changes him from child to father, from observer to painter – "the town of Winesburg had disappeared and his life there had become but a background on which to paint the dreams of his manhood."[15]

Contemporary American fiction has approached the limits of literary reflexiveness. At the end of Part One of Donald Barthelme's *Snow White* (1967), the narrative, such as it is, pauses for a series of fifteen playful questions about the work we are in the process of reading. In addition to being asked whether we like the story so far and how we would rate it on a scale of one to ten in comparison with all the works of fiction since the War, we are also directed by some of the questions to an irreverent awareness of some of its themes and techniques. Invoking the jargon of literary criticism, the interrogator, for example, demands:

3. Have you understood, in reading to this point, that Paul is the prince-figure? Yes (   ) No (   )
4. That Jane is the wicked stepmother-figure? Yes (   ) No (   )
5. In the further development of the story, would you like more emotion (   ) or less emotion (   )?
6. Is there too much *blague* in the narration? (   ) Not enough *blague*? (   )
7. Do you feel that the creation of new modes of hysteria is a valid undertaking for the artist of today? Yes (   ) No (   )
8. Would you like a war? Yes (   ) No (   )
9. Has the work, for you, a metaphysical dimension? Yes (   ) No (   )[16]

Snow White enacts the *nouveau roman* program of reader participation to the point of parody. And it self-consciously mocks the prevailing literary self-consciousness.

Vladimir Nabokov's *Pale Fire* (1962) is even more thoroughly reflexive. "Kubla Khan" and *The Road to Xanadu* at once, *Pale Fire* is John Shade's "Pale Fire," a poem in four cantos, as well as the elaborate critical commentary on that poem – and index to that commentary – by one Charles Kinbote. In a double mirror effect, Kinbote's recital, which, among other things, purports to be an account of the creation of "Pale Fire," emerges as a fictional narrative itself, and a counterpoint to his flights of fantasy is to be discovered in the "realism" of Shade's poem. The tormented reader is made ever mindful of a dazzling literary contrivance, one which at every moment challenges his assumptions about art.

With the intense reflexiveness of *Pale Fire* and *Snow White*, America has come of age in a manner unforeseen by Van Wyck Brooks. In an era in which a five-volume study of Henry James appears, James's demand for aesthetic sophistication now seems less urgent. Abandoned is the New World primitivism which so awed the Old. And, as earlier in France, theorists in the United States have abetted developments in literary self-consciousness. Raymond Federman's *Surfiction: Fiction Now . . . and Tomorrow* is a collection of essays which appropriately includes several French contributions. The volume is in effect a manifesto for a new kind of fiction compatible with the "post-realist era." Its authors call for the creation of "surfiction," which Federman, a fictionalist himself and, incidentally, an immigrant from France, defines as "that kind of fiction that tries to explore the possibilities of fiction."[17] One of his essayists, Jerome Klinkowitz, studies this phenomenon as "superfiction" in two other books.[18] With such younger writers as Federman, John Irving, Steve Katz, Ishmael Reed, Gilbert Sorrentino, and Ronald Sukenick, American literature has entered the laboratory of the novel with fervor and typewriter.

II   THE DO-IT-YOURSELF SELF

Although the sophistication necessary for a self-begetting novel was some time in developing, another essential element has been present in America from the moment of the earliest European settlements. Perry Miller writes of "that quality in *Leaves of Grass* that does make it so peculiarly an American book: its extreme self-consciousness."[19] This distinctive national self-consciousness to which Miller alludes is not so much a pensive ego reflecting back on itself as an ardent desire to create a self – and a nation. Abandoning an obsolete identity in Europe, pilgrims of every persuasion have been acutely aware of the need to construct another life in the wilderness across the Atlantic.

The North American continent was conceived of as virgin land,[20] a *tabula rasa* upon which to begin writing a new history. In contrast to the ancient intricacies of European systems, the American Revolution comes as a fresh and wilful intrusion. It is a rejection of the past in favor of what can be devised in the present for the future. Emerson's "shot heard round the world" is so because it attempts to establish a new world; it is a stubborn effort to create a fresh society seemingly *ex nihilo*. If "it presents the spectacle of men trying to live from a blueprint,"[21] it anticipates Henry David Thoreau's determination to go to the woods because he "wished to live life deliberately."[22] American literature is uniquely concerned with the intentional creation of a home, a nation and a self where nothing had existed before. Such an orientation has much in common with the self-begetting novel's attempt to beget a novel self where a dying one had existed before.

The word *individualism* is yet another import from France. However, in this case, significantly, it was coined by a Frenchman, Alexis de Tocqueville, in an attempt to interpret, in his book *De la démocratie en Amérique*, what he observed in the youthful United States of the 1830s. It seemed a spirited, enterprising world of private initiative dedicated to constructing new institutions and new lives. Frederick Jackson Turner's influential 1893 essay "The Significance of the Frontier in American History" likewise stresses the individual as central to the national mystique. Turner regards the pioneer mentality as a major force in American history and culture. Like Huck Finn, the folk myth posits the existence of a "territory ahead" free of the hierarchies and conventions of Aunt Sally's civilization. There individual worth and effort determine success. The frontier psychology implies a radical egalitarianism in which the individual, building his own life, constructs the community, and not vice versa.

Related to this is the popular, and populist, notion of "the self-made man." George Herman Ruth shared its qualities with Benjamin Franklin and Abraham Lincoln. Born again as "Babe," he batted himself out of an orphan home into a new stadium still known as "The House That Ruth Built." The rapid ascent from humble origins to captainship of industry and/or government reenacts the "American dream," the patent delusion that any child can grow up to be President of the United States. The resourceful narrator of Ralph Waldo Ellison's *Invisible Man* (1952) is an acid caricature of this myth of the self-made man. An outcast even among blacks, he is forced to depend on his own wits for mere survival. Yet that does not prevent him from declaring: "Though invisible, I am in the great American tradition of thinkers. That makes me kin to Ford, Edison, and Franklin."[23] Valid or not, though, the American dream, like the self-begetting novel, insists on the self as sovereign and creator.

The product of a society which extols the values of individualism, American literature is often a portrait of solitude. The protagonist in American fiction – Natty Bumppo, Ishmael, Huck Finn, Jake Barnes, or the Invisible Man – is characteristically a lone wanderer, celibate and aloof from the web of society. He is thus, like des Esseintes, Roquentin or Jake Donaghue, responsible for himself only to himself. This emphasis on the individual outside of a social context is what leads Richard Chase to claim that the tradition of the American novel is in truth that of the romance rather than the novel;[24] and in his Preface to *The House of the Seven Gables*, Hawthorne, more concerned with the distinction between imagination and the community, proudly agrees that he writes romances. According to Lionel Trilling's criterion of "manners," "a culture's hum and buzz of implication,"[25] American fiction, examining the enterprising individual, is generally not novelistic. Leslie Fiedler's clinical analysis of the psychopathology of American culture and literature proceeds from a similar starting point.[26] American literature becomes a dramatization of the fantasies of an adolescent not yet integrated into the community.

The theme of initiation is certainly widespread, found in such works as *The Deerslayer, Huckleberry Finn, In Our Time, The Bear, The Catcher In The Rye* and *The Adventures of Augie March*, However, the individual is generally more often confirmed in his autonomy than assimilated into a larger structure. A sequence including *The Declaration of Independence*, the Hartford Convention and the Doctrine of Nullification could be interpreted to demonstrate "the proposition, implicit in much American writing from Poe and Cooper to Anderson and Hemingway, that the valid rite of initiation for the individual in the new world is not an initiation *into* society, but, given the character of society, an initiation *away from it*."[27] The dense complexities of civilization east of the Atlantic or the Alleghenies are rejected in favor of a sovereign self emancipated from the burden of history.

An Easterner, Henry David Thoreau, is nevertheless a striking example of this kind of self. *Walden* (1854) is the account of its narrator's solitary self-sustaining life in the woods: "When I wrote the following pages, or rather the bulk of them, I lived alone, in the woods, a mile from any neighbor, in a house which I had built myself, on the shore of Walden Pond, in Concord, Massachusetts, and earned my living by the labor of my hands only."[28] By retiring from society, Thoreau is able to reconstruct himself entirely on his own. Like Descartes, he recognizes the necessity of simplifying, of wilfully paring away everything for which he is not responsible, and "Economy" is appropriately the first chapter of his record. There is to be nothing accidental about his existence, and, fully conscious of his intentions, he declares as his program "to live deep and suck out all the marrow of life, to live so sturdily and Spartan-like as to put to rout all that was not life" (p.62).

To impress us with his mastery over his own renovated existence, Thoreau constructs a persona who is clearly but "a sojourner in civilized life" (p.1) and who is distinct from the portrait of Thoreau available in contemporary documents. He insists on the need to be *extra vagant*, dividing the word thus to stress its Latin etymology in "wandering beyond." Marching to the beat of a different drummer, the narrator of *Walden* is a magnificent eccentric. Distancing himself from us through shocking opinions and outrageous puns, the cantankerous speaker is an original and proud of it.

A study of the extensive textual revisions in *Walden* reveals that not only did the historical Thoreau become a sovereign self but the literary representation of that identity is a conscious contrivance.[29] For the purposes of the narrative, the entire experience of more than two years is very neatly shaped into one year. We follow the course of the seasons and, at the conclusion of the work, we hear the pond ice cracking and look forward to the rebirth of spring and the self. Horatio Alger never succeeded so well.

Similarly, Nick Carraway, narrator of F. Scott Fitzgerald's *The Great Gatsby* (1925), is quite American in his reverence for individual autonomy: "Almost any exhibition of complete self-sufficiency draws a stunned tribute from me."[30] Nick's West Egg neighbor, who inhabits an enormous mansion all by himself, has managed to succeed entirely on his own, becoming in the process something of an outlaw. Reminiscent of the self-begetting novel's autogenous heroes, Jay Gatsby is a self-made pioneer. He debuted obscurely as James Gatz of North Dakota but was able to transform himself brilliantly. An awesome example of auto-creation, this great Gatsby incarnates the frontier spirit. Reluctant to concentrate on the past (it is difficult for the narrator to piece together details of Gatsby's personal history), he directs his individual efforts toward realities yet to be constructed. "Gatsby believed in the green light, the orgiastic future that year by year recedes before us."[31] Coming as the naïve extension into the twentieth-century of a long American tradition, his belief proves tragic.

Gatsby's self-propelled transformation from James Gatz to Jay Gatsby is somewhat similar to the onymity Marcel, Léon Delmont and Darley attain through their narratives. And James Fenimore Cooper's leather-stockinged stalker of the wilderness goes beyond the Appalachian region and its decreasing elbow room, in the process outgrowing such appellations as Natty Bumppo, Deerslayer and Hawkeye. *The Deerslayer* (1841) is an account of the young frontiersman's initiation in battle, and in solo combat he earns the right to be called Hawkeye rather than Deerslayer. Each avatar demands a fresh christening. A recognition of this fact impelled the earliest European settlers, preparing to commence their lives, to labor at devising names for landmarks within their New England, their New Amsterdam, or their New Spain. The "New Deal," "New Frontier," and "New American Revolution" were fashioned later.

It is appropriate that a number of American authors in the nineteenth-century began to adopt pseudonyms. The decision to concoct another name for themselves in truth announces an attempt to create another self. "Mark Twain" was Samuel Langhorne Clemens's most formidable invention. Van Wyck Brooks, in *The Ordeal of Mark Twain* (1920), contends that Twain, beset by the crass Gilded Age culture represented by Olivia Clemens and Elmira, New York, was only partially successful in remaking himself; and Justin Kaplan's *Mr. Clemens and Mark Twain* (1966) traces the struggle between Samuel Clemens and his personally fashioned proxy, Mark Twain, for control of his identity.

As Roger Asselineau demonstrates,[32] when the young Walter Whitman began to project himself as "Walt Whitman," he was creating a persona in his own life as much as "Song of Myself" does in his poetry. Whitman's eccentric dress and behavior suggest as self-willed a manner as that of a Parisian dandy. Facing the title page of the first edition of *Leaves of Grass* – its author's name, incidentally, appeared only within the text of "Song of Myself" – Whitman insisted on placing an engraving of his inimitable hirsute self, hat on and collar open. In *A Vision*, William Butler Yeats suitably selects Whitman as an example of what he labels "artificial individuality."[33]

Asselineau divides his study into two major sections: "The Creation of Personality" and "The Creation of a Work." When Whitman transfigured himself into "Walt," he was simultaneously constructing an ego and an opus. Furthermore, the two activities were closely complementary; through his writing, the Whitman of 1850–55 was able to assume the identity of poet at the same time as his poetry concerned itself with the theme of self-begetting.

> Let us simply say that Whitman decided to create a book and in the same stroke he created himself. His entire life was thereby changed. Nature has imitated art, thus verifying Oscar Wilde's paradox. He was tormented, unstable, frustrated, and his work permitted him to recover his equilibrium and attain serenity. Poetry saved him. Thanks to it he could emerge from the dark and tempestuous chaos in which he was struggling and gain access to an orderly, peaceful universe where light triumphs over shadows.[34]

Such a summary is as applicable to Marcel and to Marcel Proust, whose novels beget both self and a novel.

Within the American tradition of self-begetting, Ralph Waldo Emerson is himself what he might have termed a "representative man." An ordained minister at the start of a promising ecclesiastical career, the young Emerson in 1832 abruptly resigned his prestigious position in Boston's Second Unitarian Church. As his heretical "Divinity School Address" (1838) later shockingly affirmed, he was abandoning institutional religion in favor of the autocracy of the individual conscience. For the rest of his life, Emerson had to contend with the problem of devising a vocation for himself in a society in which the church had hitherto automatically adopted those with his talents and interests.

In "The American Scholar" (1837), Emerson deals in more secular terms with the theme of creating one's own life. Addressing the Phi Beta Kappa Society at Harvard, he, like Milton in "Aeropagitica," insisted on the thinker's need for and right to independence.

> In self-trust all the virtues are comprehended. Free should the scholar be, – free and brave. Free even to the definition of freedom, "without any hindrance that does not arise out of his own constitution." Brave; for fear is a thing which

a scholar by his very function puts behind him. Fear always springs from ignorance.[35]

Emerson is especially encouraged by what he considers:

> . . . the new importance given to the single person. Every thing that tends to insulate the individual, – to surround him with barriers of natural respect, so that each man shall feel the world is his, and man shall treat with man as a sovereign state with a sovereign state, – tends to true union as well as greatness.[36]

In addition to championing the solitary figure as a "sovereign state," "The American Scholar" demands national emancipation of the New World from the Old. The American of the future must boldly renounce servitude to "the courtly muses of Europe," and become a creator on his own.

The notion of "self-reliance" is clearly central to all of Emerson's works, and not simply his 1841 essay of that name. It is likewise a major element in the American literary tradition, one which links it to the preoccupations of the self-begetting novel. Emerson's "Self-Reliance" is yet another of his celebrations of the nonconformist who freely rejects ochlocracy. For him, as for Joyce and Proust, "a man is the word made flesh."[37] Emerson can thus exhort us again and again, as he does in "Nature" (1836): "Build therefore your own world. As fast as you conform your life to the pure idea in your mind, that will unfold its great proportions."[38]

This categorical imperative characterizes a large American family of self-made politicians, businessmen, authors and fictional creations, all of whom, like Gatsby, sprang from their Platonic conception of themselves. It also expresses an expansionist frontier admiration for the pioneer resolutely appropriating the wilderness.

The quality of self-reliance which Emerson urges for each individual is particularly needed in the poet. However, in "The Poet" (1843), he laments:

> I look in vain for the poet whom I describe. . . . We have yet had no genius in America, with tyrannous eye, which knew the value of our incomparable materials, and saw, in the barbarism and materialism of the times, another carnival of the same gods whose picture he so much admires in Homer; then in the Middle Age; then in Calvinism.[39]

He continues with a rather uncharacteristic catalogue of American races, regions and occupations. Yet in the next decade a native poet began to emerge who was to become a national cataloguer and who seems precisely to fill the void described.

Emerson's assertion "America is a poem in our eyes"[40] could aptly have served as epigraph to Walt Whitman's grandiloquent essay "Democratic Vistas" (1867), a prose tribute to the creation of the New World. And, in fact, after reading a copy of the first edition of *Leaves of Grass* sent him by the younger poet, Emerson wrote back on 21 July 1855:

> I find it the most extraordinary piece of wit and wisdom that America has yet contributed. . . . I give you joy of your free and brave thought. . . . I greet you at the beginning of a great career, which yet must have had a long foreground somewhere, for such a start.[41]

It is tempting to regard Emerson as a kind of John the Baptist, a prophet of self-reliance preparing the world for the entrance of Whitman, the poet of self-begetting and the self-begetting poet. According to a conversation later reported by John T. Trowbridge, Whitman himself acknowledged his relationship to the older writer: "I was simmering, simmering; Emerson brought me to a boil"[42] Presumably, however, a simmering pot eventually comes to a boil by itself.

When Walter Whitman became Walt, the figure his friend William D. O'Connor deified as "the good grey poet," he became the New World's definitive autogenous hero. Henry Miller, a later disciple of this poet of the body and the soul, aptly recognizes that "Whitman remade himself from head to foot."[43] In the retrospective "A Backward Glance O'er Travel'd Roads" (1884), Whitman describes *Leaves of Grass* – his life's work and, in an important sense, his life – as "an attempt, from first to last, to put *a Person*, a human being (myself, in the latter half of the Nineteenth Century, in America,) freely, fully and truly on record."[44] Whitman's omniverous ego expresses itself in all of his productions, but it is most evident in "Song of Myself." The very first word of that long poem is "I," and we are never in suspense about the work's epic theme: "I celebrate myself, and sing myself." This is to be no *Prelude* to a more significant work. It is instead its author's most ambitious achievement precisely because it is an attempt to embody a creative self.

Sounding his "barbaric yawp," the speaker identifies himself in section 24 of the poem as:

> Walt Whitman, a kosmos, of Manhattan the son,
> Turbulent, fleshy, sensual, eating, drinking and breeding,
> No sentimentalist, no stander above men and women or apart from them,
> no more modest than immodest.

This characterization is, at least in part, a fiction, but, like the rest of the poem, it represents an effort to construct a self, an activity inseparable from the construction of the poem. The personality of the poem, "a kosmos," emerges as the sum total of all the disparate experience evoked. As in "Crossing Brooklyn Ferry," distance and time avail not, and the speaker's vignettes present him walking the hills of Judea with Jesus (sect. 33), defending the Alamo (sect.34), and sailing beside John Paul Jones (sect.35). Whitman's poet thrives through absorption. Like his child who went forth every day, everything he looks upon he becomes. And his vision comprehends a huge range of reality – president, trapper, fugitive slave, prostitute. Walt's interminable lists define himself. If his incorporation of old and young, rich and poor, North and South, life and death, city and wilderness seems contradictory, the speaker serenely accepts this.

> Do I contradict myself?
> Very well then I contradict myself,
> (I am large, I contain multitudes) (sect.51)

Both Walt and his poem contain multitudes which, paradoxically, are simply extensions of the self. "One's-self I sing, a simple separate person,/Yet utter the word Democratic, the word En-Masse."[45] Whitman's protagonist is an individual whose distinct identity, like Blake's grain of sand, entails everything. The "I" is inescapable in almost every line of Whitman's poetry. But he is also directly addressing a "you" whom he persistently attempts to embrace in a fusion of the subjective and the objective. Once that is achieved and we are able to catch up with him, the self, as in *A la recherche*, becomes the world, and both are comprised in a work of literature.

Walt also resembles his "noiseless, patient spider" who builds the surrounding universe by launching forth filaments out of himself. The spider image portrays the individual as engendering the world. And Walt explicitly projects himself as a poet creating the work we are reading. At the conclusion of one of his extensive catalogues of motley occupations, this "poet of the woman the same as the man" (sect.21) self-consciously proclaims: "And of these one and all I weave the song of myself" (sect.15).

But as author of "Song of Myself" and numerous other poems in which the self is celebrated, Walt is also explicitly and triumphantly the author of himself. He thereby becomes what Stephen Dedalus longs to be, both creator and creation, parent and offspring – "Maternal as well as paternal, a child as well as a man" (sect.16). Walt, "hankering, gross, mystical, nude" (sect.20) often depicts himself in sensual detail cast in the role of lover. However, he just as frequently becomes an embryo or an eternal child passively nursed by the land or the sea and set in a cradle endlessly rocking.

As both father and son, active and passive, poet and poem, Walt blends the tradition of the self-begetting author with that of the American self-made man. Whitman's strophes depict the neo-Biblical drama of a world and an Adam being created. But the American poet goes on to commit the pantheist heresy of asserting absolute identity between creator and creation. If the self comes to comprise all of the world, the vehicle for this act of comprehension, the poem, becomes indistinguishable from the self it creates. And Whitman is able to conclude convincingly: "this is no book/Who touches this touches a man."[46]

In Shakespeare's Sonnet 18, the speaker, confident of the life-preserving powers of his verse, declares: "So long as men can breathe or eyes can see,/So long lives this and this gives life to thee." Whitman's poetry endows his only begotten narrator with life. At the same time, the objective existence of "Song of Myself" and the other components of *Leaves of Grass* demonstrates the continuing vitality of that created self. In "When Lilacs Last in the Dooryard Bloom'd," the speaker, in an apostrophe to a thrush, confides: "for well dear brother I know,/If thou wast not granted to sing thou would'st surely die." Walt the chanter portrays himself not only as begetting himself but as sustaining and nourishing that self through poetry.

The metaphor of the journey informs "Song of Myself." Walt conceives of himself as a walker – "I tramp a perpetual journey" (sect.46) – and everything he encounters during his imagined travels contributes to his poem and to his personality. Although he is later to glance backward o'er travel'd roads, Whitman is even more thoroughly committed to the unexplored "open road" than is his descendant Jack Kerouac.

This notion of the journey emphasizes the dynamic nature of the ego which the poet projects. Whitman's self is a nomad, forever in motion. No distinction exists between traveler and road, and as long as the possibilities of experience are not exhausted the wanderer – and his embodiment, the poem – must remain incomplete. "There is no stoppage and never can be stoppage" (sect.45), we are told, but then, in one of his multitudinous contradictions, the poet provisionally halts "Song of Myself" with the statement "I stop somewhere waiting for you" (sect.52). Presumably when we have overtaken the impetuous poet he will begin moving once more.

In this journey which we are invited to share and a record of which we at the same time read in the poem, Walt emerges as a journeyman more than a master. We see his vocation forming but never fully formed. After all, "a leaf of grass is no less than the journey-work of the stars" (sect.31).

Leaves of Grass is the happy title Whitman applied to his growing mass of collected poems, from the first edition in 1855 through each successive edition until his death in 1892. During those four decades, Whitman was regularly composing new poems, revising old ones, and readjusting their positions within the dynamic framework of his always incomplete book. The organic metaphor implied by *Leaves of Grass* conveys this sense of the book as process rather than static product. Since the expanding volume is designed to be an incarnation of Walt Whitman, its title appropriately emphasizes the vitality of its subject and reinforces the idea of journey down an open road. *Leaves of Grass* was, and is, a perpetual Work in Progress. It is a loose cluster of primitive lays which eventually cohere as an epic.

Continually begetting itself, it is likewise author of a sizeable family in American literature. Ezra Pound reluctantly made his famous "pact" with Walt Whitman and, in 1909, admitted:

> Mentaly I am a Walt Whitman who has learned to wear a collar and a dress shirt (although at times inimical to both). Personaly I might be very glad to conceal my relationship to my spiritual father and brag about my more congenial ancestry – Dante, Shakespeare, Theocritus, Villon, but the descent is a bit difficult to establish.[47]

Like his "spiritual father's" *Leaves of Grass*, Pound's *Cantos* is an open form which was growing for most of the century. Additions to the *Cantos* which slipped into print from time to time indicated that the poet – approaching ninety – and his massive poem were still alive. Pound devoted, and entrusted, his life to the *Cantos*. Charles Olson's *Maximus Poems*, John Berryman's *Dream Songs*, and Henry Miller's multi-volume prose project, *The Rosy Crucifixion*, represent similar phenomena. Although not asymptotic in the manner of *Leaves of Grass* or, for that matter, *The Canterbury Tales*, Hart Crane's *The Bridge* and William Carlos Williams's *Paterson* revive the Whitmanesque ambition of producing an epic poem capable of representing life in America. When Allen Ginsberg in a poem entitled "America" outrageously announces: "It occurs to me that I am America," he is constructing an ego which in another work appropriately greets Walt Whitman in "A Supermarket in California." And in such "non-fiction novels" as *The Armies of the Night* (1968), *Miami and the Siege of Chicago* (1969), *Of a Fire on the Moon* (1970) and *The Prisoner of Sex* (1971), Norman Mailer has created "Norman," a Whitmanesque narrator-protagonist grand enough to attempt literary control over the bewildering American experience he encounters.

The self-made literary man tends to express himself in a form approaching autobiography. Autobiography is manifestly the most reflexive of genres, and Americans as different as Benjamin Franklin, Henry Adams, Gertrude Stein, William Carlos Williams, and Malcolm X have distinguished themselves in it. Perhaps autobiography is in fact the logical extension of a native impulse toward realism; it presents the narrator focusing his attention on the subject for which he has done the most research.

American literature has tried to erect the autobiographer's encounter with the self into a universal principle. In "To The Reader," discussing the question of whether *Look Homeward, Angel* is autobiographical, Thomas Wolfe claims that "all serious work in fiction is autobiographical." And Emerson discusses Dante as if the Italian poet were a self-begetting novelist. "Dante's praise is that he dared to write his autobiography into colossal cipher, or into universality."[48] Henry Miller expands on Emerson in a Whitmanesque demand for the simultaneous creation of a self and a work of art:

> The autobiographical novel, which Emerson predicted would grow in impor-
> tance with time, has replaced the great confessions. It is not a mixture of truth
> and fiction, this genre of literature, but an expansion and deepening of truth.
> It is more authentic, more veridical, than the diary. It is not the flimsy truth of
> facts which the authors of these autobiographical novels offer but the truth of
> emotion, reflection and understanding, truth digested and assimilated. The
> being revealing himself does so on all levels simultaneously.[49]

III   THE GREAT AMERICAN NOVEL

Whitman's nationalistic, epic pretensions anticipate the popular myth of "The Great American Novel" – the consummate, sprawling work embodying a country that immodestly spanned a continent, from the Atlantic to the Pacific. In contrast to Europe's devious evolution, the United States was viewed as having been constructed *ex nihilo* quite deliberately and within a brief period of time. The analogy to a work of art was patent. "The United States themselves are essentially the greatest poem."[50] And, in his Preface to the 1855 edition of *Leaves of Grass*, Whitman emphasizes the need to create a poet persona who will be equivalent to both his national poem and his poetic nation.

> The American poets are to enclose old and new for America is the race of
> races. Of them a bard is to be commensurate with a people. To him the other
> continents arrive as contributions . . . he gives them reception for their sake
> and his own sake. His spirit responds to his country's spirit . . . he incarnates
> its geography and national life and rivers and lakes. Mississippi Columbia
> and Ohio and Saint Lawrence with the falls and beautiful masculine Hudson,
> do not embouchure where they spend themselves more than they embouchure
> into him.[51]

Whitman continues with one of his typically interminable catalogues of the varied regions of the country. However, what is remarkable about Whitman's self-consciousness here is that it is a consciousness of the creative self as embodiment of the national work of art. To the European convention of the fictive fiction-maker is added the distinctively American element of triple identification among creator, creation and nation.

Following the Civil War, with the success of the Transcontinental Railroad and the urge to reunite the severed regions of the country, the idea of The Great American Novel became a public obsession. It was to be a means of restoring confidence in a badly maimed national psyche.

An 1868 editorial in *The Nation* urged enactment of copyright laws which would have the effect of patronizing native authors by protecting their books against competition with pirated, less expensive European works. At the same time, it patriotically issued the call for what it termed "The Great American Novel" – "a single tale which paints American life so broadly, truly, and sympathetically that every American of feeling and culture is forced to acknowledge the picture as a likeness of something which he knows."[52] It was a bustling, pragmatic age, and the consummate work was to take the form of realistic prose.

Significant in references to The Great American Novel is use of the definite article. It was to be "a single tale." Every native son could dream of someday being elected President of the United States or of writing The Great American Novel. However, although several members of each generation realize that supreme political fantasy, by definition only one person in the entire history of the Republic can compose *The* Great American Novel. It is conceived of as the New World's Book of Books, subsuming and rendering obsolete everything else.

The idea of the G.A.N. becomes what Frank Kermode would term a "fiction of the end."[53] Although superb books may be written at any time, once The Great American Novel emerges the novel henceforth is truly dead. There will no longer be a need for it. However well-wrought, *Absalom, Absalom!* could follow *Huckleberry Finn*, which could follow *Moby-Dick*, which could follow *The Scarlet Letter*. T. S. Perry's observation in the *North American Review* of 1872 that "The great novel is yet unwritten"[54] is thus at once distressing and encouraging. In terms of the apocalyptic nature of the G.A.N., it must be eternally valid.

When this idea of The Great American Novel is explicitly incorporated into the structure of a specific work, the myth of the G.A.N. enters the tradition of the self-begetting novel. The G.A.N. is not necessarily reflexive, though. In fact, several of its champions seem to contend that this magnum opus commensurate with America must be committed to a "realism" which would exclude Proustian self-consciousness. The ambitious productions of such writers as Frank Norris, Theodore Dreiser, John Dos Passos, Thomas Wolfe and James T. Farrell can be viewed as deliberate bids at The Great American Novel. But they generally aim at immortality obliquely. Their novels do not directly treat the attempt to create the G.A.N.

In fact, T. S. Perry, in an early discussion of the traits of the great American novelist, maintains:

> The less conscious he is of trying to be an American, the more truly will he succeed in being so. Self-consciousness does not make a strong character, and so it is with this quality of the novelist.[55]

Although he goes on to claim: "The real novelist, he who is to write the 'great American novel,' must be a poet," Perry's disapproval of self-consciousness in literature would disqualify Walt Whitman from "greatness," as it would any novelist who projects the struggle to fashion The Great American Novel into his fiction. Frank Norris similarly advocates finding literary directions by indirections. Recognizing the hypothetical nature of the G.A.N., Norris reminds us that "The Great American Novel is not extinct like the Dodo, but mythical like the Hippogriff, and that the thing to be looked for is not the Great American Novelist, but the Great Novelist who shall also be an American."[56] Norris minimizes the adjective "American," suggesting that for him Whitmanesque solemnities about the nation are impertinent. But he pointedly retains the definite article, affirming the view that we await the event of one particular novel.

However, if the G.A.N. is as likely to come trotting along as a hippogriff, then it should not matter that some novelists self-consciously appropriate the theme of attempting The Great American Novel into their own efforts. John Barth's *The Sot-Weed Factor* (1960) follows Ebenezer Cooke, poet laureate of Maryland, through numerous adventures in England and the colonies during the late seventeenth-century. Cooke was an actual historical character, and *The Sot-Weed Factor* comically attempts to reconstruct the experiences which led him to create his poem "The Sot-Weed Factor," published in 1708. Barth's novel is thus the account of a poem's genesis. To the extent that both poem and novel, even mock-heroically, encompass much of colonial history, they become candidates for the epithet "Great American," or at least "Great Maryland." And in 1923 William Carlos Williams published in Paris a short, reflexive prose work entitled *The Great American Novel*. Narrated in the first-person by a would-be author, it is a mannered, plotless meditation on the nature of the G.A.N. and of "the American grain." Of interest as a stage in Williams's development, *The Great American Novel* is, nevertheless, neither great nor a novel.

Clyde Brion Davis's *"The Great American Novel −−"* (1938) is probably more instructive as illustration of a fusion of the self-begetting tradition with the national myth. *"The Great American Novel −−"* was the second novel by the forty-four year old former newspaperman Davis.[57] Its narrator, a journalist with literary aspirations, is portentously named Homer Zigler. We follow Homer's progress chronologically, from childhood through middle-age. A *Künstlerroman* as well as a *Bildungsroman*, *"The Great American Novel −−"* traces Homer's jobs at various newspapers and his simultaneously developing ambition to write The Great American Novel. Homer's career takes him to cities throughout the United States, and the novel's five sections are in turn located in and entitled "Buffalo," "Cleveland," "Kansas City," "San Francisco," and "Denver." Davis's novel, at least, does convey a sense of the continental sweep necessary to the G.A.N.

The account which we read of Homer's life is cast in the form of a diary kept for thirty years. The present tense perspective of Homer's diary forces us to see how flagrantly obtuse he is. His total inability to understand himself or Frances Harbach causes him to marry the wrong girl, and again and again, not content with merely suggesting his unreliability to us, Homer comes out with judgments on public issues which we, with our wider perspective, recognize as outrageously wrongheaded. Shortly before the 1908 presidential election, he naïvely anounces: "I am confident that Taft will be the worst defeated presidential candidate in history."[58] Later, in July 1914, Homer is confident: "It is apparent now to thinking people that science has advanced so far that another giant war is practically impossible" (p.178). Dramatic irony can be more subtle.

Despite Homer's artlessness, he does undergo a development, one which is connected to his education as an artist. From the time he is thirteen, Homer cherishes the hope of writing fiction. And the existence of his diary is evidence of his interest in literature. It is to serve as a kind of training ground for him. In his first journal entry, Homer notes:

> My ambition to become a novelist no longer is a vague thing. It is very real. I am directing my thoughts and my reading to the purpose of preparing myself for that career and that is my reason for writing this record (p.8).

Yet an unsympathetic family and the daily rigors of newspaper writing force Homer to suppress his artistic aspirations and incessantly to postpone writing the novel he believes he can create.

Frances Harbach and Syra Morris function as literary advisors for Homer and encourage him in his project. Indeed his plans somehow do become more sophisticated; Irving Bacheller is Homer's earliest literary idol, but he is eventually replaced by Sherwood Anderson and Theodore Dreiser. During his sojourn in Kansas City, Homer begins to outline his goals as a novelist:

> I want my novel to be all-inclusive. I want my novel to be America. I want it to hold the high purpose and sufferings of the Pilgrim fathers. I want it to hold the romance of the Spanish conquistadores and of the French padres who plunged through the terrors of an unknown land for king and church (p.64).

He continues for another paragraph with a Whitmanesque catalogue of varied elements in American history. It is a classic description of the aims of The Great American Novel. Conceiving of only one novel, *the* novel, Homer longs to be Whitman's bard commensurate with his people.

With nothing less than the exacting criteria for the G.A.N. to satisfy, he sets about sketching the tentative lines of a plot. His intended novel will be entitled *Restless Dynasty*. Beginning shortly after the War of 1812 in the Lake Champlain area, it is to trace the family of Jeremiah Williams through six generations and a broad span of American history and geography. *Restless Dynasty* gestates in Homer for many years, but when, many years later, he summarizes a revised version to Syra Morris, reviewer for the *Denver Call*, where he is now working, she is enthusiastic. "She feels 'Brutal Dynasty' actually may become the Great American Novel she and her fellow critics have been looking for so long" (p.305).

But *"The Great American Novel --"* concludes without *Brutal Dynasty* ever being written. The aging Homer Zigler is fired from his position at the *Denver Call*. About to enter the hospital for major surgery, Homer determines that after his recovery he will finally begin work on his novel and thereby transform himself from journalist into artist. He entrusts his diary to Syra's safekeeping, and, in the final sentences of Clyde Brion Davis's novel, states:

> It isn't that I am afraid of dying, but I must admit, of course, there always is danger in a serious operation of this sort. I really am not worrying about my operation at all. I know I shan't die because I am only beginning to live. I am now only starting my life's work (p.309).

Homer thus views his expected debut as novelist through the conventional image of rebirth through art. However, *Brutal Dynasty* does not materialize for us, and it is questionable whether Homer does in fact survive his operation. His assurance that he is only now beginning to live and to undertake his life's work may be as ill-founded as his political predictions. Yet Homer's literary legacy is preserved in the form of his diary, the work we have just finished reading. The diary embodies him, and if we want Homer to recommence his pathetic life we need only turn back to the first page of *"The Great American Novel --"*.

In a freakish coincidence, *"The Great American Novel --"* was published in the same year as *La Nausée*. Despite vast differences in style, tone, and achievement, both novels are set in diary form. Both center on narrators who eventually decide to write a novel but both also conclude in ambiguity over death and rebirth. Roquentin's diary is found and presented to us by anonymous editors, and it is perhaps Syra Morris who is responsible for the preservation of this account of Homer Zigler's life. Davis and Sartre each create a novel whose self-begetting remains in question.

Homer's ambitions for The Great American Novel cannot be satisfied by *Brutal Dynasty*, which we never see, but rather, if at all, by the journal which he leaves behind and which becomes the text of *"The Great American Novel --"*. Homer, whose life in some ways parallels that of his author, has, as a newspaperman in cities throughout the United States, been a "post of consciousness" for most of the significant events of early twentieth-century American history. According to the folk notion of The

Great American Novel, the New World epic, he would seem to be as likely as anyone to breed Norris's hippogriff. Yet the quotation marks and the dashes in the title *"The Great American Novel --"* suggest that Davis, at least, is skeptical about his protagonist's success. And, now obscure and out of print, Davis's novel itself makes a curious candidate for the definitive national book. It is, at least, a useful reminder that self-consciousness in literature need not entail artistic sophistication. The tradition of the self-begetting novel can produce plain children as well as chic.

IV   MILLER'S TALE

Tropic of Capricorn (1939) is a fictional projection of Henry Miller's early experiences in New York, and *Tropic of Cancer* (1934) portrays him as another American in Paris. Both novels are narrated in the first person by a writer who is very much aware that he is designing himself into the center of his story. In fact, in an angry reply to Edmund Wilson's review of *Tropic of Cancer* in *The New Republic*, Miller establishes the kind of equation between book and self found in Proust and Whitman:

> I have painstakingly indicated throughout the book that the hero is myself. I don't use "heroes,' incidentally, nor do I write novels. I am the hero, and the book is myself . . .[59]

Within his fiction itself, Miller characteristically pays direct tribute to his two self-begetting predecessors. In *Tropic of Cancer*, he describes discussions among American expatriates in France who, like the narrator of the book in which they appear, are still haunted by the country they left behind. They evoke the figure of Walt Whitman, the bard who succeeded in creating a personality commensurate with his nation and, in the process, *the* definitive work of literature.

> And inevitably there always crept into our discussions the figure of Whitman, that one lone figure which America has produced in the course of her brief life. In Whitman the whole American scene comes to life, her past and her future, her birth and her death. Whatever there is of value in America Whitman has expressed, and there is nothing more to be said. The future belongs to the machine, to the robots. He was the Poet of the Body and the Soul, Whitman. The first and the last poet (*Cancer*, p.216).

On the other side of the Atlantic, in *Tropic of Capricorn*, a thick slice of rye bread echoes Proust's *madeleine* episode. One of the references of the "cancer" image is to the fact that "The cancer of time is eating us away" (*Cancer*, p.1), and Miller's Henry, like Proust's Marcel, "knew very well I was pissing my time away" (*Capricorn*, p.279). It is appropriate, then, that one of the narrator's frequent asides permits him to launch into a rhapsody over Proust's victory in "transforming the negative reality of life into the substantial and significant outlines of art" (*Cancer*, p.146). Among British novelists, it is fittingly Lawrence Durrell with whom Miller has long had a relationship of mutual admiration.

The Alexandria Quartet and *A la recherche* resemble art colonies, and Miller's *Tropics*, for all the difference in tone, contain even more artists than whores. Almost all of Henry's acquaintances in Paris – Van Norden, Carl, Boris, Borowski, Sylvester – are portrayed as writers of some sort. Kruger is a sculptor and Elsa a musician. Aesthetic reflections are interspersed, often incongruously, with other activities. Van Norden habitually seduces virgins by beginning with a lecture on Ezra Pound's *Cantos*; and Miller's comic touch is evident in the *Cancer* scene in which Henry attends a concert and neglects the music entirely to speculate instead on what intercourse would be like if he were a woman.

Back in New York, Henry's job with the Cosmodemonic Telegraph Company brings him into daily contact with legions of human beings of every variety. Each one has a story within him and is anxious to tell it to Henry.

> In a year, reckoning it modestly, I received twenty-five thousand tales; in two years fifty thousand; in four years it would be a hundred thousand, in ten years I would be stark mad. Already I knew enough people to populate a good-sized town (*Capricorn*, p.66).

If he could populate a good-sized novel with them all, it would have to be The Great American Novel. Like Lessing's Anna, Henry is troubled by the surfeit of writers. Even Monica wants to join the ranks.

> But a kid like that thinking about becoming a writer! Well, why not? Everybody had illusions of one sort or another. Monica too wanted to be a writer. Everybody was becoming a writer. A writer! Jesus, how futile it seemed! (*Capricorn*, p.81).

Henry does, in any case, contemplate writing a kind of Horatio Alger novel about the telegraph messengers. He is, of course, the most important, if not the only, character in Miller's novels, and he considers himself large enough to contain the multitudes of his fictional cosmos. Henry's work in New York relaying messages and his position as proofreader in Paris both point to his emergence as literary creator.

Taken as a sequence, *Tropic of Capricorn* and *Tropic of Cancer* trace the development of an artist from his earliest experiences in America to his later years in France and the moment when he will be able to write the novels which portray him. Throughout Henry is conscious of his destiny and his place in the story. Early in his pilgrim's progress, Henry's New York confidant Kronski assures him:

> I think someday you're going to be a great writer. . . . Listen, when I hear you
> talk sometimes, I think to myself – if only that guy would put it down on paper!
> Why you could write a book that would make a guy like Dreiser hang his head
> (*Capricorn*, pp.86–7).

On a three-week vacation from Cosmodemonic, Henry does attempt
to give birth to his novel about the messengers. It is an ambitious failure.

> I thought that a man, to be a writer, must do at least five thousand words a
> day. I thought he must say everything all at once – in one book – and collapse
> afterwards. I didn't know a thing about writing. I was scared shitless. But I
> was determined to wipe Horatio Alger out of the North American conscious-
> ness. I suppose it was the worst book any man has ever written. It was a
> colossal tome and faulty from start to finish (*Capricorn*, p.34).

This rehearsal for *Tropic of Capricorn* itself suggests some of the monu-
mental qualities of *The Great American Novel*.

Later, in the setting of Paris, Henry conceives an even more universal
project. He and Boris brazenly dream of composing the conclusive
literary work that will do for the modern world what the G.A.N. would
for America.

> It is to be a new Bible – *The Last Book*. All those who have anything to say will
> say it here – *anonymously*. We will exhaust the age. After us not another book –
> not for a generation, at least. Heretofore we had been digging in the dark, with
> nothing but instinct to guide us. Now we shall have a vessel in which to pour
> the vital fluid, a bomb which, when we throw it, will set off the world. We shall
> put into it enough to give the writers of tomorrow their plots, their dramas,
> their poems, their myths, their sciences. The world will be able to feed on it for
> a thousand years to come. It is colossal in its pretentiousness. The thought of it
> almost shatters us (*Cancer*, p.24).

Tropic of Cancer certainly is not the last word in literature. But its
structure of permanent digression into a wide range of human experience
and thought suggests the kind of encyclopedic, resourceful work that
would be. It is hyperbole to declare that nothing that is human is alien to
Henry: but this vernacular hero does succeed in humanizing much that
was previously alien to literature. And the effort is integrally related to
the narrator's pervasive reminder that what we read is contrived. It is
closer to naïve reflexiveness than to naïve realism.

Henry liberally employs the familiar metaphor of the artist giving
birth to a work of art. For example, in the description of the moment in
Far Rockaway when he suddenly perceives his kinship with Dostoevsky
and begins "to realize that there must come a time when I should begin,
when I should put down the first word, *the first real word*," Henry
explains: "I felt all the books I would one day write myself germinating

inside me: they were bursting inside like ripe cocoons" (*Capricorn*, p.211). This conceit – poetic and personal – of literature gestating within him becomes a veritable epic simile in *Cancer*.

> Women get up to offer me their seats. Nobody pushes me rudely any more. I am pregnant. I waddle awkwardly, my big stomach pressed against the weight of the world (*Cancer*, p.23).

If a novel is being begotten, so, inevitably, is a novelist. The imagery of birth becomes as applicable to the new self Henry is creating as to his new work of art. In the middle of *Capricorn*, Henry announces: "At the point from which this book is written I am the man who baptized himself anew" (p.230). The creation of that book has had no small part in the rebirth of this American Adam. In the process, Henry must reenact the venerable paradox that in order to find the self he must first lose it. Although *Tropic of Capricorn*, Miller's American novel, represents a recovery of time past, it is only constructed when he discards personal history and departs New York to forge a fresh identity in Paris: "I did not open my eyes wide and full and clear until I struck Paris. And perhaps that was only because I had renounced America, renounced my past" (*Capricorn*, p.49).

Capricorn, incidentally, concludes on a note somewhat reminiscent of the ending of *A Portrait*. About to forsake his homeland and enter a foreign nation and another novel, Miller's narrator issues his own artificer's manifesto. A new life and a new art will begin with the self. "I shall neither serve nor be served. I shall seek the end in myself" (p.348).

Faithful to the tradition which renders des Esseintes, Marcel, Roquentin and Jake Donaghue thoroughly alone in the world, Henry projects himself as a solitary figure. He is confident of containing multitudes, but this is because he is the only "round" character in his narrative. The many supernumeraries who flit in and out of the novels simply assist in the process of defining – and creating – Henry's identity. Henry lacks permanent attachments to any person, occupation or nation. "I haven't any allegiance, any responsibilities, any hatreds, any worries, any prejudices, any passion. I'm neither for nor against. I'm a neutral" (*Cancer*, p.138). However, this rootlessness is a prerequisite for artistic creation, and, taking his solitary way, Henry sees himself transformed into an artist. "An artist is always alone – if he *is* an artist. No, what the artist needs is loneliness" (*Cancer*, p.60).

To make himself into somebody, Henry must begin as a blank, "an Arabian zero rather, the sign from which spring endless mathematical worlds, the fulcrum which balances the stars and the light dreams and the machines lighter than air and the lightweight limbs and the explosives that produced them" (*Cancer*, pp.223–4). New York memories of his Hindu friend Nanantatee, whom he called "Mister Nonentity," are evoked by Henry's realization in Paris: "What a zero I have become, what a cipher, what a nullity" (*Cancer*, p.72). It is from this point of absolute negation that he is able to begin from scratch to create a new self that will absorb the entire world. After all, "Out of nothingness arises the sign of infinity" (*Cancer*, p.227). Departing temporarily from the organic metaphor of reproduction, Henry writes of his identity as if it were a mechanical invention he has manufactured: "I remember the day I brought the machine to a dead stop and how the other mechanism, the one that was signed with my own initials and which I had made with my own hands and my own blood slowly began to function" (*Capricorn*, p.284).

The act of naming is almost as significant here as it is in Cooper's *Leatherstocking Tales*. The narrator of the novels must name as well as beget himself. Henry is inexplicably referred to as "Sunny Jim" by his father; the explanation that this "was because I was full of 'Force,' full of vim and vigor" (*Capricorn*, p.248) seems intentionally frivolous. At another point, he becomes one "Gottlieb Leberecht Müller," "the name of a man who lost his identity" (*Capricorn*, p.227). And throughout much of *Cancer* the hero is simply "Joe." In fact, everyone in the Parisian limbo of lost souls becomes "Joe" until transmuted into something more distinctive.

> I call him Joe because he calls me Joe. When Carl is with us he is Joe too. Everybody is Joe because it's easier that way. It's also a pleasant reminder not to take yourself too seriously (*Cancer*, p.93).

However, the begetting of a self is a very critical matter in Henry Miller's novels. His persona, the man who can confess "I have never found a man as generous as myself, as forgiving, as tolerant, as carefree, as reckless, as clean at heart" (*Capricorn*, p.229), has the bravado of Whitman. The *Tropic* novels are a prose "Song of Myself," and the male chauvinist adventurism for which Kate Millet[60] indicts Miller is another expression of an aggressive ego out to remake the world into a personal fiction. Again, we are forcefully reminded that the object of writing is a quest for the self: "For there is only one great adventure and that is inward toward the self, and for that, time nor space nor even deeds matter" (*Capricorn*, p.12). To that end, distinctions between fact and fiction dissolve, and Henry can renovate himself at the same time he fabricates a work of art to contain himself.

> To some this may seem like an invention, but whatever I imagine to have happened did actually happen, *at least* to me. History may deny it, since I have played no part in the history of my people, but even if everything I say is wrong, is prejudiced, spiteful, malevolent, even if I am a liar and a poisoner, it is nevertheless the truth and it will have to be swallowed (*Capricorn*, p.13).

The book becomes Henry's body as much as it does for Whitman, or even for Marcel. He swallows the world in order to feed his new self.

> The word must become flesh; the soul thirsts. On whatever crumb my eye fastens, I will pounce and devour. . . . If I am a hyena I am a lean and hungry one: I go forth to fatten myself (*Cancer*, p.90).

Amidst his epic catalogue of sexual exploits, Henry moves in a fictional world saturated with literature. Whitman had cautioned readers of *Leaves of Grass*: "No one will get at my verse who insists upon viewing them as a literary performance, or attempt at such performance, or as aiming mainly toward art or aestheticism."[61] And, at the very outset of *Tropic of Cancer*, Henry is even more fiercely contemptuous of art. Describing the book he is writing and we are reading, he declares:

> This is not a book. This is libel, slander, defamation of character. This is not a book in the ordinary sense of the word. No, this is a prolonged insult, a gob of spit in the face of Art, a kick in the pants to God, Man, Destiny, Time, Love, Beauty . . . what you will (pp.1–2).

Such disclaimers and such militant anti-traditionalism are traditional. The strategy of producing art by assaulting a bourgeois notion of "beauty" extends at least as far back as Baudelaire and Dostoevsky. As Proust emphasizes, in order to create *the* Book, an author must consciously absorb and transcend all previous books. If successful, "it will be the triumph of the individual over art" (*Cancer*, p.10). Nevertheless, in the self-begetting works of Proust, Whitman, and Miller, when the individual triumphs so does a new work of art.

Henry Miller the author of fiction and Henry Miller the fictional author are both only occasionally abashed bibliophiles. *The Books In My Life* (1950) is yet another version of Miller's life, this one based on the premise: "My encounters with books I regard as my encounters with other phenomena of life or thought."[62] In it, in addition to listing "The Hundred Books Which Influenced Me Most" and "Books I Still Intend to Read," Miller projects the grandiose scheme of cataloguing every single book he can recall having read. Yet the tormented lycée teacher Henry can declare in *Cancer*: "Every man with a bellyful of the classics is an enemy to the human race" (p.248).

Miller, like Emerson and Whitman, is committed to a dynamic rather than a static model of art and the ego. Emerson, in "The Poet," affirms that "the quality of the imagination is to flow, and not to freeze,"[63] and Whitman echoes: "A great poem is no finish to a man or woman but rather a beginning."[64] Similarly, the narrator of *Cancer* declares: "I love everything that flows, everything that has time in it, and becoming" (p.232).

The incessant digressions of *Tropic of Capricorn* and *Tropic of Cancer* provide them with rhapsodies on sundry themes rather than linear plots. They lack the self-begetting novel's tidy circular pattern of concluding with the narrator's decision to write the novel in which he appears. Instead, almost each paragraph of Miller's fiction destroys and resurrects a self and a work of literature. As in *A la recherche*, "Everything that happens will happen twice" (*Capricorn*, p.348). This self-conscious fiction will not permit us to rest with prefabricated versions of self or art. As a result, we at every point witness self and art being thrust into life.

7 Beckett's Trilogy

Now cease, my lute. This is the last
Labour that thou and I shall waste,
And ended is that we begun.
Now is this song both sung and past;
My lute, be still, for I have done.
Sir Thomas Wyatt, "My Lute Awake!" ll. 36–40

I BECKETT AND THE FRENCH TRADITION

When, several years after abandoning his native Ireland, Samuel Beckett began writing novels, plays and poems in a foreign language, French, he was creating a new self as wilfully as was Walter Whitman when he begot "Walt." Joseph Conrad and Vladimir Nabokov, also linguistic refugees, were more or less forced out of Polish and Russian, respectively, if not into English. But Beckett's transition from English to French was a freely determined, deliberate action. If he did not invent his own language, as he praises both Dante and Joyce for having done,[1] Beckett did at least consciously re-position himself within a self-begetting literary tradition. His enthusiasm for both Descartes and Proust was demonstrated anew when, after having lived for some time in France and as a disciple of James Joyce, he composed his extraordinary fictional trilogy. *Molloy* (1951), *Malone meurt* (1952) and *L'Innommable* (1953) are highly self-conscious extensions of the French tradition. It is true that Beckett's novels are "an amalgam of Joyce and Proust"[2] and that "three major deities presided, Janus-like, at the birth of Beckett the artist: Joyce, Descartes, and Proust."[3] However, if Beckett's trilogy adopts the themes and strategies of the self-begetting novel, it also represents a *reductio ad absurdum* of it.

Long before he became a French novelist and entered the stable of *Les Editions de minuit*, Beckett's preoccupations matched those of *Discours de la méthode* and *A la recherche*. Beckett did considerable research on René Descartes for his 1931 M.A. from Trinity, and the extensive footnotes to his first published creation, the 1930 poem "Whoroscope," make it clear that its narrator is Descartes and that abtruse allusions throughout the work are to details of the seventeenth-century self-begetting philosopher's life. Beckett characteristically alters the Cartesian em-

phasis and has his protagonist declare: "Fallor, ergo sum!" (l.73). Egg
imagery pervades the poem. The poet is fascinated with the odd fact,
culled from Adrien Baillet's *La Vie de Monsieur Descartes*, that the author
of *De la Formation du foetus* "liked his omelette made of eggs hatched from
eight to ten days; shorter or longer under the hen and the result, he says,
is disgusting" ("Whoroscope," Notes). As Beckett presents Descartes,
"The shuttle of a ripening egg combs the warp of his days" (Notes), and
this poem, which begins with reference to a rotten egg and concludes
with the narrator on his deathbed in Sweden, anticipates the obsession
with creation and extinction in Beckett's self-begetting trilogy.

In addition, just as Iris Murdoch's critical study of Sartre preceded
her own *Under the Net*, Beckett's first book, published in 1931, was
appropriately a monograph entitled *Proust*. The young literary scholar
traces, among other things, how "The whole of Proust's world comes out
of a teacup";[4] but the epigraph he borrows from Leopardi, *E fango è il
mondo*, would reduce everything to mud, years before Bouville was
begotten and The Unnamable, covered with "liquefied brain,"[5] became
conscious of a dense reality defying consciousness.

Molloy, Malone meurt and *L'Innommable* are thoroughly conscious of
their status as works of literature, of their place in literary history, and of
their relationships to one another. Each is a first-person account, and the
narrator of each novel explicitly presents himself as a writer. Molloy, in
his mother's bed, scribbles the pages that we read; Moran, at the behest
of Youdi, writes a report on his activities; Malone creates his world by
means of his pencil and his exercise book; and The Unnamable admits:
"It is I who write, who cannot raise my hand from my knee" (p.301). As
much as for Dante and Joyce, these are portraits of the artist.

Although Moran moves from his bed to his desk to compose the
second half of *Molloy*, both Molloy and Malone lie in bed as they write
their stories. These "horizontal narrators"[6] recall Proust and Descartes.
Molloy's obsession with his mother, whom he spends the first half of the
novel seeking and in whose bed he finally awaits death, is perhaps
suggestive of Proust's attachment to his mother. In any case, Molloy,
cloistered, bedridden and dying, is regularly visited by a mysterious
stranger who pays him and snatches away his manuscripts as rapidly as
they are completed. Molloy's situation and that of Malone, in a hospital
room filling his exercise book in order to occupy the time before his
impending death, clearly echo Proust's deathbed race to finish his huge
novel, whose separate volumes were appropriated by the publisher
before thorough revisions.

And if Molloy and Malone suggest Proust's devotion to his sheets,
they likewise carry to extremes Descarte's tendency to *faire la grasse
matinée*; "Whoroscope" emphasizes the fact that the French philosopher
"remained in bed till midday all his life" (Notes). Moran describes his as
"a methodical mind" (p.98), and Malone, outlining a deliberate pro-

gram of inventory and narration for the remainder of his life, similarly revives Descarte's celebrated *méthode*. But Molloy, seeking to understand the self and its relationship to the universe, concludes that clear and distinct ideas, the amino acids of Descarte's universe, are inadequate for the task. Ultimately even more reductive than Roquentin's direct parody of the *cognito*, Molloy's variations on the Cartesian theme subvert confidence in the self's ability to reconstruct the world: "I think so, yes, I think that all that is false may more readily be reduced, to notions clear and distinct, distinct from all other notions. But I may be wrong" (p.82).

Often reading like philosophical meditations, Beckett's three novels force us again and again to examine their status as works of art. The four author figures who narrate these three volumes self-consciously interrupt – or delay – their stories with reflections on procedure and with value judgments on their own performances, so that the works often resemble a discourse on the possibilities for fiction. Like Butor's Léon, who consciously devises fictions to personalize his unknown fellow passengers, Malone and The Unnamable concoct stories which they recognize as mere stories but which they nevertheless intend as aids to self-knowledge. Malone, in particular, is quite disgusted by the blatant sham of his Saposcat narrative, and he halts it at various points with such exclamations as "What tedium" (p.189) and "This is awful" (p.191). Huxley and Durrell introduce musical terminology into their "counterpoints" and "quartets" in order to draw attention to the power of their artifices. But Molloy, likening his reflexive narrative to a musical form, "the long sonata of the dead" (p.31), thereby mocks the pretensions of art instead of asserting poetry's conventional claim to be an immortalizer.

Furthermore, the trilogy form of *Molloy, Malone meurt* and *L'Innommable* is inherently reflexive. Each of the novels points outside of itself to the other two. Yet in doing so it exposes its own artifice and the vanity of all fiction. For such novelists as Balzac, Zola and Faulkner, the creation of multiple works sharing identical themes, characters and settings augments the realistic illusion. *La Comédie humaine*, the Rougon-Macquart cycle, and the Yoknapatawpha series create the semblance of an autonomous, sprawling universe. Their characters lead lives independent of ours, and we may occasionally catch a glimpse of their careers as we move from book to book. Even in Proust's seven-volume novel, this device of *retour des personnages* serves primarily to underscore the effects of time on various individuals. Through the full spatial and temporal span of Proust's work, we are struck by the changes in Marcel and the many figures he encounters during a complete career.

The separate units of Durrell's tetralogy, on the other hand, hover about the same personalities and incidents but thereby assault each other's reliability through conflicting perspectives. However, *The Alexandria Quartet* ultimately posits the reality of Alexandria, a state of mind and a network of relationships about which it is possible to develop a deepening understanding. Beckett's trilogy, on the contrary, again and again emphasizes the fact that each volume is simply another feeble contrivance. When reference is made in one novel to characters already encountered in another, the effect is not to create a sovereign realm peopled by independent beings. Instead, each narrator in the trilogy reveals himself to be as hopelessly inadequate as the predecessor he self-consciously replaces.

The second section of *Molloy*, in which Moran is assigned the formidable mission of tracking down Molloy, whose personal account we have just read, is itself an example of fiction reflecting back on itself. As much as any literary critic who has just encountered the bizarre figure of Molloy, Moran desperately attempts to analyze the subject of the previous narrative, distinguishing in the process "three, no, four Molloys. He that inhabited me, my caricature of same, Gaber's and the man of flesh and blood somewhere awaiting me" (p.115). *A la recherche de Molloy* throughout his own story, Moran at one point reveals himself an even more thorough student of the Beckett canon. He refers to several characters from various works preceding *Molloy*: "What a rabble in my head, what a gallery of moribunds. Murphy, Watt, Yerk, Mercier and all the others" (p.137). In turn, Moran's successor as narrator, Malone, explicitly and slightingly invokes the Beckett figures, now including both Molloy and Moran, who existed before *Malone meurt*. Anticipating his own death, which he manipulates to coincide with that of his own fictional creation, Macmann, Malone declares: "Then it will be all over with the Murphys, Merciers, Molloys, Morans and Malones, unless it goes on beyond the grave" (p.236). The accumulation of literary inventions does, in fact, continue after Malone's death. The Unnamable, who adds Mahood and Worm to the expanding collection, views his predecessors, among whom Malone is now numbered, floating past him.

It is a potentially infinite series of recapitulations and additions. All of these characters whose names begin with "M" or "W" are obvious literary devices. They are feeble, because onymous, avatars of an unnamable narrator who does not hesitate to play his hand while realizing it is holding only cards. Beckett's multi-volume fiction shares with Balzac the sense of an open form, of a reality which has not yet been exhausted despite exhausting attempts. But its effect, like that of Claude Mauriac's tetralogy, is far less exhilarating and more reductive. When art examines itself here, the examination is itself a disease.

II   AFTER THE FIRST DEATH

The solitude of des Esseintes and kin ends in the solipsism of Beckett's Ms. It is "talking of the craving for a fellow" (p.15) that Molloy begins his epic quest for his mother. But journey's end – and narrative's beginning – finds him alone in his mother's bed and as aloof from human contact as he was when imprisoned in a room in Lousse's house. The fable of A and B inserted at the very outset of *Molloy* suggests isolated, anonymous figures who can at best stop to gaze at each other before continuing their separate ways. Malone is truly man alone. He and Macmann are quarantined from all but a very few visitors more effectively than if they had merely retired to a cork-lined chamber. When Macmann is finally removed from his bed, Lemuel takes him to an island, and Mahood, who finishes his life ensconced by himself in a jar, is an islander, if not an island: "The island, that's all the earth I know" (p.327). No man is anything but an island here, and both Molloy and Moran appropriately recount masturbation experiences.

In his study of Proust, Beckett observed: "For the artist, who does not deal in surfaces, the rejection of friendship is not only reasonable, but a necessity. . . . And art is the apotheosis of solitude."[7] Beckett's own portraits of the artist therefore proceed toward The Unnamable's realization that "there was never anyone but me" (p.403). Marcel's retirement from the world is merely the starting point for his resurrection of the self and the world, but the isolated individual manipulating his private alphabet is both the alpha and the omega of the trilogy's solipsistic world.

In the self-begetting tradition, the lone artist's withdrawal is in preparation for a jubilant birth to follow. However, for Beckett's unfertile protagonists birth is a remote trauma and death a tease. More so than for the Proustian characters Beckett employed the phrase to describe, the narrators of the trilogy suffer from "the sin of having been born."[8] Family life and the continuity of generations is depicted in the novels through the figures of Molloy and his mother, Moran and his son, and the Louis and Mahood households. The attitude here toward the bonds of kinship is more akin to that of W. C. Fields than, for example, to Renaissance reverence for the family as exemplar of the ethic "From fairest creatures we desire increase." Moran's disgust for his neighbor's aberdeen Zoulou, in fact, suggests Fields's misanthropic hostility toward pets and children, and he even confesses: "It's a strange thing, I don't like men and I don't like animals" (p.105).

Moran has an adolescent son with precisely the same name as his, a parody of reproduction as perpetuation of the self. Very conscientious in the paternal role he adopts toward young Jacques, Moran scrupulously disciplines his son for the least breach of conduct, such as violating the prohibition against bringing his stamp collection along on the journey. And Moran sternly but dutifully administers an enema when he believes that, whether appreciated or not, it is for Jacques's own good. Moran pictures himself as fulfilling the responsibilities of fatherhood; he sacrifices his own comfort for the sake of a child who will be enriched with all of the advantages his author never enjoyed: "I had not struggled, toiled, suffered, made good, lived like a Hottentot, so that my son should do the same" (p.122). It is the bourgeois ideal of selflessly creating a better world for one's offspring, and in the novel it is demolished as thoroughly as is Moran's systematic life of regular meals, weekly church services, and a cultivated garden.

Moran as father sees himself imparting wisdom through discipline.

> But I was a better judge than he of what he could and could not. For I knew what he did not yet know, among other things that this ordeal would be of profit to him. *Sollst entbehren,* that was the lesson I desired to impress upon him, while he was still young and tender (p.110).

All of Moran's claims to superior understanding and experience prove a sham. He confesses not knowing the first thing about tracking down Molloy. And, during the hunt for Molloy, on which he embarks leading Jacques by the hand, Moran's pose as teacher collapses just as decisively as he does, leaving him at the mercy of his son.

Moreover, the father's solicitude for his heir is exposed as grounded in paranoia. Moran's authoritarian treatment of Jacques is the defensive reflex of a man who feels mortally threatened by his son and humiliated by him in the eyes of neighbors. Convinced that his son detests him and is constantly plotting against him, Moran refuses to accept Jacques's uncorroborated testimony about anything, even his son's claim to have been at mass on the Sunday morning of Gaber's fateful visit. In his account, Moran characterizes his son as a disgrace to the father – "He was not worthy of me, not in the same class at all" (p.104). With such a perversion of the ideal parent–child relationship, begetting and educating become a farce devoid of any redeeming product. "Cold comfort that is, to feel superior to one's son, and hardly sufficient to calm the remorse of having begotten him" (p.104). As Moran himself admits, from such creatures increase is undesirable.

Procreation is certainly not spared the reductive gaze Beckett fixes on civilization's other sacred cows. Seized by a cattle breeder and accused of trespassing on his property, Moran resourcefully contrives the explanation that he is on a pilgrimage.

> He asked me where to. He was lost. To the Turdy Madonna, I said. The Turdy Madonna? he said, as if he knew Turdy like the back of his hand and there was no Madonna in the length and breadth of it. But where is the place in which there is no Madonna? Herself, I said. . . . It's thanks to her I lost my infant boy, I said, and kept his mamma. Such sentiments could not fail to please a cattle breeder. Had he but known! I told him more fully what alas had never happened. Not that I miss Ninette. But she, at least, who knows, in any case, yes, a pity, no matter. She is the Madonna of pregnant women, I said, of

pregnant married women, and I have vowed to drag myself miserably to her niche, and thank her (p.173).

As Moran's account, especially the sigh "Had he but known!", implies, it is a fiction. This is only the reference to a Ninette, and Jacques, not Moran's wife, is very much in evidence in the novel. Elsewhere, projecting what others think of him, Moran again suggests that his son is the consequence of a birth which in fact killed the mother. "He is taken for a widower, the gaudiest colours are of no avail, rather make things worse, he finds himself saddled with a wife long since deceased, in child-bed as likely as not" (p.125). If indeed the son is alive and the mother is dead, then Moran's story to the farmer is merely the child of fancy. The Turdy Madonna merits as little veneration as the activity it allegedly champions, and death and birth are once again connected, this time by an umbilical cord.

Furthermore, while the natural order of reproduction is subverted as effectively in the trilogy as in "Whoroscope," with its rotten eggs, self-begetting is hardly more successful. The institution of the family and the relationships between generations fail to camouflage the inviolable solitude of the individual. The lone self is the starting point for the universe of these novels. But, although Molloy eventually replaces his mother, it is in neither a bridal nor a maternity bed but a deathbed. His epic journey moves toward a return to a barren womb, a tomb. Granted that the individual has somehow begotten himself, the result has been defective, and self-slaughter now takes priority over birth. From Molloy's opening declaration of intentions – "What I'd like now is to speak of the things that are left, say my goodbyes, finish dying" (p.7). – to The Unnamable's endless yearning to have done with everything, Beckett's protagonists clamor for the final silence. In addition to the deathbed situations of Molloy, Malone and Macmann, physical deterioration is evident in the developing paralyses of both and in Mahood's quadraplegy. The major ambition of such disintegrating selves is death, not birth.

But "To decompose is to live too" (p.25). And the self's fascination with death is paradoxically what perpetuates it. As Malone remarks about Louis's butchering of a pig, "The end of a life is always vivifying" (p.212). When the time comes for Malone's own death, he depicts it in terms of explicit birth imagery. Very like a womb, the room in which he is immured seems to have its own muscular expansion and contraction. "The ceiling rises and falls, rhythmically, as when I was a foetus" (p.283). And the metaphor is extended even further: "I am being given, if I may venture the expression, birth to into death, such is my expression. The feet are clear already, of the great cunt of existence" (p.283).

For each of the trilogy's characters, the urge to escape from the self ironically and frustratingly merely reaffirms its identity. The Unnamable regards himself as a nonentity, but he is nevertheless the fulcrum of the universe.

> . . . perhaps that's what I feel, an outside and an inside and me in the middle, perhaps that's what I am, the thing that divides the world in two, on the one side the outside, on the other the inside, that can be as thin as foil, I'm neither one side nor the other, I'm in the middle, I'm the partition, I've two surfaces and no thickness, perhaps that's what I feel, myself vibrating, I'm the tympanum, on the one hand the mind, on the other the world, I don't belong to either (p.383).

Miller's Henry recognizes that infinity is generated out of ciphers, and it is the negative capability of figures like Marcel and Darley that permits them to create a self and a world. However desperately Beckett's figures long for simple negation, they cannot escape the death–rebirth pattern.

Epistemological dramas, Beckett's novels reenact the Cartesian parable of self-discovery. Consumed by "a passion for truth" (p.34), Molloy and each of the other Ms confront the most fundamental problems of man's existence and his relationship to what he observes. Stopped by a policeman and asked: "What are you doing there?" (p.20). Molloy finds himself incapable of responding to any question on the elementary level expected of him, and a Kafkaesque ordeal of interrogation results. Moran poses for himself sixteen questions "of a theological nature" and seventeen "concerning me perhaps more closely" (pp.166–8). "What was God doing with himself before the creation?" wonders Moran in the first group, a parody of medieval speculation over angels on the head of a pin, while in the second group, he asks: "What would I do until my death?" If he could but answer these questions, he would know what God and man is. Similarly, The Unnamable, like an epic poet, begins his account by inquiring: "Where now? Who now? When now?" (p.291). Inquiry is creative here.

The narrative world of the novels springs from an individual asking himself such comprehensive questions. Unlike Descartes, though, Beckett's narrators emphasize their status as wordsmiths. Writing becomes an extension of thinking, and both create the self – even, and especially, when they multiply rather than resolve questions. *Scribo ergo sum* could be the motto of any of the trilogy's fictive authors. Moran recognizes that his report recreates time past: "For in describing this day I am once more he who suffered it, who crammed it full of futile anxious life, with no other person than his own stultification and the means of not doing what he had to do" (p.122).

And Malone and Macmann live only as long as Malone transcribes his story. Malone's pencil is his only potent limb, and when it slips out of his hands, he and his narrative universe effectively cease to exist for forty-eight hours (p.222). Beckett's narrators are driven by as strong a compulsion to write as is Roquentin, who admits: "I cannot put down my pen" (*La Nausée*, p.242). Each M, even though anxious to make an end to life and literature, begets both by his need to express such anxieties. A record of rebellion against the self-begetting tradition merely prolongs the self, the novel and the tradition.

III THE MANIA FOR SYMMETRY

During his description of how he kicked the charcoal-burner on both sides of the torso equally, Molloy confesses: 'I always had a mania for symmetry" (pp.84–5). A network of dualities very neatly pervades the trilogy. Beckett's either/or – or neither/nor – strategy is based on the recognition that the mind and the literary creation function according to the principle of divide and conquer. The assumption is that reality is indivisible, but, paradoxically, the only way this insight can be expressed is through the binary operations of language, an unavoidable distortion. Although Marcel and Léon learn to create an integral world, the provisional counterpoint of Guermantes and Méséglise and of Paris and Rome is a necessary though erroneous means toward that end. Henry, likewise, must establish an arbitrary distinction between Cancer and Capricorn before arriving at his final, unified vision: "The heating and cooling system is one system, and Cancer is separated from Capricorn only by an imaginary line." (*Tropic of Cancer*, p.331).

Although Molloy represents a savage force within Moran threatening to assert itself and to transform him into "uproar, bulk, rage, suffocation, effort unceasing, frenzied and vain" (p.113), Moran views the object of his hunt as "Just the opposite of myself" (p.113). Their novel is almost equally divided between Molloy's account and Moran's. Later, Worm, a creature born under the sign of the inverted M, is portrayed as "the anti-Mahood" (p.346). The narrators demonstrate a psychic need to manufacture dualisms. "As soon as two things are nearly identical I am lost" (p.156), remarks Moran, and a measure of Molloy's more advanced state of dissolution is the extreme difficulty he displays in distinguishing east from west and his right foot from his left. Malone's existence is defined for him by the contrasting activities of ingestion and excretion as much as by birth and death: "What matters is to eat and excrete. Dish and pot, dish and pot, these are the poles" (p.185). His Moll has a representation of the two thieves hanging from her ears. And, as Hugh Kenner points out in his discussion of "The Cartesian Centaur," Molloy or Moran on a bicycle is an emblem of one of the trilogy's most pervasive polarities, one which again invokes Descartes as Muse: mind versus matter.[9] Two becomes almost as important a number within Beckett's system as three is within Dante's.

One of the most fundamental oppositions within the trilogy is embodied in Molloy's notion of his two contradictory clowns. "For in me there have always been two fools, among others, one asking nothing better than to stay where he is and the other imagining that life might be slightly less horrible a little further on" (p.48). This tension between an expansive and a contractive impulse is present in each of Beckett's characters, and it is responsible for creating the narratives in which they appear. The Unnamable's ambivalent "I can't go on, I'll go on" (p.414) not only resumes the earlier anti-heroes' vacillation between assertion and effacement. In addition to posing the conflict between a life instinct and a death instinct, it reflects two attitudes toward writing. Each narrator is torn between utter silence and unlimited garrulity; there is no middle ground. However, it is an awareness of this dichotomy that creates the discourse. Molloy, who declares at the outset that he wants to finish speaking but who proceeds with a long, rambling story, likewise sees it as an issue of all or nothing: "I always say either too much or too little" (p.34). Words convey understanding of the self and the world, or else they are patent falsehood, and Malone can conceive only of either total knowledge or total ignorance: "either you know all or you know nothing" (p.232).

Moran poses the choice of either advancing with his umbrella as prop and thereby getting wet or else of stopping and sheltering himself under the umbrella. However, he concedes: "It was a false dilemma, as so many dilemmas are" (p.171). Anything with two horns is a fantasy, and it is only a unicorn that is real. Mme Louis very carefully sorts her lentils into two distinct groups. "But suddenly with a furious gesture she swept the two together, annihilating thus in less than a second the work of two or three minutes" (p.214). The result is somewhat less than tragic, since any differentiation is arbitrary in the first place.

The ultimate reality posited by the trilogy is thus a unity. It is something incomprehensible and ineffable because it, like Moran's bees, refuses to submit to the dualistic categories of the intelligence. While contemplating his bees, Moran is transported into a state of near mystical ecstasy. The dance of the bees is so complex as to become simple. It is, in any case, inscrutable, serving as an awesome example of a mystery unamenable to the methodical human mind.

And in spite of all the pains I had lavished on these problems, I was more than ever stupefied by the complexity of this innumerable dance, involving doubtless other determinants of which I had not the slightest idea. And I said, with rapture, Here is something I can study all my life, and never understand. . . . But for me, sitting near my sun-drenched hives, it would always be a noble thing to contemplate, too noble ever to be sullied by the cogitations of a man like me, exiled in his manhood. And I would never do my bees the wrong I had done my God, to whom I had been taught to ascribe my angers, fears, desires, and even my body (p.169).

Like the God of the Old Testament, the inexhaustible phenomenon is what it is. The Lord is One, and reality is only distorted when it is anthropomorphized with two arms, two legs and two horns.

A major dualism for the novels' epistemology is that of subject and object, observer and observed: Moran and Molloy. As Moran asymptotically turns into Molloy, this distinction collapses. As any mystic knows, subject and object are identical. However, when it becomes a question of accommodating such a vision, of translating it into the language of a divisive mind, lines are drawn and lies are told. As long as Moran continues to accept the cognitive paradigm of subject and object to be apprehended, he can no more know Molloy than A can know B. Although the "real" Molloy exists somewhere, he must settle for "my caricature of same" (p.178).

When knowledge becomes self-knowledge, as it is in fact throughout the trilogy, the individual futilely attempts the epic action of transposing himself totally into the object of his own consciousness. Yet the self remains as much an inaccessible fugitive from its own grasp as Albertine is from Marcel's. Whenever one of Beckett's narrators tries to depict himself fully, something escapes, namely the element which does the depicting. However persistently the self tries to represent itself as object, a residue remains as subject. Genuine self-consciousness becomes a fiction, a truth of which the novels are quite conscious.

The Unnamable is the trilogy's most complete portrait of the necessarily incomprehensible identity. Unlike Marcel, Léon, Darley or Henry, The Unnamable never does earn a name for himself. He truly contains multitudes, and to define him would be to limit him. The mother of his predecessor calls her son "Dan," but Molloy claims: "I don't know why, my name is not Dan" (p.17). When asked by the policeman, Molloy is unable to provide his name. And, anticipating The Unnamable's resistance to language, Molloy acknowledges: "And even my sense of identity was wrapped in a namelessness often hard to penetrate, as we have just seen I think" (p.31). Each of the narrators in the cumulative trilogy fails at capturing all of himself in language. A later narrator must replace him and thereby add to what little he has accomplished. The Unnamable is aware that he comes along as the outermost in a series of voxes within voxes. He recognizes that the self-portraits of Molloy, Moran and Malone are inadequate approximations of the same self. Like Mahood and Worm, each has served, without complete success, as The Unnamable's "vice-exister" (p.315), his "surrogate" (p.392). Yet no mere proxy is more than an approximation, and The Unnamable stands as the representation of that which cannot be represented. Moran speaks of "the inenarrable contraption I called my existence" (p.114), but the phrase most directly applies to The Unnamable. He is an integral, transcendent reality whom no arbitrary categories can fully enclose. He can never begin to tell us about himself. But neither can he end.

IV   NOT MIDNIGHT

Samuel Beckett has been canonized by Claude Mauriac as one of the apostles of *alittérature*. Mauriac's own novel is framed by the statements "The marquise went out at five o'clock" and "The marquise did not go out at five o'clock." And Moran's account likewise begins with the statement "It is midnight. The rain is beating on the windows" and concludes with his admission: "It was not midnight. It was not raining."

The effect of such assertions and denials is to subvert fiction at the same time as it is being created. It works in the same way as the name "Mag," which Molloy applies to his mother.

> I called her Mag when I had to call her something. And I called her Mag because for me, without my knowing why, the letter g abolished the syllable Ma, and as it were spat on it, better than any other letter would have done. And at the same time I satisfied a deep and doubtless unacknowledged need, the need to have a Ma, that is a mother, and to proclaim it, audibly. For before you say mag you say ma, inevitably (p.17).

According to Molloy, the abusive title "Mag" also contains within it the affectionate "Ma." Similarly, in the process of attempting to destroy art, Beckett's narrators also create it.

Writing his report, Moran echoes Symbolist and Dadaist scorn for mere "literature" when he states: "But it is not at this late stage of my relation that I intend to give way to literature" (p.151). He even contends: "It seemed to me that all language was an excess of language" (p.116). Definition is, by definition, an abomination, and Molloy sees himself a victim of the false dilemma either falsify or remain quiet: "I am merely complying with the convention that demands that you either lie or hold your peace" (p.88). "Reality" emerges as pre-verbal; in Moran's words, "Not one person in a hundred knows how to be silent and listen, no, nor even to conceive what such a thing means. Yet only then can you detect, beyond the fatuous clamour, the silence of which the universe is made" (p.121). If the universe is, indeed, naturally silent, then all literature becomes mere sound and fury or even blasphemy. Under such conditions, Molloy's text declares "that you would do better, at least no worse, to obliterate texts than to blacken margins, to fill in the holes of words till all is blank and flat and the whole ghastly business looks like what it is, senseless, speechless, issueless misery" (p.13). Fiction once again becomes falsehood, a fact which both Plato and the fictive authors of the trilogy fill their manuscripts to explain.

Beckett's novels project a mistrust of art even more radical than Roquentin's contempt for the consolation his Aunt Bigeois derives from Chopin. If art is traditionally a creator and an immortalizer, it is also a murderer here. Life is dynamic and ineffable, and fixed literary forms become lethal. In its succession of acid self-portraits of the artist, the trilogy reenacts the stoning of Orpheus.

These novels are as obsessed with a self-effacing authenticity as is Mauriac's Carnéjoux. The fictional context of *La Marquise* is shattered at the end, and the novelist Carnéjoux merges with the historian Desprez as admittedly inadequate chroniclers of Parisian experience. Malon self-consciously arranges it so that his life and his death coincide with those of his creation, Macmann. But The Unnamable's later, larger perspective makes it clear that, despite his lucidity, Malone is merely artful.

What remains is a commitment to the non-human, non-verbal world of objects. Like Whitman's animals ("they are so placid and self-contained . . . . They do not sweat and whine about their condition"), objects are genuine because they are aloof from man's artificial systems. Molloy arranges his sixteen sucking stones in various intricate patterns in his pockets and according to what he calls "the principle of trim" (p.71). Yet despite his ingenious efforts, Molloy admits that one sucking stone is as good, or as bad, as another: "deep down it was all the same to me whether I sucked a different stone each time or always the same stone, until the end of time. For they all tasted exactly the same" (p.74). And so he proceeds to demolish the elaborate design he has spent the previous eight pages constructing: "And the solution to which I rallied in the end was to throw away all the stones but one, which I kept now in one pocket, now in another, and which of course I soon lost, or threw away, or gave away, or swallowed" (p.74).

The Ms worship, or at least are obsessed by, such objects as sucking stones, sticks, hats, and bicycles. The curious trinket, resembling a crucifix, which Molloy pilfers from Lousse, induces awe precisely because it, like Moran's bees, is hopelessly unintelligible.

> . . . I could never understand what possible purpose it could serve, nor even contrive the faintest hypothesis on the subject. And from time to time I took it from my pocket and gazed upon it, with an astonished and affectionate gaze, if I had not been incapable of affection. But for a certain time I think it inspired me with a kind of veneration, for there was no doubt in my mind that it was not an object of virtu, but that it had a most specific function always to be hidden from me. I could therefore puzzle over it endlessly without the least risk. For to know nothing is nothing, not to want to know anything likewise, but to be beyond knowing anything, to know you are beyond knowing anything, that is when peace enters in, to the soul of the incurious seeker (pp.63–4).

Roquentin anticipates some of this obscurantist reverence for the non-human world which forever eludes the nets of language. One of his epiphanies clearly resembles The Unnamable's sense of futility over trying to pin words on recalcitrant things.

Les choses se sont délivrées de leurs noms. Elles sont là, grotesques, têtues, géantes et ça paraît imbécile de les appeler des banquettes ou de dire quoi que ce soit sur elles: je suis au milieu des Choses, les innommables. (*La Nausée*, p.177).

[Things are freed from their names. They are there, grotesque, stubborn, huge, and it seems idiotic to call them benches or to say anything about them. I am in the middle of Things, the unnamables]

"To restore silence is the role of objects" (p.13), contends Beckett's brand of *chosisme*, and silence is the supreme value in his clamorous universe. The art objects fashioned by each of the trilogy's writers paradoxically aspire to silence through words.

It is an endless effort, one which insures eternal life for a suicidal narrative. At the very outset of his account, Molloy naïvely believes: "now it's nearly the end" (p.8), and the journeys of both Molloy and Moran describe a circle; "life seems made up of backsliding" (p.61). The stories of Molloy and Moran each recount how they came to write what we are reading – how Molloy moved toward his mother's bed, where he fills his pages, and how Moran ended up at his desk composing a report for Youdi. Beckett's novels, consistent with the self-begetting tradition, thus account for their own origins and propel the reader back to the first page after he has read the last.

More important, however, is the fact that there can never be a complete first reading of the trilogy. Beckett's narrators all share the same contradictory ambitions. On the one hand, they want to exhaust everything, to say all there is to say. But, exhausted, they also want to have done with it, to shut up, even though this would mean compromising with their vision of the truth: "For if you set out to mention everything you would never be done, and that's what counts, to be done, to have done" (p.41). An ugly duckling attempting a swan song, each M prolongs his existence and that of the work in which he appears in the very act of attacking both.

"The search for the means to put an end to things, an end to speech, is what enables the discourse to continue" (p.299) is one of The Unnamable's most lucid remarks. His own discourse, like *La Marquise*, turns into a dense, unpunctuated flow of words which conceivably – or rather inconceivably – could never end. Positing the primacy of unity and silence, the trilogy's fragmented chatter runs from volume to volume, until The Unnamable's last recorded syllables: "I can't go on, I'll go on."

Beckett's novels thus reenact the lying Cretan paradox exhibited by Plato's *Phaedrus*, a dialogue which ironically concludes by attacking the value of all discourse. The trilogy is just such a "self-consuming artifact,"[10] striving for what Roland Barthes describes as "The terminal agraphia of Rimbaud or of certain surrealists – plunged into obscurity for that very reason – that unsettling abandonment of literature."[11] Barthes reads the history of Western literature as an evolution in formal self-awareness. While Beckett falls short of the neutral writing, "le degré zéro de l'écriture," which Barthes posits as the term of his historical continuum, Beckett, like Mallarmé, "expresses well that fragile moment of History in which literary language survives only the better to sing its need to die."[12]

Unlike Marcel, who comes to believe in literature as a glorious triumph, a means of recreating himself, Beckett's fictive authors profoundly mistrust the self and its talk. Yet in expressing their desire for extinction, they merely prolong their agonies despite themselves. The Unnamable is a reluctant immortal. Words cannot exhaust his infinite variety, but words explaining this fact sustain his narrative. A new self and a new novel come to life through Marcel's belief in the potency of art. Beckett mocks the Proustian devotions, but his blasphemy is as self-begetting as is Marcel's fervor. The trilogy faithlessly perpetuates itself and the tradition of the self-begetting novel.

Some Reflexive Fictions

Henry Adams, *The Education of Henry Adams*
S. Y. Agnon, *A Guest for the Night*
John Barth, *Chimera*
     Lost in the Funhouse
     The Sot-Weed Factor
*Samuel Beckett, *Molloy*
     Malone meurt
     L'Innommable
Jorge Luis Borges, *Ficciones*
Mikhail Bulgakov, *The Master and Margarita*
*Michel Butor, *La Modification*
Roland Cailleux, *Une Lecture*
Miguel de Cervantes, *Don Quixote*
Geoffrey Chaucer, *The House of Fame*
Julio Cortázar, *Rayuela*
Dante Alighieri, *Divina Commedia*
*Clyde Brion Davis, *"The Great American Novel ——"*
William Demby, *The Catacombs*
René Descartes, *Méditations*
José Donoso, *El obsceno pájaro de la noche*
*Lawrence Durrell, *The Alexandria Quartet*
Irvin Faust, *Foreign Devils*
John Fowles, *Daniel Martin*
William Gaddis, *Recognitions*
André Gide, *Les Faux-Monnayeurs*
     Le Journal des Faux-Monnayeurs
     Paludes
William Golding, *Free Fall*
Witold Gombrowicz, *Ferdydurke*
Stephen Hudson, *A True Story*
Aldous Huxley, *Point Counter Point*
Joris-Karl Huysmans, *A Rebours*
John Irving, *The World According to Garp*
Henry James, *Stories of Writers and Artists*

James Joyce, *A Portrait of the Artist as a Young Man*
    Ulysses
    Finnegans Wake
Jack Kerouac, *The Subterraneans*
Siegfried Lenz, *Die Deutschstunde*
*Doris Lessing, *The Golden Notebook*
Norman Mailer, *The Armies of the Night*
    Advertisements for Myself
Bernard Malamud, *The Tenants*
*Claude Mauriac, *La Marquise sortit à cinq heures*
Thomas Mann, *Doktor Faustus*
*Claude Mauriac, *La Marquise sortit à cinq heures*
*Henry Miller, *Tropic of Cancer*
    Tropic of Capricorn
Alberto Moravia, *L'Attenzione*
*Iris Murdoch, *Under the Net*
Vladimir Nabokov, *Pale Fire*
    The Real Life of Sebastian Knight
    Speak, Memory
Novalis, *Heinrich von Ofterdingen*
Flann O'Brien, *At Swim-Two-Birds*
Charles Olson, *Maximus Poems*
Robert Pinget, *Quelqu'un*
Ezra Pound, *Hugh Selwyn Mauberly*
*Marcel Proust, *A la recherche du temps perdu*
James Purdy, *Cabot Wright Begins*
Raymond Queneau, *Le Chiendent*
Rainer Maria Rilke, *Die Aufzeichnungen des Malte Laurids Brigge*
Philip Roth, *The Great American Novel*
    My Life as a Man
Ernesto Sabato, *El túnel*
Marc Saporta, *Composition no. 1*
Nathalie Sarraute, *Les Fruits d'or*
    Entre la vie et la mort
*Jean-Paul Sartre, *La Nausée*
    Les Mots
Wallace Stegner, *All the Little Live Things*
Laurence Sterne, *The Life and Opinions of Tristram Shandy, Gentleman*
Henry David Thoreau, *Walden*
Miguel de Unamuno, *Niebla*
Paul Valéry, *Monsieur Teste*
Gore Vidal, *1876*
Evelyn Waugh, *The Ordeal of Gilbert Pinfold*
Walt Whitman, *Leaves of Grass*
William Wordsworth, *Prelude*

Notes

CHAPTER 1

1. *Beyond Psychology* (New York: Dover, 1941), p.114.
2. Ibid., p.123. See also Rank, *Modern Education*, trans. Mabel E. Maxon (New York: Alfred A. Knopf, 1932), pp.192–4.
3. Ibid., p.213.
4. James Joyce, *A Portrait of the Artist as a Young Man* (New York: Viking, 1956), p.231.
5. "Dante . . . Bruno . Vico . . Joyce," *Our Exagmination Round His Factification for Incamination* (London: Faber and Faber, 1938), p.8.
6. (New York: Random House, 1961), p.21.
7. *A Portrait*, p.94.
8. "Intervention à Royaumont," *Répertoire* I (Paris: Les Editions de Minuit, 1960), p.273.
9. *Le Journal des Faux-Monnayeurs* (Paris: Editions Eos, 1926), p.55.
10. *Point Counter Point* (New York: Harper & Row, 1956), pp.301–2.
11. *At Swim-Two-Birds* (Harmondsworth, Middlesex: Penguin, 1967), p.40.
12. André Gide, *Les Faux-Monnayeurs* (Paris: Gallimard, 1925), p.243.
13. Jean-Paul Sartre, *La Nausée* (Paris: Gallimard, 1938), p.144.
14. *Proust and Three Dialogues* (London: John Calder, 1965), p.39.
15. Henry A. Grubbs, "Sartre's Recapturing of Lost Time," *Modern Language Notes*, LXXIII (Nov 1958), p.522.
16. See *Le Journal des Faux-Monnayeurs*.
17. "Préface" to Aldous Huxley, *Contrepoint* (Paris: Plon, 1953), trans. Jules Castier, p.iv.
18. *Ulysses*, p.208.
19. Interview with Jean Cau, *L'Express* (7 May 1959), cited in Victor Brombert, "Lawrence Durrell and His French Reputation," *The World of Lawrence Durrell*, ed. Harry T. Moore (Carbondale: Southern Illinois University Press, 1962).
20. "Présentation des *Temps modernes*," *Les Temps modernes*, I, 1 (1 Oct 1945), pp.11–13; and "Qu'est-ce que la littérature?" in *Situations II* (Paris: Gallimard, 1948), p.208.
21. "Les Œuvres d'art imaginaires chez Proust," *Répertoire II* (Paris: Les Editions de Minuit, 1964).
22. *Proust par lui-même* (Paris: Editions du Seuil, 1959).
23. *Proust and Three Dialogues*.
24. *Sartre: Romantic Rationalist* (New Haven: Yale University Press, 1953).
25. *Clea* (New York: Pocket Books, 1961), p.134.

26. *Tropic of Capricorn* (New York: Grove, 1961), p.126.

27. Richard Macksey, "The Artist in the Labyrinth: Design or *Dasein*," *Modern Language Notes*, LXXVII, 3 (May 1962), p.241.

28. *Les Faux-Monnayeurs*, p.105.

29. F. Scott Fitzgerald, *The Great Gatsby* (New York: Scribner, 1925), p.99.

30. *Clea*, p.275.

31. *Tropic of Cancer* (New York: Grove, 1961), p.23.

32. *Fear and Trembling and The Sickness Unto Death*, trans. Walter Lowrie (Garden City, New York: Doubleday, 1954), p.38.

33. *Partial Magic: The Novel as a Self-Conscious Genre* (Berkeley: University of California Press, 1975), p.xi.

34. *Contexts of Criticism* (Cambridge: Harvard University Press, 1957), p.79.

35. *The Liberal Imagination: Essays on Literature and Society* (New York: Viking, 1950), p.209.

36. *Essais critiques* (Paris: Editions du Seuil, 1964), p.254.

CHAPTER 2

1. Marcel Proust, *A la recherche du temps perdu*, ed. Pierre Clarac & André Ferré (Paris: Editions Gallimard, 1954), I, 64. All references to the novel are to volume and page number of this three-volume Pléiade edition.

2. Hence the scorn for "realistic" fiction, "qui se contente de 'décrire les choses,' d'en donner seulement un misérable relevé de lignes et de surfaces" [which contents itself with "describing things," with merely giving a wretched list of lines and surfaces] (III, 885). The focus of the novel's attention and style is on juxtapositions. Consequently, relationships take precedence over that which they relate, a reversal of the preoccupations of classic Western philosophy.

3. *Etudes sur les temps humain* (Edinburgh: Edinburgh University Press, 1949), p.392.

4. *Thomas Mann: The Ironic German* (Cleveland: World Publishing Company, 1961), p.272.

5. *Marcel Proust: The Fictions of Life and Of Art* (New York: Oxford University Press, 1965), p.194.

6. "Tradition and the Individual Talent," *The Sacred Wood* (New York: Barnes & Noble, 1960), p.52.

7. See *The Maxims of Marcel Proust*, edited and translated by Justin O'Brien (New York: Columbia University Press, 1948).

8. *A Portrait of the Artist as a Young Man*, p.215.

9. *Mensonge romantique et vérité romanesque* (Paris: Grasset, 1961), p.235.

10. *Les Voix narratives dans "A la recherche du temps perdu"* (Geneva: Droz, 1965), p.16.

11. "Le 'je' proustien," *Bulletin de la Société des Amis de Marcel Proust et des Amis de Combray*, No. 9 (1959), 69–82.

12. "The Narrator, Not Marcel," *The French Review*, XXXIII, No. 4 (Feb 1960), 389–92.

13. Suzuki, p.74.

14. Waters, p.390.

15. *Du Temps perdu au Temps retrouvé. Introduction à l'œuvre de Marcel Proust* (Paris: Belles Lettres, 1950), p.248.
16. *Marcel Proust and the Creative Encounter* (Chicago: University of Chicago Press, 1972), p.3.
17. Ibid., p.241. However, in the later *An Age of Fiction*, co-authored with Margaret Guiton (New Brunswick: Rutgers University Press, 1957), Brée appears to recant. There, contending that *La Nausée* is not a self-begetting work, she nevertheless suggests that Proust's novel is. "Sartre, unlike Proust, does not imply his own novel is the very novel his narrator will write" (p.207).
18. Brée, *Du Temps perdu*, p.27.
19. Ibid., p.29.
20. *Muller*, p.22.
21. Brée, *Du Temps perdu*, p.28.
22. *Poulet*, p.400.
23. "Quatre Images de Marcel Proust," *Portraits in Œuvres complètes de Robert Brasillach* (Paris: Club de l'honnête homme, 1964), p.211.

CHAPTER 3

1. Jean-Paul Sartre, *La Nausée* (Paris: Gallimard, 1938). All page references are to this edition.
2. Claude-Edmonde Magny, "The Duplicity of Being," trans. James O. Morgan, in *Sartre: A Collection of Critical Essays*, ed. Edith Kern (Englewood Cliffs, New Jersey: Prentice Hall, 1962),p.24.
3. Georges Poulet, "La 'Nausée' de Sartre et le 'Cogito' cartésien," *Studi Francesi*, 15 (Sep–Dec 1961), p.458.
4. "'Some of These Days': Sartre's *Petite Phrase*," *Contemporary Literature*, 2, No. 3 (Summer 1970), 377.
5. Poulet, *Studi Francesi*, p.462.
6. Germaine Brée and Margaret Guiton, *An Age of Fiction*, p.207.
7. Nevertheless Francis Jeanson, *Sartre par lui-même* (Paris: Editions du Seuil, 1955), p.122, and Iris Murdoch, *Sartre: Romantic Rationalist*, p.18, insist on reading *La Nausée* in terms of Sartre's subsequent denunciation of aesthetic salvation.
8. *Les Mots* (Paris: Gallimard, 1964), p.210.
9. *Qu'est-ce que la littérature?* in *Situations II* (Paris: Gallimard, 1948). p.313.
10. See Jean Isère, "Sartre vs. Proust," *Kenyon Review*, IX (Spring 1947), 287–9; H. C. R. Stockwell, "Proust and Sartre,"*Cambridge Journal*, VII (May 1954), 476–87; Henry A. Grubbs, "Sartre's Recapturing of Lost Time," *Modern Language Notes*, LXXIII (November 1958), 515–22; Robert G. Cohn, "Sartre vs. Proust," *Partisan Review*, XXVIII (Sep–Nov 1961), 633–45; Roger Shattuck, "Making Time: A Study of Stravinsky, Proust, and Sartre," *Kenyon Review*, XXV (Spring 1963), 248–63; Reinhard Kuhn, "Proust and Sartre: The Heritage of Romanticism," *Symposium*, XVIII (Winter 1964), 293–306; Zimmerman, op. cit., 375–81. Edith Kern's *Existential Thought and Fictional Technique: Kierkegaard, Sartre, Beckett* (New Haven: Yale University Press, 1970) discusses links to Beckett as well.

11. "Présentation des *Temps modernes*" in *Les Temps modernes*, I, No. 1 (1 Oct 1945), pp.11–13.
12. Sartre, *Situations II*, p.208.
13. See Isère and Cohn for detailed examinations of Sartre's charges against Proust and refutations of them.
14. Kuhn, p.302.
15. Grubbs, p.522.
16. Sartre, *Situations II*, p.129.
17. *Situations I* (Paris: Gallimard, 1947).

CHAPTER 4

1. "Le Réalisme mythologique de Michel Butor,"*Critique*, 129 (Feb 1958), pp. 99–118.
2. Michel Butor, *La Modification* (Paris: Union générale d'éditions, 1957). All references are to this edition.
3. For an historical survey of the use of the second person, see Bruce Morrissette, "Narrative 'You' in Contemporary Literature," *Comparative Literature Studies*, II, 1 (1965), pp.1–25.
4. In an interview with Paul Guth in *Le Figaro littéraire*, 607 (7 Dec 1957), Butor declared: "I needed an interior monologue below the level of the language of the character himself, in an intermediary form between the first and third person." See also Pierre Deguise, " Michel Butor et le 'nouveau roman'," *French Review*, XXXV, No. 2 (Dec 1961), pp. 155–63; Bernard Pingaud, "Je, Vous, Il," *Esprit*, 26, No. 7–8 (July-Aug 1958), pp. 91–9; and Jean Roudaut, *Michel Butor ou le Livre futur* (Paris: Gallimard, 1964).
5. "Il n'y a pas d'école Robbe-Grillet" in *Essais critiques* (Paris: Editions du Seuil, 1964), p.103.
6. Robert Pinget, *Quelqu'un* (Paris: Les Editions de Minuit, 1965), p.195.
7. Marc Saporta, *Composition no. 1* (Paris: Editions du Seuil, 1962), unnumbered first page.
8. Simone de Beauvoir, *et al.*, *Que peut la littérature?* (Paris: Editions du Seuil, 1966), p.119.
9. Ibid., p.120.
10. Georges Charbonnier, *Entretiens avec Michel Butor* (Paris: Gallimard, 1967), p.59.
11. Relevant or not, the Feast of Saint Cecile is 22 November. The martyr, a virgin, was decapitated in Rome in 232 A. D.
12. *Répertoire II* (Paris: Les Editions de Minuit, 1964), pp. 252–92.
13. See, for example, *Hérold* (Paris: Editions G. Fall, 1964), and "Claude Monet ou le Monde renversé" and "Les Mosquées de New York ou Mark Rothko" in *Répertoire III*.
14. Giovanni-Paolo Pannini (1691–1765). He died in Rome.
15. Roudaut, p.84.
16. "Une Autobiographie dialéctique," *Répertoire I* (Paris: Les Editions de Minuit, 1960), p.262.
17. "Victor Hugo romancier," *Répertoire II*, p.240.
18. "Le Roman comme recherche," *Répertoire I*, p.8.

19. Ibid., p.7.
20. *Pour un nouveau roman* (Paris Les Editions de Minuit, 1963).
21. "Intervention à Royaumont," *Répertoire I*, p.272.
22. "Le Roman comme recherche," p.11.
23. Ibid., p.11.
24. Ibid., p.11.
25. *Répertoire I*, pp.79–94.
26. *Que peut la littérature?* p.118.
27. "La Critique et l'invention," *Répertoire III*, p.18.
28. "Littérature et méta-langage," *Essais critiques*, p.107.
29. Ibid., p.106.
30. "Ecrivains et écrivants," *Essais critiques*, p.149.
31. Jean Ricardou, *Problèmes du nouveau roman* (Paris: Editions du Seuil, 1967), pp.171–93.
32. Jean Thibaudeau, "Le roman comme autobiographie," *Théorie d'ensemble*, ed. Philippe Sollers (Paris: Editions du Seuil, 1968), p.215.
33. Philippe Sollers, *Drame* (Paris: Editions du Seuil), cover-note.
34. Ricardou, pp.11–16.
35. *The French New Novel* (London: Oxford University Press, 1969), p.4.
36. Robbe-Grillet, p.134.
37. Madeleine Chapsal, *Les Ecrivains en personne* (Paris: René Julliard, 1960), p.58.
38. *The New Novel* (New York: Farrar, Straus, and Giroux, 1971).
39. See *Yale French Studies*, No.24 (1959).
40. Claude Mauriac, *La Marquise sortit à cinq heures* (Paris: Editions Albin Michel, 1961). All references are to this edition.
41. "Le Temps immobile," *L'Alittérature contemporaine* (Paris: Editions Albin Michel, 1958, revised 1969), pp.365–81.
42. *L'Alittérature contemporaine*, p.12.
43. Jean-Paul Sartre, "Préface" in Nathalie Sarraute, *Portrait d'un inconnu* (Paris: Robert Marin, 1948), p.7.
44. Ibid., pp.7–8.
45. Jean Pierre Faye, *Le récit hunique* (Paris: Editions du Seuil, 1967), pp.36–55.
46. *Le récit hunique*, pp.286–304.
47. *L'Alittérature contemporaine*, p.341.
48. Faye, p.36.
49. *L'Alittérature contemporaine*, p.11.
50. Northrop Frye, *Anatomy of Criticism* (Princeton: Princeton University Press, 1957), p.49.

CHAPTER 5

1. Aldous Huxley, *Point Counter Point*, p.302.
2. Lawrence Durrell, *Clea*, p.119. Clea is the fourth volume of *The Alexandria Quartet*. The first three are *Justine, Balthazar*, and *Mountolive*. All references to the *Quartet* are to the Pocket Books editions, published simultaneously.
3. Harry Levin, *The Gates of Horn*, p.76.
4. Ibid., p.74.

5. Victor Brombert, "Lawrence Durrell and His French Reputation," *The World of Lawrence Durrell*, ed. Harry T. Moore (Carbondale, Illinois: Southern Illinois University Press, 1962), p.174.
6. Joseph Conrad, *The Secret Agent* (Garden City, N.Y.: Doubleday & Co., 1953), p.144.
7. Ibid., p.199.
8. *The Novelist As Philosopher: Studies in French Fiction, 1935–1960* (New York: Oxford University Press, 1962).
9. In René-Marill Albérès, "Romanciers italiens," *La Table Ronde*, Sep 1957, pp.9–24.
10. *The Intellectual Hero: Studies in the French Novel, 1880–1955* (Philadelphia: Lippincott, 1961), p.11.
11. Frank MacShane, *The Life and Work of Ford Madox Ford* (New York: Horizon Press, 1965), p.119.
12. *A Portrait of the Artist as a Young Man*, p.34.
13. *Ulysses*, p.248.
14. George D. Painter, *Marcel Proust: A Biography* (London: Chatto & Windus, 1965), II, p.341.
15. Quoted in Harry Levin, *James Joyce: A Critical Introduction* (Norfolk: New Directions, 1941), p.134.
16. Hugh Kenner, *Dublin's Joyce* (Bloomington: University of Indiana Press, 1956), p.112.
17. Eugene M. Waith, "The Calling of Stephen Dedalus," *College English*, XVIII (Feb 1957), p.256.
18. *A Reader's Guide to James Joyce* (London: Thames and Hudson, 1959), p.176.
19. "Joyce's Categories," *Sewanee Review*, LXI (Summer 1953), p.427. He is perhaps referring to William Troy's 1934 essay "Stephen Dedalus and James Joyce" included in *Selected Essays* (New Brunswick: Rutgers University Press, 1967), pp.89–93. Troy sees a dramatic turning-point in Stephen's life when he smashes the chandelier in Bella Cohen's brothel: "at this moment Stephen Dedalus, as we have known him up to this scene, vanishes from existence, and the author of *Ulysses* is born" (pp.92–3).
20. "The Eighteenth-Century Method," *The Athenaeum*, No.4671 (7 Nov 1919), p.1164.
21. Aldous Huxley and Stuart Gilbert, *Joyce the Artificer: Two Studies of Joyce's Method* (London: Chiswick Press, 1952).
22. (New Haven: Yale University Press, 1953).
23. *Under the Net* (New York: The Viking Press, 1954), p.61. All references are to this edition.
24. *Sartre: Romantic Rationalist*, p.75.
25. Ibid., p.15.
26. "Against Dryness: A Polemical Sketch," *Encounter*, XVI, No.1 (Jan 1961), pp.19–20.
27. Ibid., p.20.
28. Jacques Vallette, "*Justine, Balthazar*, et Lawrence Durrell, "*Mercure de France*, No. 1143 (Nov 1958), p.539.
29. "One Vote for the Sun," in *The World of Lawrence Durrell*, p.152.
30. Kenneth Young, "A Dialogue With Durrell," *Encounter*, XIII No. 6 (Dec 1959), p.62.

31. Jacques Vallette, "Mountolive," *Mercure de France*, No. 1147 (Mar 1959), p.518.
32. Lawrence Durrell, "The Kneller Tape," in *The World of Lawrence Durrell*, p.167.
33. *The Golden Notebook* (New York: Ballantine Books, 1968), p.62. All references are to this edition.
34. Doris Lessing, "The small personal voice," in *Declaration*, ed. Tom Maschler (New York: E. P. Dutton & Co., 1958), pp.193–4.
35. Ibid., p.188.

CHAPTER 6

1. "The New Tradition in Fiction," in *Surfiction: Fiction Now . . . and Tomorrow*, ed. Raymond Federman (Chicago: Swallow Press, 1975), p.37.
2. *Anti-intellectualism in American Life* (New York: Alfred A. Knopf, 1963), p.39.
3. "Preface to 'The Lesson of the Master,'" in *The Art of the Novel* (New York: Charles Scribner's Sons, 1934), p.277.
4. *The Letters of Henry James*, ed. Percy Lubbock (New York: Charles Scribner's Sons, 1920), Vol. I, p.408. Letter of 17 Aug 1908.
5. "Henry James," *Little Review*, V (Aug 1918), p.46.
6. *Image and Idea* (Norfolk, Connecticut: New Directions, 1949), p.20.
7. Ibid., p.9.
8. *The Education of Henry Adams* (Boston: Houghton Mifflin, 1961), p.432.
9. Henry Adams does, in fact, resemble Proust in his account of a developing consciousness "already littered and stuffed beyond hope with the millions of chance images stored away without order in the memory" (p.353). His portrait of diplomatic intrigues among American and British officials during a period of crisis for both nations gives the impression that everything existed solely for the creation of *The Education*, that "there was only one student to profit by this immense staff of teachers" (p.149). Henry, like Marcel, apparently wastes his entire life but is redeemed by his Life.
10. 'Much Madness Is Divinest Sense."
11. *The American Adam* (Chicago: University of Chicago Press, 1955).
12. "Rappaccini's Daughter," in *Mosses From an Old Manse, The Centenary Edition of the Works of Nathaniel Hawthorne* Vol. X (Columbus, Ohio: Ohio State University Press, 1962–74), pp.91–2.
13. "The Custom-House," ibid., Vol. I, p.36.
14. *Winesburg, Ohio* (New York: Viking Press, 1960), p.56.
15. Ibid., p.247.
16. *Snow White* (New York: Bantam Books, 1968), p.82.
17. "Surfiction – Four Propositions in Form of an Introduction," *Surfiction: Now . . . and Tomorrow*, p.7.
18. *Literary Disruptions: The Making of a Post-Contemporary American Fiction* (Urbana: University of Illinois Press, 1975); *The Life of Fiction* (Urbana: University of Illinois Press, 1977).
19. "The Shaping of the American Character," in *Whitman: A Collection of Critical Essays*, ed. Roy Harvey Pearce (Englewood Cliffs, New Jersey: Prentice-Hall, 1962), p.134.

20. See, of course, Henry Nash Smith, *Virgin Land: The American West As Symbol and Myth* (Cambridge: Harvard University Press, 1950).
21. Perry Miller, p.136.
22. *Walden and Civil Disobedience*, ed. Sherman Paul (Boston: Houghton Mifflin, 1957), p.62.
23. *Invisible Man* (New York: New American Library, 1947), p.11.
24. *The American Novel and its Tradition* (Garden City: Doubleday, 1957).
25. "Manners, Morals, and the Novel," in *The Liberal Imagination*, p.206.
26. *Love and Death in the American Novel* (New York: Criterion Books, 1960).
27. Lewis, p.115.
28. Thoreau, p.1.
29. See James Lyndon Shanley, *The Making of Walden* (Chicago: University of Chicago Press, 1965).
30. F. Scott Fitzgerald, p.9.
31. Ibid., p.182.
32. *L'Evolution de Walt Whitman* (Paris: Marcel Didier, 1954).
33. *A Vision* (New York: Macmillan, 1961), p.113.
34. Asselineau, p.18.
35. "The American Scholar," *Selections from Ralph Waldo Emerson*, ed. Stephen E. Wicher, p.74.
36. Ibid., p.79.
37. "Self-Reliance," ibid., p.162.
38. "Nature," ibid., p.56.
39. "The Poet," ibid., p.238.
40. Ibid., p.238.
41. "Letter to Walt Whitman," ibid., p.362.
42. Asselineau, p.54.
43. *Stand Still Like The Hummingbird* (New York: New Directions, 1962). p.109.
44. "A Backward Glance O'er Travel'd Roads," *Leaves of Grass and Selected Prose*, ed. Sculley Bradley (New York: Holt, Rinehart and Winston, 1962), p.486.
45. "Inscriptions," ibid., p.1.
46. "So Long," *Leaves of Grass*, p.412.
47. "What I Feel About Walt Whitman," in *A Century of Whitman Criticism*, ed. Edwin Haviland Miller (Bloomington, Indiana: Indiana University Press, 1969), p.126.
48. "The Poet," op. cit., p.238.
49. *The Books In My Life* (Norfolk, Connecticut: New Directions, 1950), p.169.
50. Whitman, p.453.
51. Ibid., p.454.
52. J. W. DeForest, "The Great American Novel," *The Nation*, VI (9 Jan 1868), p.28.
53. See *The Sense of An Ending: Studies in the Theory of Fiction* (New York: Oxford University Press, 1967).
54. "American Novels," *North American Review*, CXV (Oct 1872), p.378.
55. Ibid., p.378.
56. *The Responsibilities of the Novelist and The Joyous Miracle*: Vol. III, *Collected Works* (New York: Doubleday, Doran & Co., 1928), p.67.
57. Some brief biographical information on Davis can be found in a publisher's

pamphlet: Herbert Gorman, *The Man With The Seeing Eye* (New York: Rinehart and Company, 1946).

58. Clyde Brion Davis, *"The Great American Novel – –"* (New York: Farrar and Rinehart, 1938), p.76.
59. *New Republic,* LXXXV, No. 1224 (18 May 1938), p.49.
60. See *Sexual Politics* (New York: Doubleday and Co., 1970).
61. "A Backward Glance O'er Travel'd Roads," op. cit., p.487.
62. *The Books In My Life,* p.12.
63. "The Poet," op. cit., p.237.
64. "Preface to 1855 Edition," op. cit., p.470.

CHAPTER 7

1. "Dante . . . Bruno . Vico . . Joyce," in *Our Exagmination Round His Factification For Incamination of Work in Progress,* pp.1–22.
2. Melvin J. Friedman, "The Novels of Samuel Beckett: An Amalgam of Joyce and Proust," *Comparative Literature,* XII, 1 (Winter 1960), pp.47–58.
3. Lawrence E. Harvey, *Samuel Beckett: Poet and Critic* (Princeton: Princeton University Press, 1970), p.406n.
4. Samuel Beckett, *Proust and Three Dialogues,* p.34.
5. Samuel Beckett, *Three Novels* (New York: Grove Press, 1965), p.293. All references are to this one-volume edition of the Trilogy, in which Beckett himself translated *Malone Dies* and *The Unnamable* and translated *Molloy* in collaboration with Patrick Bowles.
6. Hugh Kenner, *Samuel Beckett: A Critical Study,* p.199.
7. *Proust and Three Dialogues,* p.64.
8. Ibid., p.67.
9. Kenner, pp.117f.
10. See Stanley Fish, "Literature in the Reader: Affective Stylistics," *New Literary History,* II, 1 (Autumn 1970), pp.137–8.
11. *Le Degré zéro de l'écriture suivi de Eléments de sémiologie* (Paris: Gonthier, 1965), 65–6.
12. Ibid., p.66.

Index

Van Gogh, Vincent, 7
Verfremdungseffekt, 10
Vico, Giovanni Battista, 4
Vidal, Gore, 145
Voltaire (François-Marie Arouet), 89, 103

Wagner, Richard
  Die Meistersinger, 9
.Waith, Eugene M., 84
Waters, Harold A., 20–1
Waugh, Evelyn, 75, 145
Whitman, Walt, 8, 103, 110–11, 119, 120, 127, 129
  "A Backward Glance O'er Travel'd Roads," 113, 117, 127
  "Democratic Vistas," 113
  1855 Preface, 117
  Leaves of Grass, 107, 111, 113–17, 122, 126, 141, 145

Wilde, Oscar, 111
Williams, William Carlos
  The Great American Novel, 6, 119
  Paterson, 116
Wilson, Edmund, 122
Wolfe, Thomas, 12, 118
  Look Homeward, Angel, 105, 116
  The Story of a Novel, 105
Woolf, Virginia
  To the Lighthouse, 77–8
Wordsworth, William, 145
Wyatt, Sir Thomas, 129

Yale French Studies, 71
Yeats, William Butler, 111
Young, Kenneth, 151n

Zimmerman, Eugenia Noik, 37, 148n
Zola, Emile, 4, 66, 79, 103, 131
  Germinal, 48